P9-BZU-555

CHINA

Jerry E. Jennings

Jerry E. Jennings is an author and editor of textbooks for young people. He received his education at Michigan State University and Columbia University. Mr. Jennings has done extensive research in Chinese geography and history.

Margaret Fisher Hertel

Margaret Fisher Hertel, an author and editor of textbooks, has traveled extensively in Asia. After graduating from Maryville College, she continued her education at Mexico City College. As a former teacher, Mrs. Hertel is keenly aware of the needs and interests of elementary and secondary school students.

LIBRARY OF CONGRESS CATALOG CARD NUMBER: 83-080050
ISBN: 0-88296-275-2

BOOKS IN THIS SERIES

CHINA
JAPAN
INDIA
SOUTHEAST ASIA
AFRICA
SOVIET UNION
THE UNITED STATES
AMERICAN NEIGHBORS

THE FIDELER COMPANY Grand Rapids, Michigan

CHINA

CONTRIBUTORS

Chu-yuan Cheng

Chu-yuan Cheng is Professor of Economics at Ball State University, Muncie, Indiana. He was formerly Senior Research Economist in the Center for Chinese Studies at the University of Michigan. Professor Cheng is the author of several books and numerous articles on the economy of China. His most recent book is *China's Economic Development: Growth and Structural Change.*

Earl Heuer

Earl Heuer is a specialist in Chinese studies and political science. He has taught at Grand Valley State College in Allendale, Michigan, and at Victoria University in Wellington, New Zealand. Mr. Heuer has made four trips to the Republic of China. He visited first in the summer of 1976, shortly before the death of Mao Tse-tung, and again in 1978, 1979, and 1980.

Betty-Jo Buell
Nancy Crittenden
Margaret DeWitt
Raymond E. Fideler
Deborah Hendricks
Florence Jachim
Mary Mitus
Connie Negaran
Janet M. Ott
Bev J. Roche
Marion H. Smith
Alice W. Vail
Joanna Van Zoest
Ellen Walters
Audrey Witham

People watching a swimming meet in Peking, the capital city of China. There are more than one billion people living in China. No other country in the world has such a large population.

CONTENTS

The Great Wall of China was built centuries ago to keep enemy tribes from invading China's fertile farmlands. It winds for more than fifteen hundred miles over hills and mountains in northern China.

A Global View of Asia

If you could view the earth from a space station, you would notice that its curved surface is covered mainly with water. Lying like enormous islands in the water are several great masses of land. By far the largest of these masses is Eurasia, which is located on the opposite side of the earth from North America.

Human beings have been living in Eurasia for at least one million years. Long ago, the people in the westernmost part of this landmass developed a civilization that differed greatly from the civilizations in the eastern part. As time went on, the western part of Eurasia came to be called Europe. The rest of this landmass came to be known as Asia, or the East. Geographers today generally agree that Europe and Asia are divided by an imaginary line extending from the Caspian Sea northward along the Ural Mountains to the Arctic Ocean. To the south, Europe and Asia are separated by the Caucasus Mountains and by the Black and Aegean seas. (See map at right.)

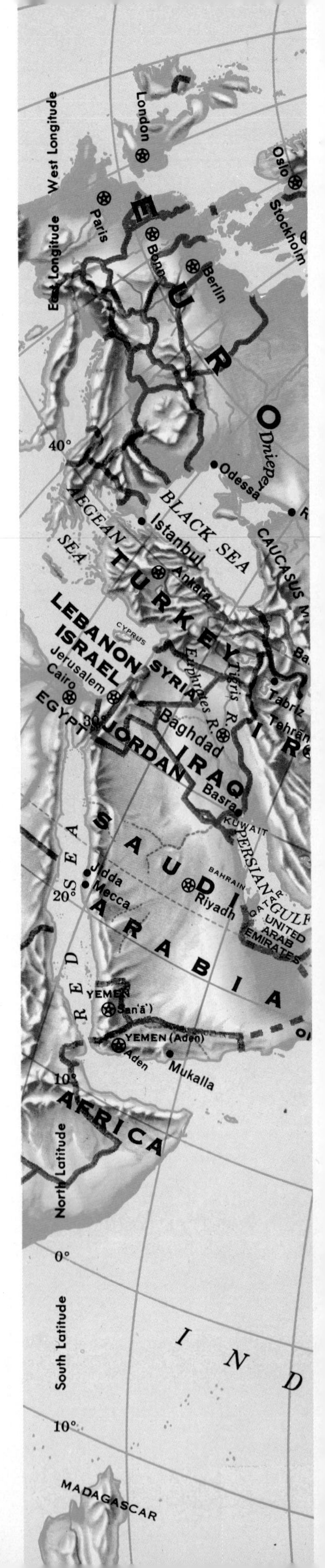

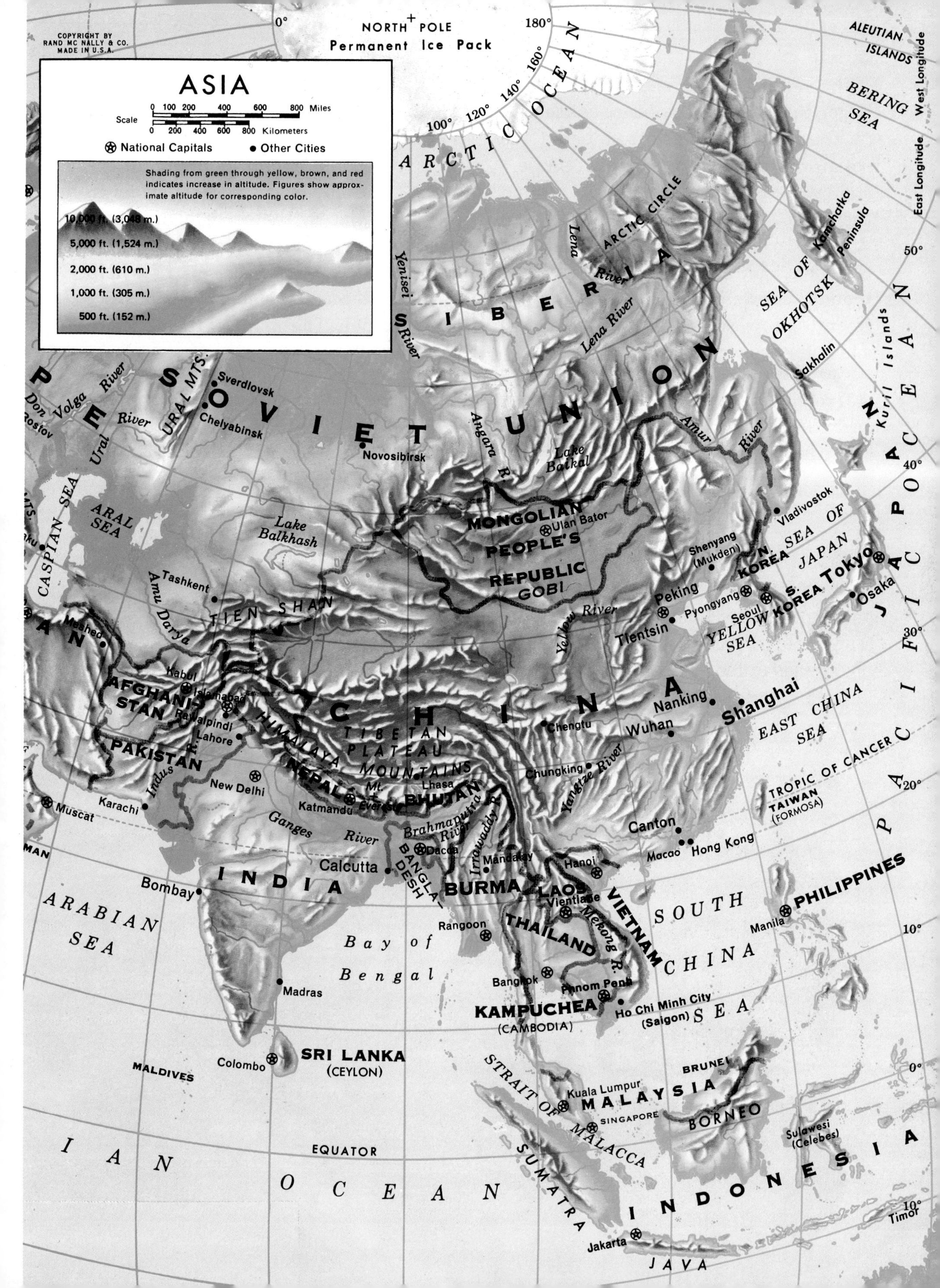

COPYRIGHT BY RAND MC NALLY & CO. MADE IN U.S.A.
ASIA
Scale
0 100 200 400 600 800 Miles
0 200 400 600 800 Kilometers
National Capitals
Other Cities
Shading from green through yellow, brown, and red indicates increase in altitude. Figures show approximate altitude for corresponding color.
10,000 ft. (3,048 m.)
5,000 ft. (1,524 m.)
2,000 ft. (610 m.)
1,000 ft. (305 m.)
500 ft. (152 m.)
NORTH POLE
Permanent Ice Pack
0°
180°
160°
140°
120°
100°
ARCTIC OCEAN
ALEUTIAN ISLANDS
BERING SEA
West Longitude
East Longitude
ARCTIC CIRCLE
Kamchatka Peninsula
SEA OF OKHOTSK
Sakhalin
Kuril Islands
Lena River
Yenisei River
SIBERIA
SOVIET UNION
Sverdlovsk
Chelyabinsk
Novosibirsk
URAL MTS.
Ural River
Volga River
Don
Rostov
Angara R.
Lake Baikal
Amur River
Vladivostok
CASPIAN SEA
ARAL SEA
Lake Balkhash
Baku
MONGOLIAN PEOPLE'S REPUBLIC
Ulan Bator
GOBI
Shenyang (Mukden)
N. KOREA
S. KOREA
Pyongyang
Seoul
SEA OF JAPAN
JAPAN
Tokyo
Osaka
Tashkent
TIEN SHAN
Amu Darya
Meshed
Peking
Tientsin
Yellow River
YELLOW SEA
Kabul
AFGHANISTAN
Islamabad
Rawalpindi
Lahore
PAKISTAN
Indus R.
HIMALAYA MOUNTAINS
TIBETAN PLATEAU
CHINA
Chengtu
Nanking
Shanghai
Wuhan
EAST CHINA SEA
Chungking
Yangtze River
NEPAL
Mt. Everest
Lhasa
BHUTAN
New Delhi
Katmandu
Karachi
Muscat
Ganges River
Brahmaputra River
Irrawaddy R.
TROPIC OF CANCER
TAIWAN (FORMOSA)
Canton
Macao
Hong Kong
Dacca
BANGLADESH
Calcutta
Mandalay
Hanoi
INDIA
Bombay
BURMA
LAOS
Vientiane
VIETNAM
Mekong R.
THAILAND
PHILIPPINES
Manila
ARABIAN SEA
Rangoon
Bay of Bengal
SOUTH CHINA SEA
Bangkok
Phnom Penh
Ho Chi Minh City (Saigon)
KAMPUCHEA (CAMBODIA)
Madras
SRI LANKA (CEYLON)
Colombo
MALDIVES
STRAIT OF MALACCA
BRUNEI
Kuala Lumpur
MALAYSIA
SINGAPORE
BORNEO
Sulawesi (Celebes)
EQUATOR
INDIAN OCEAN
SUMATRA
INDONESIA
Jakarta
JAVA
Timor
PACIFIC OCEAN
50°
40°
30°
20°
10°
0°

The world's largest continent. Asia is larger than any of the other continents on the earth. It extends from below the equator* to above the Arctic Circle,* and stretches nearly halfway around the world. About one third of the total land surface of the globe is included in this giant continent. The map on pages 6 and 7 shows that there are many different countries in Asia. Some are large and some are very small.

A continent of contrasts. The map on pages 6 and 7 also shows that Asia has a great variety of land features. In some parts of this vast continent, there are broad, level lowlands and deep valleys. In other places, there are high, windswept plateaus and ranges of towering mountains. These highland barriers help to divide the continent of Asia into six main regions. The map on the opposite page shows these regions.

*See Glossary

The Himalayas are the highest mountains in the world. Locate these and other highlands on the map on pages 6 and 7. How can you tell which areas are highlands and which are lowlands?

REGIONS OF ASIA

East Asia includes Japan, North and South Korea, and much of China. Taiwan and Hong Kong are located here also. There are more people living in East Asia than in any other part of the world.

Southeast Asia is a tropical, rainy region made up of islands and peninsulas. It includes the countries of Burma, Thailand, Kampuchea (also called Cambodia), Laos, Vietnam, Malaysia, Singapore, Indonesia, Brunei, and the Philippines.

South Asia includes the large, triangle-shaped peninsula on which the countries of India, Pakistan, and Bangladesh are located. It also includes the island countries of the Maldives and Sri Lanka (formerly Ceylon) and the three mountainous countries of Afghanistan, Nepal, and Bhutan. South Asia is one of the most densely populated parts of the world.

Chinese and Mongolian Middle Asia includes the Mongolian People's Republic as well as Sinkiang, Inner Mongolia, and Tibet, which are parts of China. It is a thinly populated region of deserts, grasslands, plateaus, and high mountains.

Soviet Asia includes the vast area known as Siberia, as well as the other parts of the Soviet Union that are located on the continent of Asia. Much of this region is thinly populated.

Southwest Asia includes Turkey, Iran, Iraq, Syria, Lebanon, Israel, Jordan, and all of the countries on the Arabian Peninsula. (See map on pages 6 and 7.) It also includes the island of Cyprus and a small part of Egypt. Three major religions—Judaism, Christianity, and Islam—began in this dry, rugged region. Some of the world's largest reserves of oil are located in Southwest Asia.

Using Natural Resources

See page 195

The picture above shows elephants moving heavy logs in Thailand. Forests are an important natural resource in some parts of Asia. Other gifts of nature found on this continent include rich mineral deposits, swiftly flowing rivers, and fertile soil. In spite of their natural wealth, most countries in Asia are very poor. Why do you suppose the people of this continent have not been able to make greater use of their natural resources?

A continent of rich resources. Some parts of Asia contain great natural wealth. Vast deposits of coal and petroleum are located on this continent. Asia is also rich in tin and other minerals needed by modern industry. It has large forests, and rushing rivers that could be used to produce hydroelectric power. In much of Asia, the land and climate are poor for growing crops. However, this continent also has large areas of fertile farmland.

A continent with a huge population. In a continent so large and so rich in natural resources, you would expect to find many people. The map on pages 12 and 13 shows that this idea is correct. More than two and one-half billion people live in Asia today. This is about six tenths of the world's population.

All parts of Asia are not equally crowded. As the map on pages 12 and 13 shows, a large part of the continent has almost no people. Other parts are densely populated. Why do you think Asia's population is distributed so unevenly? The map on pages 6 and 7 and the map below provide clues that may help you answer this question.

The home of many different peoples. Asia's people are divided into hundreds of separate groups. These groups differ greatly in their customs and ways of living. They also speak different languages. For example, there are fourteen major languages in India alone.

A continent with a long history. People have been living in Asia for hundreds of thousands of years. Some of the world's

Continued on page 14.

The amount of rainfall differs from place to place on the continent of Asia. What are some ways in which rainfall helps to determine where people live? You may wish to do research in other sources before answering this question.

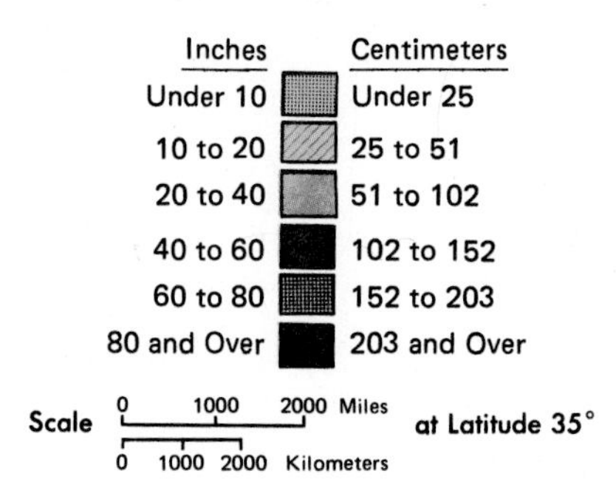

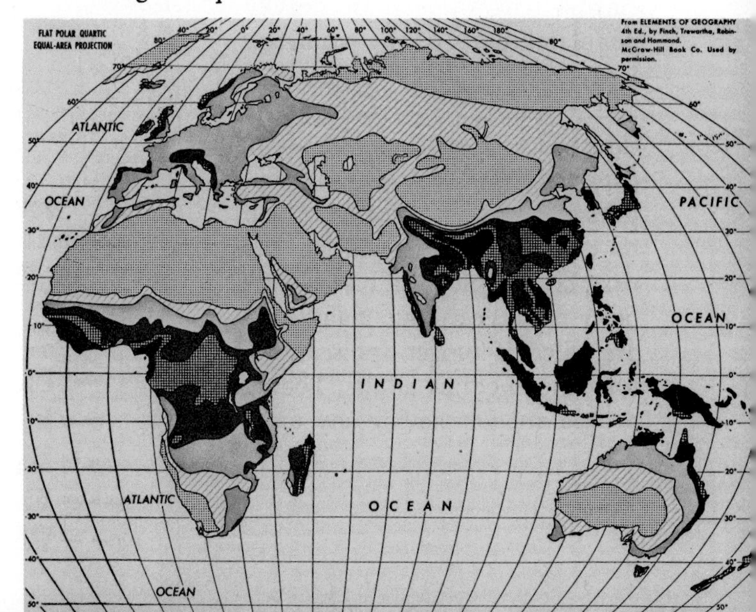

A crowded street in Ho Chi Minh City, Vietnam. About six tenths of the world's people live in Asia. Most of them are in South and East Asia. Why are these two areas so heavily populated?

WORLD POPULATION

About four and one-half billion people live in the world today. If all these people were distributed evenly over the earth there would be about seventy-nine people living on each square* mile (30 per sq. km.) of land. This is not the case, however. The map at right shows that some areas are very crowded, while others are almost empty. The three most heavily populated parts of the world are East Asia, South Asia, and Europe.

The world's population is more than twice as large as it was only fifty years ago. Larger food supplies and better medical care help to explain this increase. In the past, large numbers of babies were born each year, but many children died of hunger or disease before they became adults. Today, people are not having any more

*See Glossary

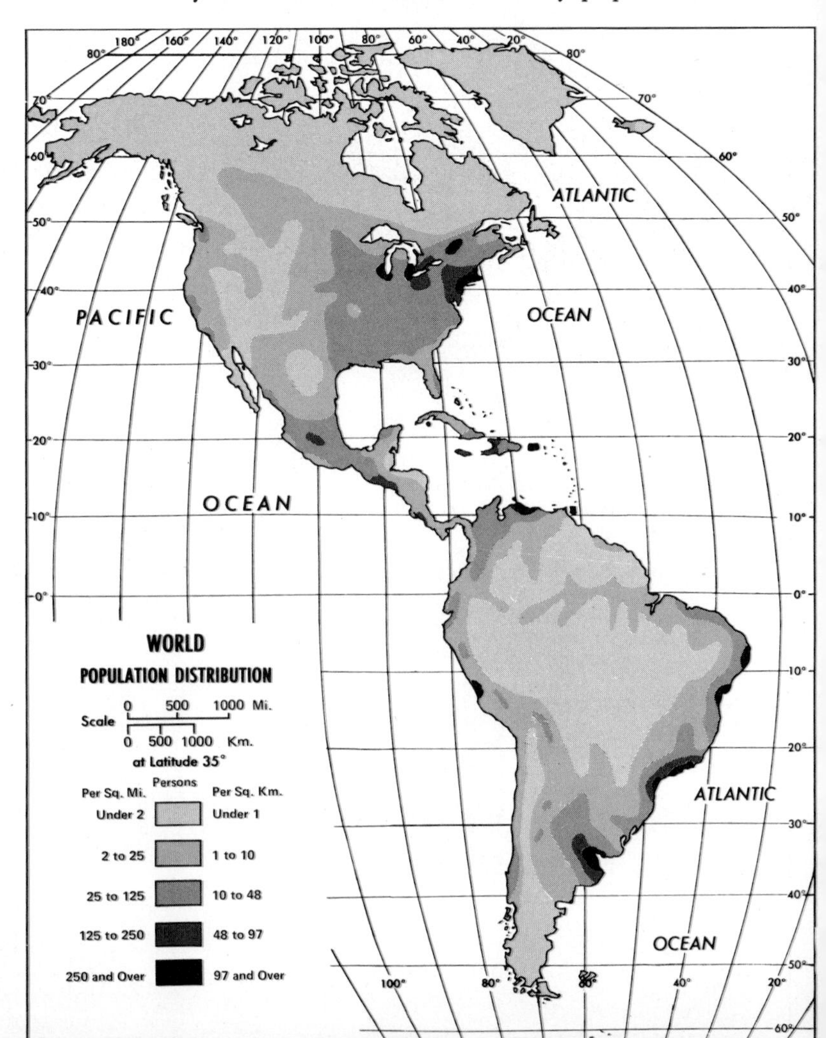

children than before. However, more children are living to become adults and to have children of their own. It is mainly for this reason that the world's population has been growing so rapidly. If it continues at its present rate, world population will probably double again within about forty years.

In the developing countries of the world, families are generally larger than they are in the developed nations. (See map on page 165.) As a result, the population of the developing countries is increasing more rapidly. For example, population is growing about three times as fast in Vietnam as it is in Japan.

The rapid growth of population is a serious problem for all the people of the world. Each year, human beings are using larger and larger amounts of the earth's resources. Many experts believe that population growth must slow down if people everywhere are to have an opportunity to meet their needs.

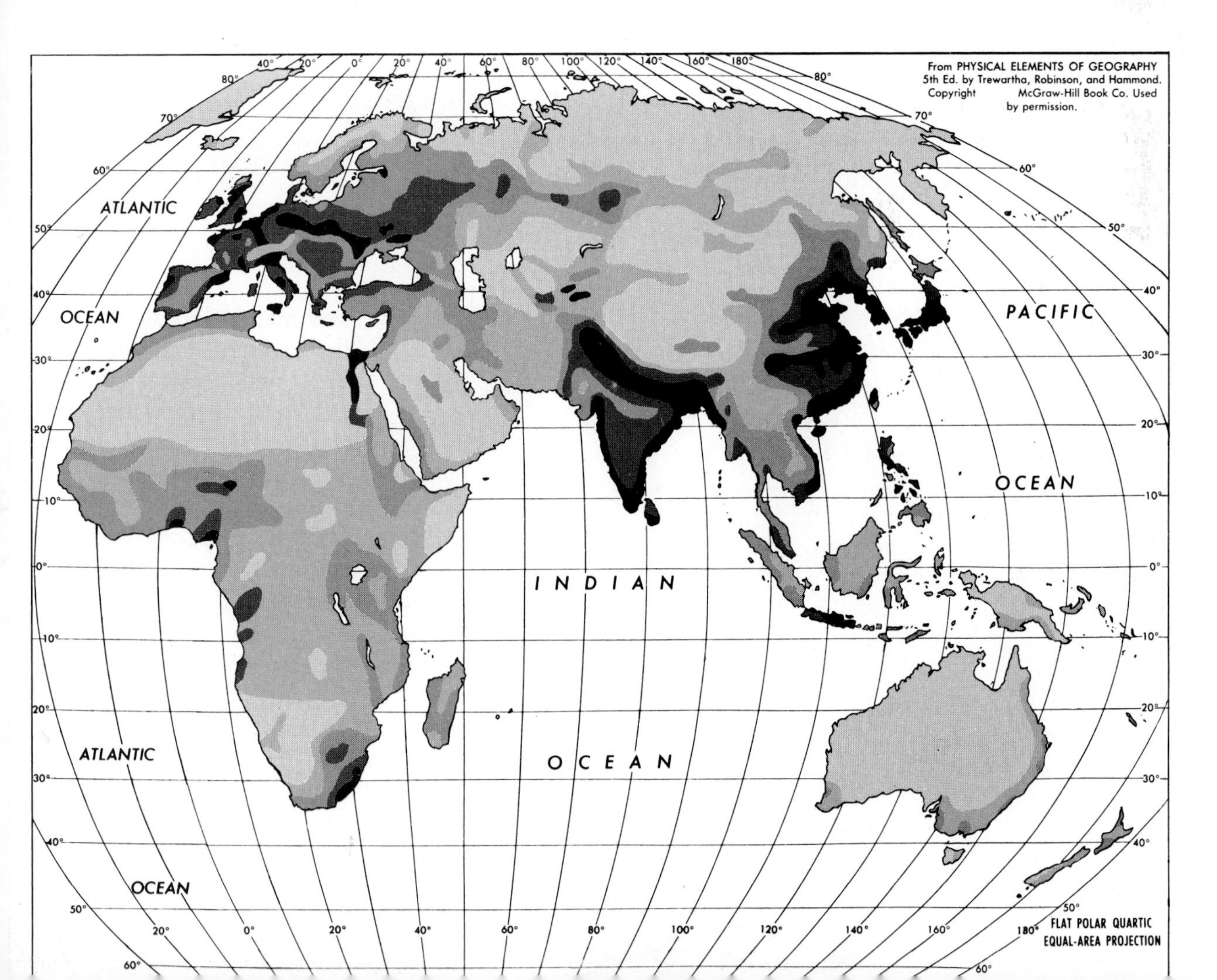

first civilizations arose here. Asia has been the home of many great artists, writers, and thinkers. All of the world's major religions developed here. People in Asia produced many inventions that still affect our lives. For example, printing was invented in China, and iron making developed in what is now Turkey. Over the centuries, many great cities grew up in Asia. These cities were famous for their wealth and beauty.

A continent that has seen great changes. During the 1800's, several powerful Western* nations took over large areas in Asia. Among these countries were Great Britain, France, and the Netherlands. They had strong national governments and a great deal of industry. In most Asian countries, the national government was very weak. Many people felt more loyalty to their own small groups than they did to the nation as a whole. Also, the Asian countries had little industry. It was these weaknesses that made it possible for Western countries to take over large areas in Asia. (See map below.)

In the early years of this century, a new feeling arose in the hearts of many Asians. They wanted to

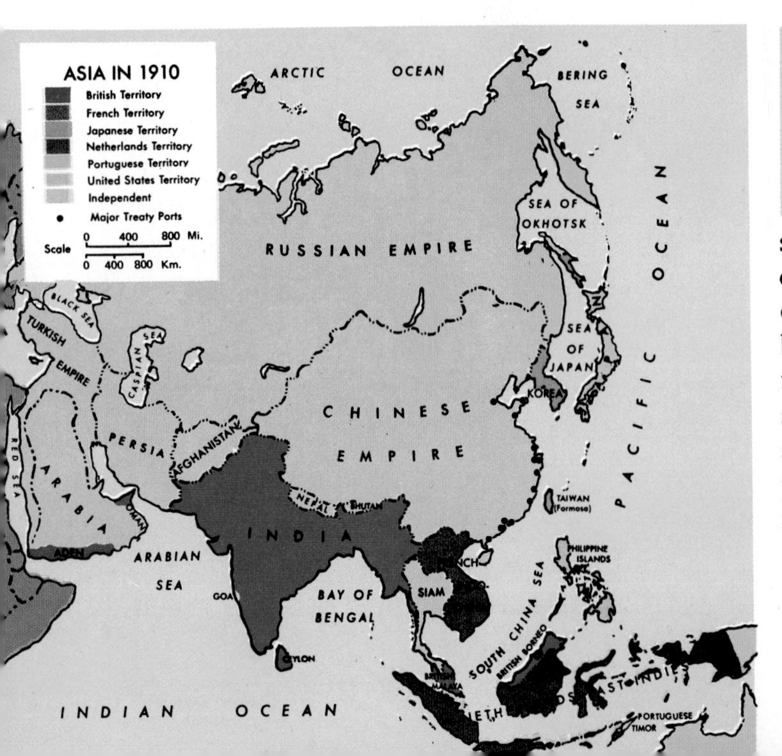

Colonialism

The map at left shows the areas of Asia that were independent in 1910 and the areas that were under colonial rule. Several countries shown as independent were actually under the influence of stronger nations. For example, the great Chinese Empire had been forced to sign treaties* that allowed foreign nations to control several of its seaports. During and after World War I and World War II, many changes took place in Asia. You may wish to make maps similar to this one in which you show Asia in 1930, in 1950, and today. Refer to pages 201-203 for help in finding the information you need.

*See Glossary

Parliament House in New Delhi, India's capital. The national lawmaking body of India meets here. In the years that followed World War II, India and many other countries in Asia became independent. What was the main reason for this? What problems did the newly independent countries face?

form strong, independent nations of their own. This feeling is known as nationalism. As time passed, nationalism helped Asians to win their freedom from Western rule. Today, Asia is the home of about forty independent nations.

To see how nationalism arose in Asia, let us look at the history of Indonesia. This country is located on a group of islands in Southeast Asia. (See map on pages 6 and 7.) In early times, Indonesia was divided into many small, quarreling states. During the eighteenth century, people from the Netherlands began taking over Indonesia. They set up a strong colonial government. Later, roads, railroads, and a shipping line were established. These brought the people into closer contact with each other. Some Indonesians had a chance to attend Western schools. There they learned new ideas about freedom and self-government. They also came to realize that the Western nations were getting most of the benefit from Southeast Asia's rich resources.

All of these things helped the growth of nationalism in Indonesia. After World War II* ended, the Indonesians refused to live under foreign rule any longer. They fought hard for their independence and won it.

A continent whose people are seeking a better way of life. Independence did not solve all the problems facing the people of Asia. Today, most Asian countries are very poor. Although they have rich resources, these resources have not been fully developed. There is little modern industry. Most of the people still make their living by farming. Millions of Asians suffer from hunger and disease. There are not enough roads, schools, or hospitals.

In the past, many Asians took their poverty for granted. They did not know that there was any other way of life. This is no longer true. In movies and foreign magazines, Asians see healthy people who have better food, clothing, and housing than they do. They also see cars, television sets, and other products commonly used in Western countries. As a result, people in Asia are now demanding a better way of life for themselves.

In this book, you will be exploring one of the most important countries in Asia—the People's Republic of China. As you do research, try to discover how China is similar to other Asian countries. Also look for ways in which it differs from them. For example, did China have to struggle for independence from foreign rule? Do China's people face the same problems as other Asians? If so, how are they trying to solve these problems and achieve a better way of life?

Plowing a rice field on the island of Java. Most of Asia's people live in small villages and earn their living by farming. They are generally very poor. In the past, Asians took their poverty for granted, but now they are demanding a better life. How did this change come about?

CHINA

An Overview of China

A country with more people than any other. In the eastern part of Asia is the enormous country of China. (See map on pages 6 and 7.) It extends from the Pacific Ocean westward more than halfway across the continent. More than one billion people make their homes in China today. No other country has such a large population.

A country with a long history. The Chinese can trace their history back about four thousand years. During much of this time, China was a great and powerful country. Travelers from distant lands came to admire the wonders of China's civilization.

Proud of their achievements, the people of China paid little attention to changes taking place in other parts of the world. By the 1800's, some of the Western* countries were developing a new way of life based on industry and trade. They became powerful enough to force China to sign treaties* giving them certain privileges. As a result, China no longer had full control over its own territory. In the years that followed, China was weakened still further by wars and revolutions.

A Communist nation. In 1949 the Chinese Communist Party gained control of China. The Communists established a strong government that allows no opposition to its rule. This government is trying to make China into a powerful and prosperous nation. As you do research in this book, try to discover how China's leaders are trying to achieve their goal.

*See Glossary

Chinese Names in This Book

The Chinese language does not have an alphabet like ours. (See pages 182-183.) Therefore, various systems have been developed for writing Chinese words in our alphabet. One system that has been widely used for many years is the Wade-Giles system. It was developed in the late 1800's. In this book, the Wade-Giles system is used for spelling most of the names of persons, cities, and geographical features such as rivers and mountain ranges.

During recent years, the Chinese government has been using a new system of writing that also has the same alphabet as ours. This system is called Pinyin. It differs from Wade-Giles in the spelling of many Chinese names. For example, China's capital city is "Peking" in Wade-Giles and "Beijing" in Pinyin. Today, Pinyin is gaining wide acceptance in the Western world. The maps on pages 20-21 and 82 give the Pinyin spellings for the names of Chinese cities and provinces. In the Glossary, you will find the Pinyin spellings of other common Chinese names.

In China the names of people are written just the opposite of the way they are in our country. The family name comes first, and the given name comes last. Thus, Mao Tse-tung would be known as "Mr. Mao" rather than as "Mr. Tse-tung."

A parade in Tien An Men Square, in Peking. China is ruled by a Communist government. What is communism? How does the way of life developed by the Communists in China differ from the way of life in our country? Use the Table of Contents to help you locate the information you need.

Pinyin† spellings of cities appearing on this map.

	Pinyin
Anshan	Anshan
Canton	Guangzhou
Changchun	Changchun
Changsha	Changsha
Chengchou	Zhengzhou
Chengtu	Chengdu
Chichihaerh	Qiqihar
Chihsi	Jixi
Chinchou	Jinzhou
Chungking	Chongqing
Foochow	Fuzhou
Fushun	Fushun
Fusin	Fuxin
Hangchow	Hangzhou
Hantan	Handan
Harbin	Harbin
Hengyang	Hengyang
Hofei	Hefei
Hsiangtan	Xiangtan
Huainan	Huainan
Huhehot	Hohhot
Kaifeng	Kaifeng
Kalgan	Zhangjiakou
Kirin	Jilin
Kueiyang	Guiyang
Kunming	Kunming
Lanchou	Lanzhou
Lhasa	Lhasa
Liaoyang	Liaoyang
Loyang	Luoyang
Luta	Luda
Mutanchiang	Mudanjiang
Nanchang	Nanchang
Nanking	Nanjing
Nanning	Nanning
Paoting	Baoding
Paotou	Baotou
Peking	Beijing
Penchi	Benxi
Pinghsiang	Pingxiang
Poshan	Boshan
Shanghai	Shanghai
Shenyang	Shenyang
Shihchiachuang	Shijiazhuang
Sian	Xian
Soochow	Suzhou
Suchow	Xuzhou
Swatow	Shantou
Taiyuan	Taiyuan
Tangshan	Tangshan
Tientsin	Tianjin
Tsaochuang	Zaozhuang
Tsinan	Jinan
Tsingtao	Qingdao
Tzukung	Zigong
Urumchi	Ürümqi
Wuhan	Wuhan
Wuhsi	Wuxi
Yenan	Yanan
TAIWAN	
Chilung	Jilong
Kaohsiung	Gaoxiong
Taichung	Taizhong
Tainan	Tainan
Taipei	Taibei

†See page 18.

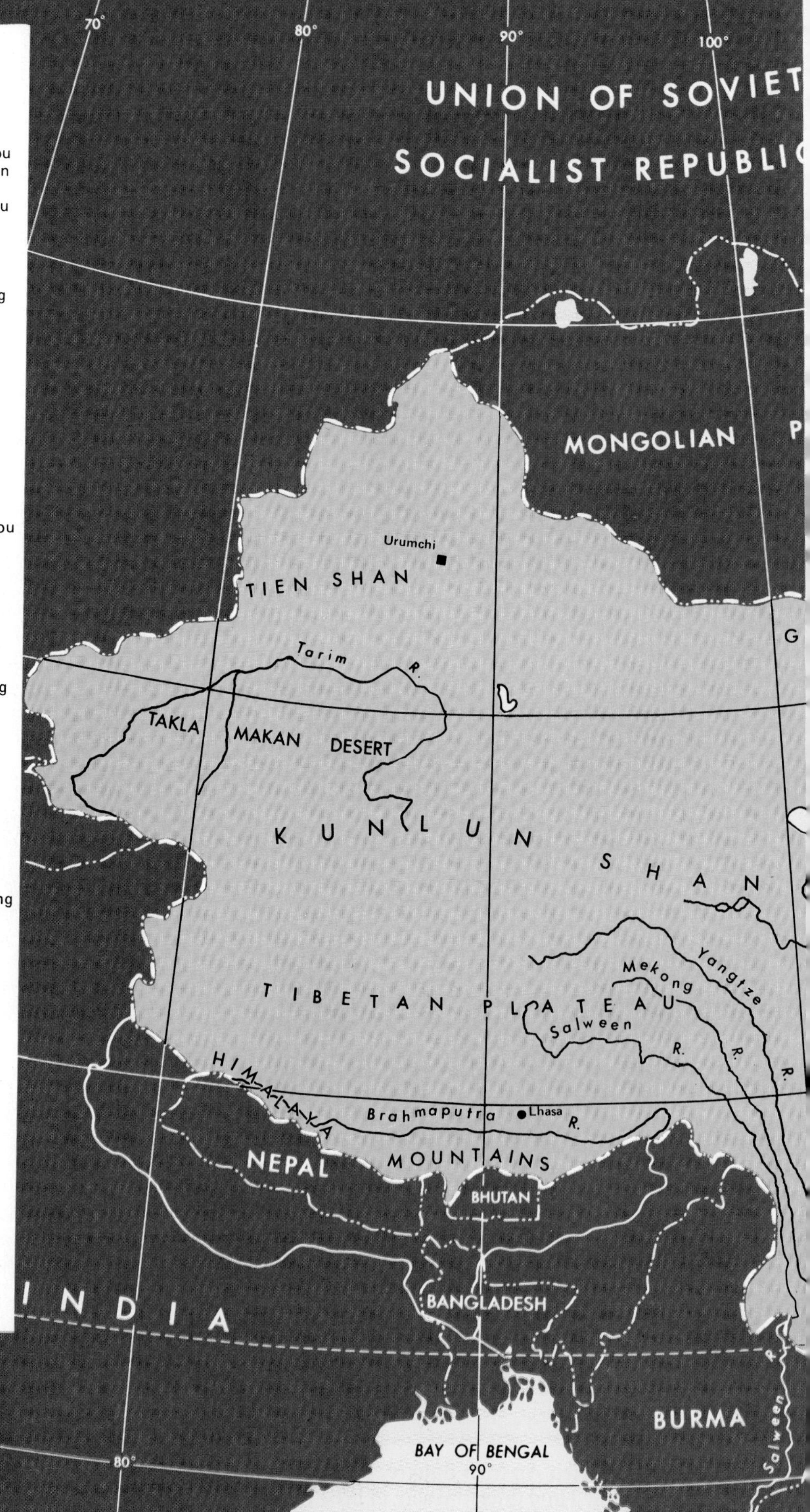

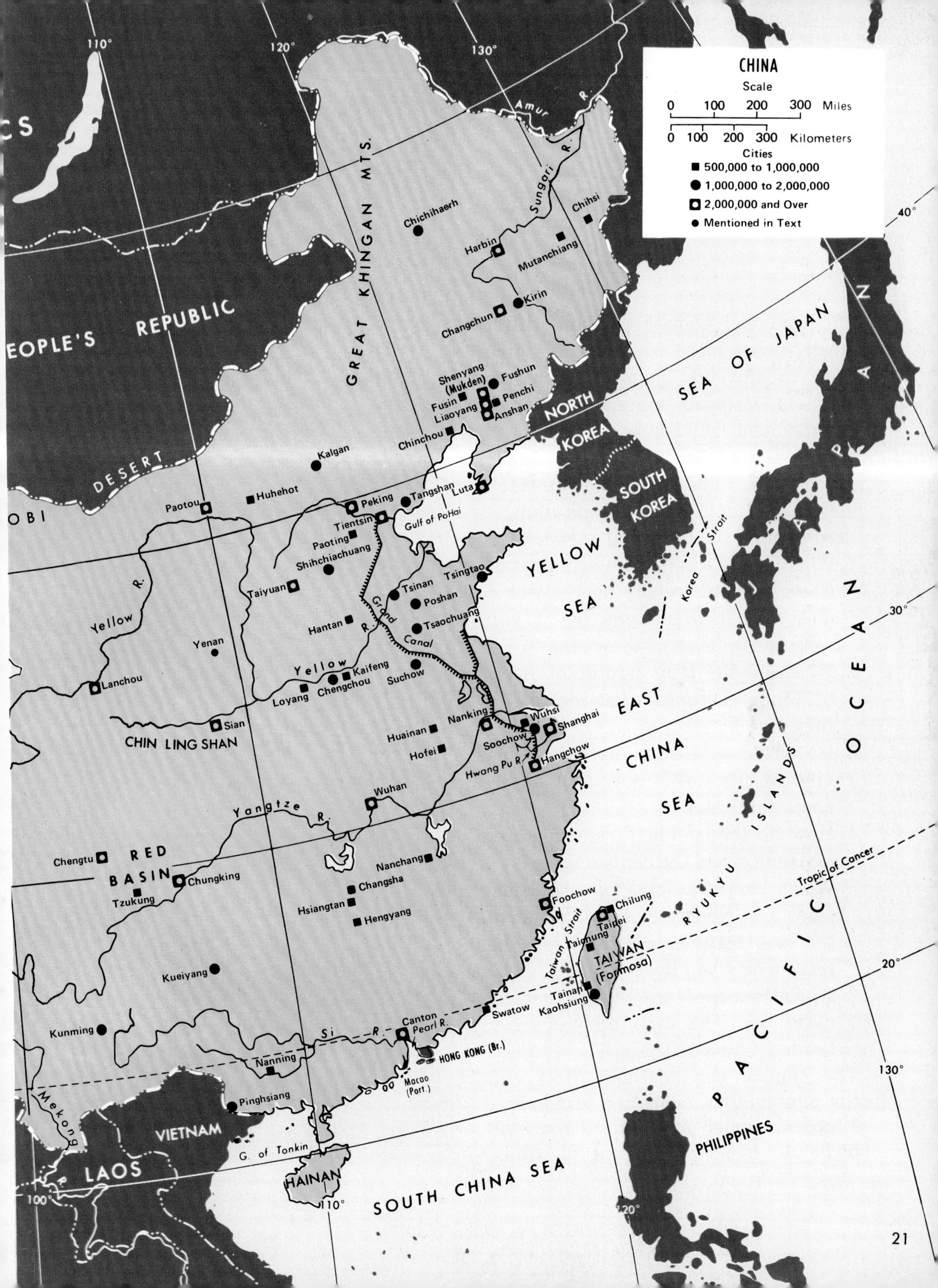
CHINA
Scale
0 100 200 300 Miles
0 100 200 300 Kilometers
Cities
500,000 to 1,000,000
1,000,000 to 2,000,000
2,000,000 and Over
Mentioned in Text
PEOPLE'S REPUBLIC
GOBI
DESERT
GREAT KHINGAN MTS.
Amur R.
Sungari R.
Chichihaerh
Harbin
Chihsi
Mutanchiang
Kirin
Changchun
Shenyang (Mukden)
Fushun
Fusin
Penchi
Liaoyang
Anshan
Chinchou
Kalgan
Luta
Tangshan
Peking
Huhehot
Paotou
Tientsin
Gulf of PoHai
Paoting
Shihchiachuang
Taiyuan
Tsinan
Tsingtao
Poshan
Tsaochuang
Hantan
Grand Canal
Yellow R.
Yenan
Kaifeng
Chengchou
Loyang
Suchow
Lanchou
Sian
CHIN LING SHAN
Nanking
Wuhsi
Shanghai
Soochow
Hwong Pu R.
Hangchow
Huainan
Hofei
Wuhan
Yangtze R.
Chengtu
RED BASIN
Chungking
Tzukung
Nanchang
Changsha
Hsiangtan
Hengyang
Kueiyang
Kunming
Foochow
Chilung
Taipei
Taichung
TAIWAN (Formosa)
Tainan
Kaohsiung
Taiwan Strait
Swatow
Canton
Pearl R.
Si R.
HONG KONG (Br.)
Macao (Port.)
Nanning
Pinghsiang
Mekong
VIETNAM
LAOS
G. of Tonkin
HAINAN
SOUTH CHINA SEA
PHILIPPINES
NORTH KOREA
SOUTH KOREA
SEA OF JAPAN
JAPAN
YELLOW SEA
Korea Strait
EAST CHINA SEA
RYUKYU ISLANDS
PACIFIC OCEAN
Tropic of Cancer
110°
120°
130°
40°
30°
20°
100°

Part 1
Land and Climate

The land and climate of China differ greatly from place to place. In some parts of this vast country, there are high, snowcapped mountains, barren deserts, and windswept plateaus. In other parts of China, there are fertile valleys and plains. As you do research in Part 1 about China's land and climate, keep in mind the following questions:

1. Where are the main highland areas of China? Where are the main lowland areas? What would you see if you were to visit each of these areas?
2. What are the most important rivers of China. Through what regions do they flow?
3. Do all parts of China have the same kind of climate? If not, what differences are there?
4. How do the land and water features of China affect the climate there?
5. Which parts of China have land features and climate that are similar to the land features and climate in the place where you live?
6. What countries are China's nearest neighbors? What large body of water borders China on the east?

The maps on pages 6-7 and 20-21, and the photographs, maps, and text in Part 1 provide much information that will be helpful in answering these questions.

A farmer plowing a field with a team of oxen in North China. If you were to travel through China, you would see many hillsides covered with terraces that resemble huge stairsteps. What is the reason for these terraces? To answer this question, do research in Chapter 14.

In China there are high mountains, fertile lowlands, and vast plateaus. The photograph above shows a lake near Kunming, on the Yunnan-Kweichow Plateau. (See the map on pages 20 and 21 and the map at right.) What kind of land features would you see if you were to visit this part of China?

1 Land

A Problem To Solve

How do the land and water features of China affect the people who live there? To solve this problem, you first need to know what kinds of land and water features are found in China. Then you will need to consider how these features have affected:

1. the history of China
2. where China's people live
3. farming
4. transportation

Chapters 2, 3, 7, 14, and 17 contain additional information that will be helpful in solving this problem.

See pages 198-200

The People's Republic of China is the world's third largest country in area. Only the Soviet Union and Canada are larger. The United States is slightly smaller than China.

The enormous country of China is separated from other nations by highlands, deserts, and water. Along its southern and western borders rise some of the world's most rugged mountains.

To the north are many miles of barren deserts, and to the east is the vast Pacific Ocean.

The map below shows that China may be divided into three main regions. The regions of North China and South China are the most important parts of this country, for it is here that most of the people live and most of the crops are grown. To the west lies the vast, bleak region of Outer China. It includes about half of the country's land, yet only about one twentieth of China's people live here. Let's charter a plane and take a tour through these three regions. We shall follow the route shown on the map below.

South China. Our plane has just left an airport in the city of Shanghai, near the east coast. The map on pages 20 and 21 shows us that Shanghai is not far from the mouth of the great Yangtze River.* The Yangtze flows across South China to the Pacific Ocean. It is one of the longest rivers in the world.

As we fly westward high above the Yangtze River, we see that it flows through a flat plain. Our pilot tells us that this lowland extends about six hundred miles inland from the sea. It was formed of soil that was washed away from land farther upstream and carried here by the river. Green rice fields and busy cities cover most of the Yangtze River Plain. There are also many lakes in this area. Crisscrossing the countryside are a number of canals, which allow small boats to travel from one city to another.

*See Glossary

China's three main regions are North China, South China, and Outer China. Which two regions have the most people? What facts help to explain this?

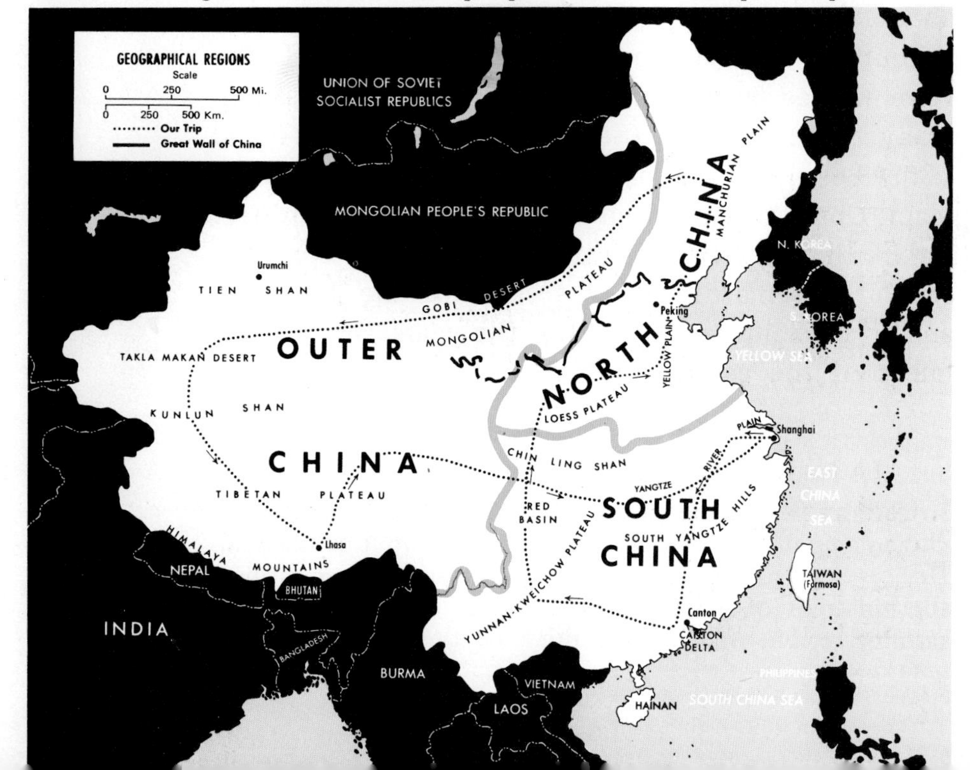

Soon our plane turns southward and we fly over the South Yangtze Hills. In river valleys between the hills we see more rice fields. Rice is also growing on terraces that rise like stairsteps on many hillsides. (See picture on pages 22 and 23.)

As we approach China's southern coast, we fly over another plain. This, too, was formed of soil deposited by rivers. It is much smaller than the Yangtze River Plain, and is dotted with hills. Here we see many fields of mulberry bushes, which are grown to provide food for silkworms. (See page 146.) In other fields, workers are harvesting rice or cutting sugarcane. This plain is called the Canton Delta, for near the center lies the great city of Canton.*

Our pilot tells us about two large islands that lie off China's coasts. One of these is Hainan, located southwest of the Canton Delta. Most of Hainan is rugged and mountainous, but a narrow plain extends along much of the coast. The other island lies east of the Canton Delta, about one hundred miles from the mainland. It is known as Taiwan, or Formosa. Forested mountains cover much of this beautiful island. Most of Taiwan's people live in the lowlands on the island's western side. In the past, Taiwan was governed as part of China. Today it has a separate government. The feature on pages 179-181 explains how this came about.

Soon we are flying northwest of the Canton Delta. Here we see jagged hills that jut up into the sky in many strange shapes. (See picture on pages 134 and 135.) Long ago, this part of South China was a high plain. Under this area there were layers of limestone,* a rock that dissolves in water. In many places, underground streams dissolved sections of the limestone and formed huge caverns. Over the years, the roofs of many of the caverns fell in. The cavern walls that

Irrigating a field in the Canton Delta. The paddles on this machine scoop up water from the canal and dump it on the field. Devices such as this one have been used by Chinese farmers for hundreds of years. The Canton Delta is an important farming region. What do you think are the reasons for this?

remained standing are the strangely shaped hills we see in this part of China today.

As we fly farther west, the land rises gradually to form a plateau. Because most of this highland region lies in the provinces* of Yunnan and Kweichow, we call this the Yunnan-Kweichow Plateau. Here we see valleys and plains. Where the land has not been plowed for crops, the countryside is green with trees and tall grass.

We fly northward across the Yunnan-Kweichow Plateau until we come to the bed of a great lake that dried up millions of years ago. This ancient lake bed is like a huge basin scooped out of the earth. It is bordered on the south by the plateau we just crossed. Mountain ranges surround it on the other sides. Because the rocks and soil of this great basin are purplish red in color, it is called the Red Basin. (See map on page 25.) The floor of the Red Basin is very hilly. We see terraced rice fields on the slopes of these hills.

North of the Red Basin, our plane rises to cross a range of rugged mountains

Terraced hillsides on the Loess Plateau. This area is made up of hills and mountains that have been partly covered with a powdery, yellow dust called loess. Where did the loess come from?

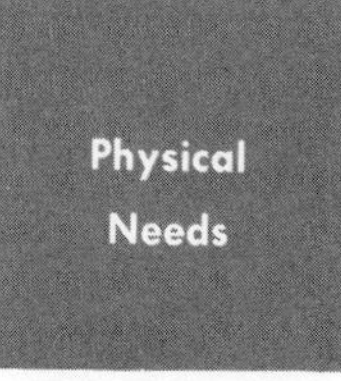

See pages 191-192

A canal on the Yellow Plain. The boats in this picture are carrying wheat that was grown in the fields nearby. The Yellow Plain is one of the most densely populated areas in China. Why do you suppose this is so? Do you think it is generally true that human beings live in the parts of the world where they are best able to meet their physical needs? Explain.

that tower as high as thirteen thousand feet above sea level. This is the Chin Ling Shan. As we fly over this range, we leave South China behind us.

North China. We are flying over North China now. Much of the countryside below us looks dusty and brown, instead of green as it was in much of South China.

The part of North China that lies just across the Chin Ling Shan is called the Loess Plateau. (See map on page 25.) It is made up of hills and mountains that have been partly covered with a powdery, yellow dust called loess. Winds have probably blown this dust out of the deserts that lie farther north. In places, the loess is three hundred feet thick. Rivers have cut deep gullies into this soft earth. In fields between the gullies and on terraced hillsides, we see wheat and millet* growing.

As we fly eastward from the Loess Plateau, we come to a huge lowland that extends all the way to the Pacific coast. This is the Yellow Plain. Many people live in this lowland, for the soil and climate are well suited to farming. China's capital, Peking, is located here.

Through the middle of the Yellow Plain flows the great Yellow River. It received its name because it is colored yellow by the silt* that it washes from the Loess Plateau. Each year, much of this silt settles to the bottom of the river, making it more shallow. Through the years, the river has often overflowed its banks and caused great damage to farms and villages nearby. For this reason, it is sometimes called "China's Sorrow." To help keep water from spilling over into their fields, the people of the Yellow Plain have built high dikes along the river's banks.

Hills and mountains rise along the northern edge of the Yellow Plain. We see the Great Wall of China winding across these highlands. (See picture on pages 4 and 5.) It was built centuries ago to protect people in the Yellow Plain from warlike tribes who lived in the grasslands and deserts farther to the north.

Northeast of the Great Wall we see another lowland, called the Manchurian Plain. This broad plain contains some of the most fertile farmland in China. It also has rich deposits of coal and other minerals. In one place we fly low enough to see power shovels scooping coal from a huge open pit. Besides farms and mines we see many cities on the Manchurian Plain. Heavy smoke rises from factory chimneys in these cities.

The Manchurian Plain is almost surrounded by mountains. The mountains to the east receive plenty of rain, and fine forests grow on their slopes. Grass covers most of the drier mountain slopes to the west.

Outer China. Now our pilot flies us over the mountains that border the Manchurian Plain on the west, and we head toward the lonely, dry region called Outer China. West of the mountains lies a high, rolling area called the Mongolian Plateau. It extends more than a thousand miles westward. In the eastern part of this vast plateau, enough rain falls for short grass to grow. As we fly across this grassland, we see flocks of sheep and goats, and herds of cattle, horses, and camels. Near them are round tents, called yurts, where groups of wandering shepherds live.

The Mongolian Plateau. Large herds of horses, cattle, and other animals graze on rolling hillsides in some parts of the Mongolian Plateau. Why are these areas used for pasturing livestock?

Farther west, the land is drier. The Gobi Desert stretches through this part of the Mongolian Plateau. In some places, the ground is covered with small stones and coarse sand. Strong desert winds have blown most of the topsoil from these wastelands.

Still farther west, we come to an even drier desert, called the Takla Makan. The part of the desert over which we are now flying is covered with great sand dunes.

To the north of the Takla Makan are snowcapped mountain peaks. This range is known as the Tien Shan, or "Heavenly Mountains." If we flew close to the Tien Shan, we could see patches of green between the mountains and the brown desert. These are oases* that get their water from mountain streams.

Our plane is flying south now. Ahead of us we see more mountain ranges. These are the rugged Kunlun Shan. (See map on page 25.) Our plane must climb very high to cross these snow-crowned mountains. In many places they rise twenty thousand feet above sea level. South of these mountains stretches the high Tibetan Plateau. Much of this area is too cold and dry even for grass to grow.

Near the southern border of the Tibetan Plateau we come to a fertile valley about twelve thousand feet above sea level. In this valley is Lhasa, the ancient capital of Tibet.* Beyond Lhasa are the lofty Himalaya Mountains. This mountain system separates China from the neighboring countries of India, Nepal, and Bhutan. One of the peaks in

The Tibetan Plateau is bordered on the south by the lofty Himalaya Mountains and on the north by the rugged Kunlun Shan. Sometimes this part of China is called the "roof of the world." Do you think this name is a good one? Explain why you think as you do.

The Yangtze River is one of the longest rivers in the world. It flows through deep gorges between the cities of Chungking and Wuhan. (See map on pages 20 and 21.) Where does the Yangtze River begin? What other important rivers begin in this same part of China?

the Himalayas is Mount Everest, the highest mountain in the world. It towers more than 29,000 feet above sea level.

From Lhasa, we begin our eighteen-hundred-mile journey back to Shanghai. On the way, our plane crosses the mountains in west central China where several important rivers begin.

Soon we are once again over South China. Below us, we glimpse the Yangtze River flowing through a rocky, steep-sided gorge.* As we come closer to Shanghai, we again see green rice fields. More and more towns and villages appear. When we compare this fertile region with the deserts and high plateaus of Outer China, we can see why most of China's people live in the eastern half of the country.

Using Natural Resources

See page 195

Chinese farmers winnowing rice. They toss the rice into the air with their shovels. The wind blows away the hulls and other waste materials, and the kernels fall to the ground. In certain parts of North China and all of South China, the climate is well suited to growing crops. Rainfall is plentiful, and there are many warm, sunny days. Would you say that rainfall and sunshine are important natural resources? Explain. Are there any other natural resources that farmers need in order to grow crops? If so, what are they?

2 Climate

A Problem To Solve

Not all parts of China have the same kind of climate. Why is this so? To solve this problem, you will need to discover how temperatures and rainfall in different parts of China are affected by:

1. mountain barriers
2. distance from the ocean
3. distance from the equator
4. winds
5. altitude above sea level

See pages 198-200

The enormous country of China has many different climates. If we were to travel through China at any season of the year, we could see green farmlands, brown deserts, and mountain peaks capped with sparkling white snow.

Climate in South China. The map on page 25 shows the three main regions of China. During the summer in South China, the weather is hot and rainy. The air is so damp in some places that books mold and leather shoes mildew overnight. Nearly everywhere, the countryside is fresh and green with trees, grass, and growing crops.

Warm winds, called the summer monsoons, help to bring this kind of weather to South China.

Rainfall in China. Which region of the country receives the most rainfall each year? Which regions receive the least?

AVERAGE ANNUAL RAINFALL

Inches	Centimeters
Under 10	Under 25
10 to 20	25 to 51
20 to 40	51 to 102
40 to 60	102 to 152
60 to 80	152 to 203
80 and Over	203 and Over

Because they come from the ocean, they are filled with moisture. When these winds blow across China, they lose much of their moisture in the form of rain.

In late summer and in autumn, fierce storms sometimes strike the coast of South China. These storms, which are called typhoons,* begin far out in the ocean. Typhoons cause great damage along China's southeastern coast. Enormous waves sink fishing boats, and sheets of driving rain flatten crops in the fields. Sometimes many people are killed.

Winter in South China is quite pleasant. In the southeastern part of this region, the temperature is cooler than in summer, but it is still warm enough to wear summer clothes most of the time. There is much less rain than in summer, but enough falls for crops to grow. Farmers work in their fields all winter long. In the northern part of South China, winter days are cooler than in the southern part. Snow sometimes falls, but in the daytime temperatures very seldom go below the freezing point.

When we look at South China on the globe, we can see one important reason why winters here are not very cold. Most of this region is nearer to the equator than the rest of China. The island of Hainan is so close to the equator that it has palm trees, banana plants, and other tropical plants.

The chilly weather that does come to South China is brought by cold winds called the winter monsoons. They blow out of the dry, frozen lands north of China. At the beginning of their journey, these winds are bitterly cold. On their long trip southward, however, they are warmed somewhat by the sun.

The winter monsoons do not reach all of South China. A high mountain range, called the Chin Ling Shan, lies just to the north of this region. This range prevents the winter monsoons from blowing across the western part of South China.

Climate in North China. Winters are colder in North China than they are in South China. As you have learned, the winter monsoons help cause this cold weather. These winds come from the cold, dry lands north of China. When they reach the Manchurian Plain, they

*See Glossary

are still bitterly cold. (See map on page 25.) Here, many of the people look quite fat, for they wear layer upon layer of thick, padded clothing to protect themselves from the cold. Farther south, winters are somewhat milder.

The winter monsoons are very dry, and they raise great clouds of yellow dust from fields and riverbeds. Sometimes these clouds of dust are so thick they hide the sun.

After a warm spring, hot summer weather comes to North China. Some days the temperature goes as high as one hundred degrees. Crops such as wheat, corn, and soybeans ripen under the blazing sun.

Most of the rain that falls in North China comes in summer. During most years, the amount of rainfall is about right for farming. Sometimes, however, there is not enough rain, and crops wither and die. In other years, there is so much rain that rivers overflow their banks and flood the land. Usually less rain falls here than in South China. The high mountains of the Chin Ling Shan help to cause this. They often prevent

A rainy August day in the South China province of Hunan. South China has hot, rainy summers and mild winters. Do you think this kind of climate is good for growing crops?

the warm, damp winds that blow across South China from bringing moisture to North China.

Climate in Outer China. The climate in Outer China is even drier than the climate in North China. Some parts of this region are dreary deserts that receive only about two inches of rainfall each year. When we compare the map on page 25 with the map on pages 6 and 7, we see that most of Outer China lies in the heart of Asia, far from any ocean. Mountain barriers prevent moisture-filled winds from bringing rain to much of the land.

If we were to travel through Outer China in July, we would need both summer and winter clothing. On the high Tibetan Plateau, summers are very cool. Still higher, on the mountain peaks, there is snow in midsummer. On the vast deserts of Outer China, the days are extremely hot. Soon after the sun goes down, however, the air becomes very cool.

Winters in Outer China are bitterly cold. Temperatures in some parts of the desert often drop far below freezing. On the Tibetan Plateau strong, icy winds blow much of the time. It is hard to realize that at the same time cold winter winds are blowing in these highlands, crops are growing in the warm sunshine of South China.

See page 194

Shoveling snow from a street in Peking. Winters in North China are generally dry, but snow falls from time to time. Whenever it snows in Peking, large numbers of people go out to shovel the snow from streets and sidewalks. Why do you suppose they do this? Do you agree with the old saying that "many hands make light work"? Explain. How do people in your own community work together to carry out important tasks?

The Gobi Desert covers part of the Mongolian Plateau in Outer China. To the west of the Gobi is an even drier desert called the Takla Makan. Why do you suppose Outer China is so dry?

Earthquakes

Earthquakes in China. Early in the morning on July 28, 1976, an earthquake struck the province of Hopeh in northeastern China. (See map on page 82.) Sixteen hours later, another earthquake struck the same area. These two quakes were so severe that the city of Tangshan in Hopeh was almost completely wiped out. The huge cities of Tientsin and Peking also suffered heavy damage. According to the Chinese government, about 242,000 people were killed in the 1976 earthquakes. Another 164,000 people were injured.

The worst earthquake disaster in history also took place in China. It is believed that about 830,000 persons lost their lives when an earthquake struck the province of Shensi in the year 1556.

Measuring earthquakes. Each year, thousands of earthquakes take place throughout the world. Most are so slight that they cause little or no damage. Some earthquakes occur in areas that are thinly populated. As a result, few people are killed or injured, and there is little damage to property. Each year, however, about a dozen earthquakes cause serious damage. Sometimes, earthquakes under the ocean create enormous waves that destroy towns or cities along the seacoast and kill thousands of people.

This picture shows damage in Peking caused by earthquakes that struck China on July 28, 1976.

In 1935, an American scientist named Charles F. Richter developed a scale for measuring the magnitude, or strength, of earthquakes. On this scale earthquakes are rated upwards from 1. Each whole number represents a strength ten times as great as the previous number. The strongest earthquakes ever recorded have been rated 8.9 on the Richter scale. The 1976 earthquakes in Tangshan rated 8.2 and 7.9, which means they were extremely severe.

The information used to calculate an earthquake's strength is obtained from an instrument called the seismograph. This instrument detects and records movements of the earth, even those that are much too slight for a person to notice. When an earthquake occurs, it causes wavelike movements through the entire earth. Seismograph stations have been built in various locations around the world to record the strength of these movements. When an earthquake occurs, scientists compare the seismograph readings at a number of different locations. In this way, they can determine just how strong the earthquake was and how large an area it affected.

What causes earthquakes? Today, scientists explain earthquakes through the theory of plate tectonics. According to this theory, the earth's outer layer consists of about twenty rigid plates that range in thickness from about forty-five to ninety miles. These plates are in slow, continuous motion. Sometimes two adjoining plates separate, slide past one another, or collide. Then the rocks at the edges break apart or crumple, causing an earthquake.

Where do earthquakes occur? The map at the top of the opposite page shows where most earthquakes strike. About three fourths of all earthquakes occur in a belt that circles the Pacific Ocean. Most of the remaining earthquakes occur in an area called the Alpine-Himalayan belt. This area extends from the mountains of western Europe all the way to eastern Asia.

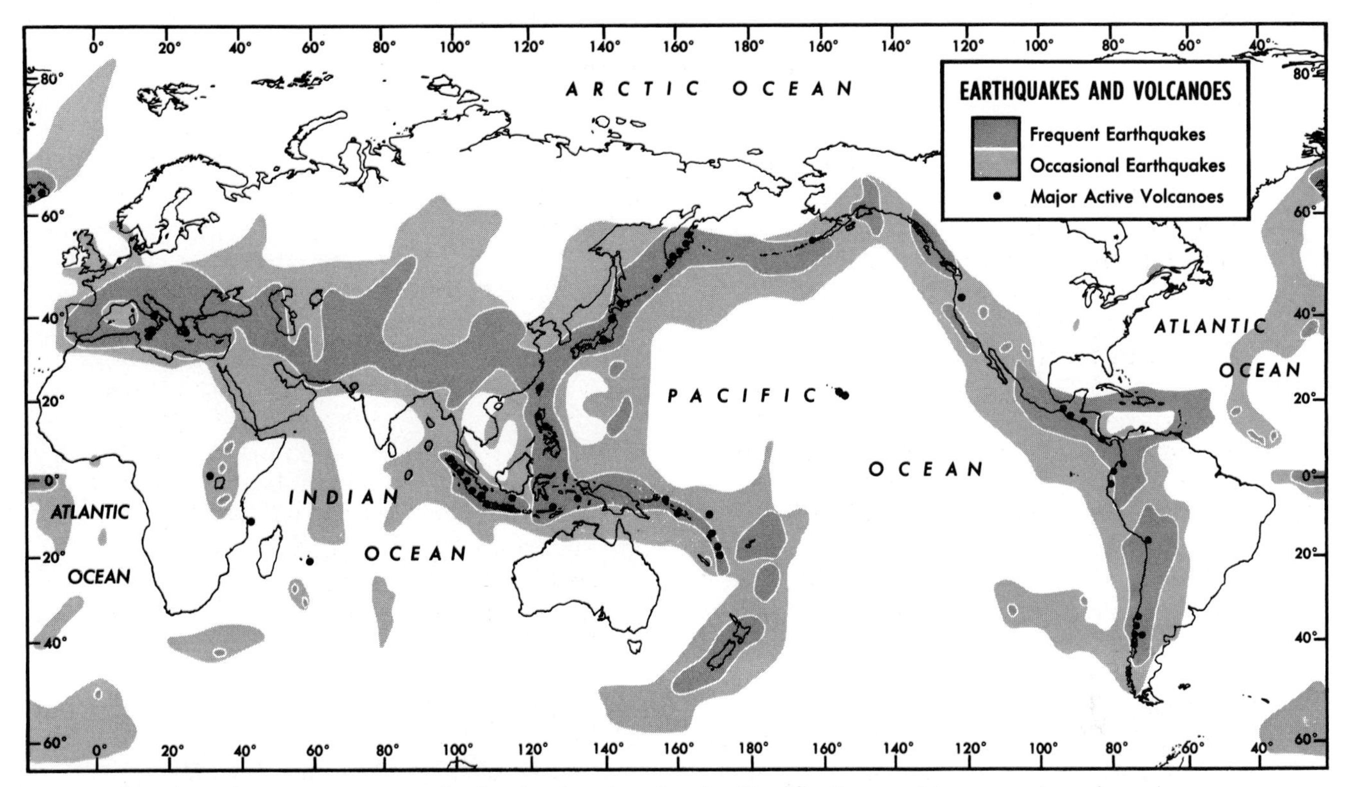

Earthquakes are common in lands that border the Pacific Ocean. Many earthquakes also occur in a mountainous zone that extends from western Europe all the way to eastern Asia.

Make a Relief Map

With a group of your classmates, make a relief map of China. Follow these steps:

1. Trace the country's outline from a large map of China. Use carbon paper to transfer this outline to a piece of heavy cardboard.
2. Using the map on pages 6 and 7 as a guide, form the highlands and lowlands of China with papier-mâché or clay.
3. After allowing it to dry thoroughly, paint your map. You may wish to use brown for high mountains, yellow for other highlands, and green for lowlands. You might use blue to show bodies of water.

Use Your Imagination

The Yangtze River is the most important river in China. Imagine that you have just taken a trip down this mighty waterway. Write a letter to a friend telling about this experience. Include information about the following:

a. where the Yangtze begins
b. where you began your trip
c. the areas through which the Yangtze flows
d. names of the large cities along its banks
e. the types of boats on the Yangtze
f. the importance of this river to the Chinese

Also, describe some of the interesting sights you saw. In writing your letter, use information in Chapters 1 and 17 of this book. Do additional research in outside sources. The suggestions on pages 201-203 will help you locate information. You may wish to illustrate your letter with pictures and a map.

Do Research About Floods

Over the centuries, rivers in China have often flooded. Do research in this book and other sources to answer the following questions:

1. What causes rivers to overflow their banks?
2. Where have some of China's most serious floods occurred?
3. What have the Chinese people done to prevent floods in their country?

When you have completed your research, organize your information and prepare an interesting oral report. (See "Making Reports," pages 204-206 of the Skills Manual.)

Part 2
History and Government

Historians sometimes say China has the world's oldest living civilization. As you do research about China's history and government in Part 2, try to find answers to the following questions.

1. When did civilization first arise in the land we now call China?
2. How did China first become united under a single government?
3. What were some of the customs and ideas that made up the way of life in old China? Why did this way of life change very little over the centuries?
4. What contributions made by the Chinese have enriched the lives of people throughout the world?
5. What changes took place in China after the arrival of people from Western* countries?
6. What form of government does China have today? How did it get this form of government?
7. How can a study of China's history help us to understand life in China today?

If you wish to do additional research in other sources, refer to the suggestions on pages 201-203 of this book.

*See Glossary

Change and Continuity

The Gate of Heavenly Purity. This building is located in a part of Peking called the Forbidden City, where China's emperors used to live. Today the Forbidden City is a public museum. The Chinese way of life has changed greatly under Communist rule. Yet many buildings and works of art from earlier times have been preserved. Why do you suppose this is so? Is it important for all people to understand and appreciate their country's history? Explain your answer.

Bronze vessels made in China during the Shang dynasty, more than three thousand years ago. Historians sometimes say that China has the world's oldest living civilization. What do you think they mean by this statement? When did civilization first begin to develop in China?

3 China Long Ago

Early people of China. No one knows for sure when people first came to the land we now call China. But scientists believe that a type of human being known as Peking man lived in caves on the Yellow Plain almost 400,000 years ago. Peking man may have been an ancestor of the people who live in China and other Asian countries today.

For thousands of years, the early Chinese lived in about the same way as people in other parts of the world. They gathered seeds and fruit and hunted wild animals for food. These hunters lived in small groups that traveled constantly from one place to another in search of game. They wore clothing made from animal skins. Their crude tools and weapons were made of stone.

Gradually, some of the people living in China learned how to plant and harvest crops. They began to grow millet,*

*See Glossary

barley, and other crops for food. They also raised animals such as pigs, sheep, and cattle. These people were China's first farmers.

After farming was introduced, people no longer had to travel from place to place in search of food. They settled down in villages and built simple houses out of wood, sun-dried mud, and other materials. From clay they made cooking pots and other vessels, which they sometimes painted in bright designs.

A great civilization arises in China. Nearly four thousand years ago, important changes began to take place in the Yellow Plain and other fertile areas of North China. Some of the people there discovered how to combine copper and tin to produce a useful metal called bronze. With this new metal, they could make better tools and weapons than ever before. The people of North China became highly skilled at crafts such as weaving and pottery making. They also developed a form of writing, with word symbols much like those used in China today. (See pages 182-183.) As the years passed, a number of small cities grew up in the lowlands of North China.

At that time, there were already three other great civilizations in the world. (See map at right.) Eventually, all three of these disappeared and were replaced by other civilizations. But the way of life developed by the early Chinese never died out entirely. For this reason, historians often say that China has the world's oldest living civilization.

It will help you understand why the Chinese civilization has been so long-lasting if you remember certain facts about China's geography. As you discovered on page 24, China is separated from neighboring countries by rugged mountains, barren deserts, and large bodies of water. As a result, the Chinese were able to develop their own special way of life without much interference from other people.

The Chinese establish a powerful empire. At the time civilization was developing in North China, much of this area was ruled by a family known as the Shang. The Shang dynasty* remained in power until about 1100 B.C. Then another group, called the Chou, became powerful enough to overthrow the Shang ruler and establish a dynasty of their own. Kings of the Chou dynasty ruled over parts of North China for more than eight hundred years.

During the Chou period, great changes took place in people's way of life. The Chinese learned how to make iron, which was better than bronze for tools

Four "cradles of civilization" were (1) the Nile River valley in Egypt; (2) Mesopotamia, the land between the Tigris and Euphrates rivers in what is now Iraq; (3) the Indus River valley in what is now Pakistan; and (4) the valley of the Yellow River in China. Do research to find out when civilization began to develop in each of these areas.

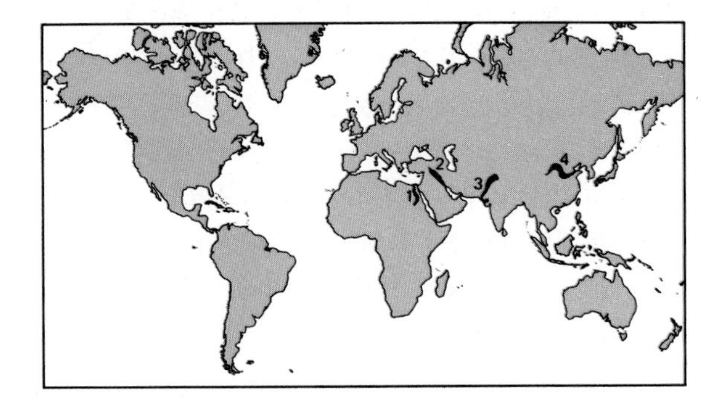

and weapons. Forests were cut down and swamps were drained to provide more farmland for the growing population. Trade increased, and cities grew larger. Writers began to produce important works of history and poetry. Great thinkers like Confucius* taught their ideas about the way people should behave. (See page 49.) These ideas have influenced Chinese life down to the present day.

As time passed, the Chou rulers lost much of their power. North China broke up into a number of small kingdoms that were constantly at war with each other. One of these kingdoms, which was ruled by the Ch'in family, became more powerful than any of the others. The Ch'in ruler Shih Huang Ti* was a highly skillful warrior. By conquering nearby territories and adding them to his kingdom, Shih Huang Ti built a great empire. For the first time, much of what is now China was united under a single government.

Many different dynasties rule over China. The Ch'in dynasty lasted for only a few years after the death of Shih Huang Ti in 210 B.C. Then it, too, was overthrown. During the centuries that followed, other dynasties gained control of China. Some of them, like the Han, the T'ang, and the Sung, ruled for hundreds of years. (See chart at right.) Others were in power for shorter periods of time. When a dynasty became weak, there was usually warfare as rival leaders fought to take over China. Sometimes these warriors gained control of certain areas and ruled them as separate kingdoms. Eventually a strong leader would unite the country once more.

Invaders from the north conquer China. To the north of China lay the vast grasslands of the Mongolian Plateau. These grasslands were the home of the Mongols and other nomads* who made their living by raising herds of livestock. The nomads were skillful horseback riders and fierce warriors. Through the years, they fought many battles against

CHINA'S MAIN DYNASTIES

Shang: Approx. 1700 B.C. to 1100 B.C.
Written records; bronze and pottery.

Chou: Approx. 1100 B.C. to 256 B.C.
First use of iron in China; Confucius teaches standards of behavior; Taoism begins.

†Period of disorder: 256 B.C. to 221 B.C.

Ch'in: 221 B.C. to 206 B.C.
Much of China united into an empire under a single ruler; Great Wall under construction.

Han: 206 B.C. to A.D. 220
Chinese Empire extended; trade with India and Southwest Asia; paper and porcelain invented.

†Period of disorder: A.D. 220 to A.D. 589
Buddhism introduced from India.

Sui: A.D. 589 to A.D. 618
Unity of the empire restored; gunpowder invented.

T'ang: A.D. 618 to A.D. 907
Peace and prosperity; printing invented; art and literature flourish; Islam introduced.

†Period of disorder: A.D. 907 to A.D. 960

Sung: A.D. 960 to A.D. 1279
China a leading sea power; landscape painting important; Genghis Khan conquers much of China.

Yüan (Mongols): A.D. 1279 to A.D. 1368
Kublai Khan extends Mongol Empire; Marco Polo visits China; Grand Canal;* trade flourishes.

Ming: A.D. 1368 to A.D. 1644
European nations send traders; arts flourish; palaces and temples built in capital, Peking.

Ch'ing (Manchus): A.D. 1644 to A.D. 1912
Stable government at first; wars with Britain and Japan; peasant uprisings.

†During these periods China was divided into warring states governed by various kings, warlords, and other rulers.

the Chinese in order to gain control of the fertile lowlands in North China.

Around A.D. 1200, a brilliant soldier named Genghis Khan became the Mongol leader. He set out to conquer neighboring peoples and bring them under his rule. Within a few years, the Mongols controlled one of the largest empires the world has ever known. This empire stretched from eastern Europe to the Pacific Ocean, and included much of North China. In 1279, Genghis Khan's grandson, Kublai Khan, conquered South China also. But China remained under Mongol rule for less than one hundred years. Then the Chinese people overthrew the invaders and set up a new dynasty called the Ming.

Genghis Khan, who established the great Mongol Empire, is shown in this ancient Persian painting. Do research to discover what present-day countries were included in the Mongol Empire.

In the 1600's, another group of foreign invaders conquered China. These were the Manchus, who lived on the Manchurian Plain. (See map on page 25.) They set up a new dynasty called the Ch'ing, which ruled over China until the beginning of the present century. In the next chapter, you will learn how the Manchu rulers finally lost their power.

Life in Old China

The people who invaded China did not bring many changes to the country. Instead of introducing new customs, they usually adopted the Chinese people's way of life. This way of life stayed much the same for centuries.

Farmers and city dwellers. Throughout China's long history, most of its people made their living by farming. Some rented small pieces of land from wealthy landowners, while others had farms of their own. Chinese peasants* lived in small villages close to their fields. They worked hard every day from sunrise to sunset, using only the simplest tools. The peasants had few opportunities to gain an education. Most of them never traveled more than a few miles from the villages where they were born.

A much smaller number of people in China lived in cities or large towns. These city dwellers worked at many different kinds of jobs. Some were soldiers or government officials. Others were merchants or craft workers. In the cities of China, there were shops and markets where people could buy all kinds of goods. There were also temples, schools, and theaters. City people usually had a more comfortable and interesting way of life than country people.

Family life. From earliest times, people in China believed that family life was very important. Most Chinese felt a greater sense of loyalty to their family than they did to the government or to any other group.

In wealthy families, sons did not move away from home when they married. Instead, they brought their brides to the family home. If the house became too crowded, new rooms were added. Grandparents, parents, aunts, uncles, and children all lived together under one roof. Some households included more than two hundred persons.

The farms on which most Chinese peasants worked were too small to support large households like these. A typical peasant family was more like an American family of today. Usually it was made up of a mother and father and their unmarried children, although it might also include grandparents and one or two other close relatives.

No matter how large or how small a household was, its members followed certain rules of behavior. Everyone honored and obeyed the oldest man in the family. Younger sons honored and obeyed their older brothers as well as their fathers and grandfathers. Women and girls honored and obeyed all the males in the family.

In old China, the family carried out many duties that are usually performed by the government in modern countries. For example, each family was supposed to provide education for all its young people. In addition, it was supposed to make sure that every family member obeyed all the laws and customs of the community.

Confucius was a great philosopher who lived around 500 B.C. For over two thousand years, China's people followed the rules of behavior recommended by Confucius. What were some of these rules?

People in old China were considered a part of their families even after they died. The Chinese believed that the spirits of their dead ancestors could have a powerful influence on their lives. To keep these spirits happy, people took food and other gifts to their ancestors' graves. We call this custom "ancestor worship."

Great thinkers of old China. In addition to observing ancient customs, the Chinese followed the teachings of certain philosophers.* The most famous of these was K'ung Fu-tzu, who is known to English-speaking people as Confucius. He lived around 500 B.C. One of his best-known teachings is, "Do not do to others what you would not want them to do to you."

Confucius believed that people were happiest when they followed rules of good behavior. Rulers should be wise and honest in order to set a good example for their subjects. Citizens should obey their rulers, just as children should obey their parents. It was important for people to study carefully the writings of ancient thinkers to learn about the right way to live.

The ideas of Confucius and his followers had a great influence on the Chinese way of life. For over two thousand years, most people in China followed the rules of behavior laid down by these thinkers.

Another group of philosophers in China had ideas that were very different from those of Confucius and his followers. These people were the Taoists. Supposedly Taoism had been founded by a wise man named Lao-tzu, born a short time before Confucius. Some historians today doubt that there ever really was such a person.

The Taoists believed that human laws and governments were useless. They felt that there was only one true law, or principle, for people to follow. This was the Tao, which in English is called the "Way." The Taoists taught that everything in nature had its beginning in the Tao. If people wished to understand the Tao, they should not try to become rich, powerful, or famous. Instead, they should live simply and naturally, as the plants and animals do. Only in this way could they find peace and harmony.

Taoism never had as much influence on the Chinese way of life as Confucianism did. But many poets and artists in China were inspired by Taoist ideas. Their works illustrate the Taoists' love for the greatness and beauty of nature.

The people of early China were also influenced by the teachings of Buddhism. This was a religion that had been started by a great thinker known as Buddha,* who lived in India about 500 B.C. Through the years, Buddhism spread to a number of countries in eastern Asia. Many Chinese became Buddhists, although most of them continued to practice ancestor worship and to follow the rules of Confucius at the same time.

Government in old China. As you have discovered, Confucius taught people to honor and obey their rulers. The Chinese honored their emperor so greatly that when they came into his presence, they knelt down and touched their foreheads to the floor. They believed it was their duty to obey the emperor's commands without question. At the same time, they expected the emperor to rule wisely and fairly. If a ruler was unjust or too weak to govern effectively, it was considered perfectly all right to overthrow him and put another emperor in his place.

The Need for Faith

See pages 191-192

The Lungmen Caves are located near the city of Loyang in North China. (See map on pages 20 and 21.) These caves are filled with Buddhist statues that were carved from stone about fifteen hundred years ago. In the past, millions of Chinese were followers of Buddhism and other religions. How did this change when the Communists came to power? Do you think that people in China today still have a need for some kind of faith? If so, how do you suppose they meet their need? Chapter 7 contains information that will help answer these questions.

A Chinese emperor with his attendants. Government officials called "mandarins" helped the emperors to rule over their vast territories. How were these officials chosen?

The Chinese emperors needed many government officials to help them run their huge empire. These officials were chosen very carefully. They had to take government examinations to show how well they knew the writings of philosophers and historians. If a man passed these difficult examinations he could become one of the most important officials in the land. Then he would be called a "mandarin," and other people would respect and obey him. Even a man from the poorest family in China could dream of becoming a mandarin. But a poor person was not likely to have enough education to pass the necessary examinations.

China's government did not interfere very much with the everyday lives of ordinary people. As long as the villagers lived in peace, the government usually let them run their own affairs.

China's contributions to the world. The people who lived in China long ago made a number of important inventions and discoveries. For example, they were the first people to learn how to make paper. They also invented printing, first with carved blocks of wood and later with pieces of movable type. The Chinese were the first to burn coal as fuel and to use paper money in place of metal coins. They discovered how to raise silkworms and make silk cloth.

They also developed a beautiful kind of pottery called porcelain. (See page 124.) Other Chinese inventions included gunpowder, rockets, and the compass.

The early Chinese are noted for their great building projects. Over a period of several hundred years, they built the longest wall in the world to protect their lands from invading nomads. This great wall is still standing today. (See picture on pages 4-5.) Chinese builders also constructed a great waterway known as the Grand Canal, which is more than one thousand miles long.

The people of ancient China loved painting, sculpture, poetry, and other forms of art. They created many beautiful works of art that are still enjoyed today. You can read more about the arts of ancient China in Chapter 11.

China and other countries. China's great civilization was admired by people in other lands. Officials from neighboring countries came to learn about China's government and to study the ideas developed by Chinese philosophers. The Chinese system of writing was adopted by people in Japan, Korea, and what is now Vietnam. These people also borrowed many Chinese customs.

A few people from distant lands in Europe traveled to China and were impressed by what they saw. In A.D. 1271, an Italian trader named Marco Polo began the long, difficult journey across Asia with his father and uncle. The travelers finally reached China, where they were welcomed by the emperor Kublai Khan. They stayed for nearly twenty years. When they returned home to the city of Venice, Marco Polo told about all the things he had seen. People did not believe his stories because they thought such a wonderful place could not exist.

The Chinese were extremely proud of their fine civilization. They called their country Chung Kuo, which means "Middle Kingdom," because they believed it was the center of the civilized world. The Chinese thought that most people who lived in other countries were barbarians.* Partly for this reason, they were slow to adopt new ideas and inventions that were developed in Europe during the 1600's and 1700's. The Chinese never dreamed that their way of life would one day be changed completely by outsiders.

4 Changes Come to China

One day in 1793, three ships sailed into the Chinese port of Tientsin. Carefully stored away in one ship was a jeweled box containing a letter from the king of England to the emperor of China. The letter asked for permission to send English trading ships to several ports in China. It also suggested that England and China carry on friendly relations with each other.

"Will the emperor agree to these requests?" wondered the ambassador who was to deliver the letter. For many years before this, European nations such as England, the Netherlands, and Portugal had been carrying on trade with a number of countries in eastern Asia. However, foreign traders were not welcome in China. These traders were allowed to come to only one Chinese port, Canton. And they were permitted to do business only with merchants chosen by the Chinese government.

Several European countries had sent ambassadors to China to try to work out a system of trading that would be more convenient for them. These efforts had not been successful. The emperor of China thought his country was so much more important than any other nation that he refused to treat the European rulers as equals.

When the English ambassador delivered the letter from his king, he received the same treatment as the others. The emperor greeted him politely. But the emperor said that the great Chinese Empire did not need anything from other countries, and he refused to grant the English king's requests.

Unwelcome outsiders force their way into China. In the years that followed, foreign traders continued to come to Canton, the one Chinese port that was open to them. There they bought tea, silks, spices, and other valuable products that could be sold for high prices in Europe and the United States.

The European traders needed a product they could sell to the Chinese in return for the goods they were buying. But there was only one foreign product that many people

See page 196

This picture, painted by a Chinese artist around the year 1800, shows the waterfront at Canton. The offices and warehouses in the background were owned by merchants from Europe and the United States. For many years, Canton was the only Chinese port open to foreign traders. Why did the Chinese have so little interest in trading with other countries? Why were Europeans and Americans so eager to buy Chinese goods? How did these differing ideas about trade eventually lead to conflict between China and the Western nations?

in China wanted. This was a dangerous, habit-forming drug called opium, which was obtained from certain kinds of poppy plants that grew in India. Through the years, many Chinese people had become addicted to opium. Because India was controlled by Great Britain at that time, it was easy for British traders to bring opium to China. The Chinese government made it unlawful to import opium, but the traders smuggled it in anyway. As time passed, the traders and the Chinese government became more and more annoyed with each other. Finally, in 1839, the Chinese government seized and burned a whole shipload of opium owned by British merchants. This led to war between Great Britain and China.

The British defeated the Chinese without much difficulty. Their modern guns and warships were more effective than the bows and arrows, spears, and old-fashioned guns used by the Chinese troops. When the war ended in 1842, China signed a treaty* that gave Britain special advantages for trading.

Now people in France, the United States, and other Western countries saw how weak China was. They easily forced the Chinese to grant them various privileges and also to give up control over certain territories. For awhile, it even looked as though several greedy nations might divide the entire country of China among themselves.

During the 1800's, thousands of foreigners came to China. In addition to business people, there were many missionaries* who wanted to teach the Chinese about Christianity. The new ideas brought by all of these people made some Chinese wonder if their ancient way of life was really the best.

China is torn by riots and rebellions. Most people in China felt angry as they watched the unwelcome foreigners flock into their country. Although the Western nations claimed they were not waging war against China, there were foreign soldiers in Chinese cities and foreign gunboats in Chinese harbors. From time to time, some of the Chinese rioted against the foreign missionaries, but they were no match for the foreign troops and gunboats.

Many Chinese were dissatisfied with their government because it had been so weak in dealing with the foreigners, and for other reasons as well. Since 1644, the rulers of China had been Manchus. Although these people lived like the Chinese, most persons in China still thought of them as outsiders. The Manchu rulers treated the Chinese people harshly and allowed them little freedom. The poor peasants were forced to pay heavy taxes to the government. Often, dishonest officials kept the tax money for themselves, instead of using it for roads, schools, and other needed improvements.

During the 1800's, there were several rebellions against Manchu rule. The most serious of these was the Taiping Rebellion, which lasted from about 1850 to 1865. It was led by the followers of a new religion that combined the ideas of Confucius with Christianity. After a long struggle, the Manchus finally defeated the rebels. At least twenty million people were killed during the Taiping Rebellion.

By the end of the 1800's, some Chinese realized that the only way China

*See Glossary

Conflict

Three important leaders of modern China were (left to right) Sun Yat-sen, Chiang Kai-shek, and Mao Tse-tung. Sun was a leader in the movement to overthrow the emperor and establish a republic in China. He founded the Kuomintang, or Nationalist Party. Later a bitter struggle developed between the Nationalists, led by Chiang Kai-shek, and the Chinese Communists, led by Mao Tse-tung. What were the causes of this conflict?

could become strong again was by becoming more modern. The young man who was emperor of China at that time agreed. He tried to start new schools and make other reforms.

The emperor did not have an opportunity to carry out his plans, however. His aunt, Empress Dowager Tzu Hsi,* wanted to keep the old way of life. In 1898 this strong, hot-tempered woman forced the emperor to give up his power and took control of the country herself.

At about the same time, groups of armed Chinese called the "Boxers" began to attack foreigners. They also killed hundreds of Chinese who had become Christians. This struggle was called the Boxer Rebellion.

Even though the Boxers received aid from some of the empress dowager's supporters, they did not succeed in driving the foreigners out of China. Instead, Britain and other countries sent troops into China to stop the rebellion. Now the empress dowager and her followers were forced to realize that China would have to change. Thousands of Chinese students were sent to other countries to learn new skills that would help them make China a modern nation.

China becomes a republic. The students who went to other countries learned new ideas about government. Many believed that China should establish a more democratic form of government, in which the people would have an opportunity to help run the country. A young doctor named Sun Yat-sen became the leader of these people. They were joined by other Chinese who wanted to bring an end to Manchu rule.

In October of 1911, people in various parts of China began to rebel against the Manchu government. Four months later, on February 12, 1912, China became a republic. Sun Yat-sen and other leaders of the rebellion agreed that a well-known general named Yüan Shih-k'ai should become president.

Instead of helping the Chinese to prepare for a democratic form of government, Yüan tried to make himself emperor. But there was so much opposition that Yüan had to give up his plans. After Yüan's death in 1916, the country was in even worse trouble. Powerful army leaders seized control of large parts of China. These "warlords" made the people pay heavy taxes, and they fought each other to gain more power. China was no longer a united country.

Two parties struggle for power. There were two groups of people who thought they had the answer to China's problems. One was a political party called the Kuomintang, or the "Nationalists," which had been started by Sun Yat-sen. The Nationalists believed that China was not yet ready for a democratic government like that of the United States. They wanted to unite China under a military government that would later make way for a democracy.

The other group that wanted to gain control of the government was the Communist Party of China. (See pages 189-190.) This party was formed by a small group of students and teachers in 1921. They were helped by an advisor from the Comintern, an international Communist organization founded by the Soviet Union. The Chinese Communists wanted to start a revolution* that would give them control of China's government.

Neither the Chinese Communists nor the Nationalists were strong enough to defeat the warlords alone. To solve this problem, the Comintern made a plan. The Chinese Communists would work with the Nationalists until the warlords were defeated. Then the Communists would throw out the Nationalists and rule China as they pleased.

At first the Comintern plan worked well. By the summer of 1923, the Chinese Nationalists and Communists were fighting side by side to defeat the warlords. The Soviet Union sent advisors, money, and weapons to help them. After the Nationalist leader Sun Yat-sen died in 1925, a young army officer named Chiang Kai-shek took his place. With the help of the Communists, Chiang succeeded in taking large portions of China from the warlords.

In 1927, Chiang did something the Communist leaders in the Soviet Union had not expected. He turned against his Communist allies. By this time, Chiang had built up a powerful Nationalist army. Under Chiang's orders, army troops moved into the city of Shanghai, where there was a strong Communist organization. The Nationalist troops killed most of the Communist leaders in Shanghai and many other Communists throughout the country. Chiang established a new capital at Nanking and then set to work to bring the rest of China under his control.

Although the Communist Party had suffered a great defeat, it was not destroyed entirely. Some of the Communists escaped to remote areas in the mountains, where they were safe from Chiang's troops. There they began to win support from the peasants by promising them a better way of life.

One of the Communist hideouts was located in the mountains of Kiangsi Province. (See map on page 82.) By 1934 this hideout was in danger of being captured by Nationalist troops. The Communists decided to move to a safer location in Shensi Province, far to the northwest.

The Communist leader was a strong-willed young man named Mao Tse-tung. He and his followers set off on a journey that is known today as the "Long March." In a year's time, they traveled on foot about six thousand miles. The Communist forces had to cross rugged mountains, barren plateaus, and swift rivers. Many died of hunger or disease, or were killed by Nationalist troops. Although more than 100,000 people took part in the Long March, only about 20,000 finally reached Shensi. These people set up a new headquarters in the city of Yenan and continued their struggle against the Nationalists.

The Japanese attack China. Chiang had brought most of China under his control, but now he faced another dangerous enemy. The island country of Japan had become a powerful industrial nation. (See map on pages 6 and 7.) Japan's military leaders wanted to control China so that Japanese manufactured goods could be sold in Chinese stores, and Japanese factories could use

Chinese soldiers defending the Great Wall against Japanese invaders. In 1931, Japan began to take over parts of China. The struggle between China and Japan later became part of World War II. What were some of the reasons why the Japanese leaders wanted to gain control of China?

coal and iron ore from Chinese mines. They also wanted to move some of their people from the crowded islands of Japan to less populated areas in China. For these reasons, Japan began to take over parts of China. This conflict later became part of World War II.*

The Chinese fought bravely, but their army was not as strong or as well-equipped as Japan's. By 1938 much of the country had been conquered, and the Nationalist government had been forced to move inland to the city of Chungking. Still the Chinese refused to surrender.

The Communists gain control of China. At the beginning of the war with Japan, the Nationalists and the Communists had agreed to put aside their rivalry and fight together against the Japanese. In 1941 this agreement was broken. From then on, China was divided into three parts. One was controlled by the Japanese, another by the Nationalists, and the third by the Communists. As the war continued, the Communists were able to take over more and more of the country.

While the war was being fought, problems arose that the Nationalist government did not solve. Factories, roads, railroads, homes, and farms were destroyed. Because the Japanese controlled China's seacoast, it was difficult to bring in from other countries the manufactured goods that China needed. Food and other necessary items became scarce. Instead of making certain that these scarce supplies were distributed fairly, government officials allowed some of their friends to store up goods and sell them at high prices. Soon only

the wealthier people could afford to buy the goods they needed.

Besides being corrupt, the Nationalist government became less democratic as time went on. Elections were not free. Newspapers and magazines could not publish articles that lacked government approval. Secret police watched the people to see that no one said or did anything against the government.

In 1941 it seemed likely that China would soon give up the fight against Japan. But this situation changed when the Japanese attacked a United States military base at Pearl Harbor, in the

Communist troops entering Shanghai in 1949, with a picture of Mao Tse-tung on their truck. After more than twenty years of struggle, the Communists finally defeated the Nationalists in 1949 and took control of China. What were some of the main reasons for the Communists' victory?

Hawaiian Islands. The United States joined World War II on the side of China and the other Allies against Japan, Germany, and Italy. During the remaining years of the war, our country sent troops and military supplies to help the Chinese in their fight against the Japanese. The war finally ended in 1945, with victory for the Allies.

The end of World War II did not bring peace to the weary, war-torn nation of China. The Communists and the Nationalists quarreled about who should take over the parts of the country that had been occupied by the Japanese. Soon the two groups were at war again. The Nationalists received little support from the people, for many Chinese were unhappy about the dishonesty and lack of democracy in the government.

The Communists, led by Mao Tse-tung, made many promises and worked hard to gain people's trust. As more and more Chinese began to support the Communists, Mao's army grew stronger. In 1949 it forced Chiang Kai-shek and the Nationalist government to flee to the island of Taiwan. (See pages 179-181.) The Communists now controlled practically all of the Chinese mainland.

See page 194

After the Communists took control of China in 1949, they made a great effort to win the loyalty of the Chinese people. Huge posters like the one in the picture above were displayed in public places throughout the country. They urged all citizens to support the government's goals. Do you think it is important for the citizens of any country to feel a sense of loyalty toward their government? What might happen if people lacked this feeling of loyalty?

5 China Under Communism

Great problems face the new leaders of China. When the Communists came to power in 1949, China was in serious trouble. The long years of war had caused much destruction. Roads and railroads had been torn up. Homes and stores had been destroyed, and many factories had been shut down.

In addition to the damage caused by warfare, there were other problems facing the country. In 1949, more than four fifths of all the people in China earned their living by farming. But many peasants owned farms that were too small to provide them with a good living. Others did not have any land of their own. They rented small plots of ground from owners who had some land to spare. Usually the peasants had to give such a large part of their crops to these landlords that they barely had enough left over to feed their families.

For years before this, people from rural areas had been moving to China's cities to look for jobs in stores or factories. But there were not enough jobs for everyone who came. Many of the newcomers could not find work at all, while others worked at jobs that paid them very little money. Because they could not afford better housing, they had to live in crowded slums.

Like most other Asian countries, China did not have enough schools or hospitals. Most of its people did not know how to read or write, and many were in poor health.

The Communists stamp out opposition and set up a strong national government. Soon after the Communists came to power in China, they began to organize a strong national government. (See Chapter 6.) The chairman of the Communist Party, Mao Tse-tung, became head of the government also. Other political parties were allowed to exist, but they could not disagree with the main goals of the Communist Party.

In China there were still large numbers of people who opposed the Communists. Many of them were landlords or business people. They were accused of crimes such as sabotage* and were brought before special courts made up largely of peasants and factory workers. No one knows how many of these "enemies of the people" were killed or put in prison

*See Glossary

during the early years the Communists were in power. But some historians claim there were millions.

Some opponents of the Communists were persuaded to change their views through a process known as "thought remolding." Neighbors, relatives, and co-workers put pressure on these people to accept Communist ideas. They were forced to confess their "errors" in public and to promise that they would be loyal to the Communist government in the future.

In addition to silencing the opposition, the Communist leaders worked to gain people's support for their goals. Newspapers and radio stations were brought under government control and were used to spread Communist ideas. The Communist Party appointed people known as cadres to work in cities and farming villages throughout China. The cadres helped to set up organizations such as youth clubs, women's groups, and workers' unions. Through these organizations, Communist ideas could be passed along to the people.

The government begins to do away with private property. As time passed, the Communist leaders of China changed the way farms and factories were owned. Large amounts of farmland were taken from the landlords and divided among the peasants, just as the Communists had promised. But most farmers still did not own enough land to raise all the food their families needed.

Gradually the Communist cadres persuaded the peasants to join their land together to form large "collective farms." Each of the many families on a collective farm was allowed to keep a small plot of land on which to raise food for its own use. The rest of the land was owned and cultivated by all of the families together. Each worker on a collective farm was paid according to the amount of work that he or she did.

At the same time, the government began to take over factories and other business enterprises in China. Some companies were allowed to continue under private owners for a time, but they had to cooperate with the government. In addition, new government-owned companies were started.

Mao orders a "Great Leap Forward." By the late 1950's, China was recovering from the long years of war, and starting to become a modern industrial nation. But Mao Tse-tung felt that more rapid progress was needed. In 1958 he started a nationwide campaign called the "Great Leap Forward." Its slogan was "Twenty years in a day."

During the Great Leap Forward, China's collective farms were joined together to form much larger units called communes. Some of the new communes had populations of more than fifty thousand people. Families in the communes were no longer allowed to raise food for their own use on small private plots. Instead of being paid according to the amount of work they did, the farm workers received food and other goods free of charge from the commune.

Life in the communes was very different from what the Chinese peasants were used to. The Communist leaders said that more work could be accomplished if certain changes were made in family life. In order to free the women to work outside their homes, nurseries were established to care for the young children. Also, most people in the communes had to eat in large mess halls rather than in their homes.

The workers in the communes were organized into huge groups called production brigades. Members of these brigades worked long hours in the fields. Sometimes they were sent many miles from home to build dams or roads or to take part in other projects. They might be gone for months at a time.

Besides establishing farm communes, the government tried to speed up the growth of industry. Factories were run day and night, and workers were urged to do more work than was good for their health. People in rural areas were encouraged to build small blast* furnaces in their backyards. (See picture, pages 136-137.) There they produced iron for making tools and other needed articles.

The Great Leap Forward brought several important benefits to China. Many dams and reservoirs were built to provide water for irrigation. Hydroelectric power plants were constructed to supply electricity to cities and factories. New roads and railroads were built to carry passengers and freight across the countryside.

In many ways, however, the Great Leap Forward was a failure. The backyard blast furnaces produced iron of such poor quality that many of them were closed down. There were not enough trains or trucks to handle the sudden increase in goods that needed to be transported. Overworked factory machines broke down, and workers became too tired to do a good job. Farm workers in the communes were bitterly unhappy about the changes that had been made in their way of life. They missed having their own small plots of land to cultivate, and they did not like to eat in the community mess halls. The production brigades moved around so much that the workers no longer felt they had homes of their own. As time passed, many people in the communes became discouraged and did less work.

To make matters worse, there were serious floods and droughts* in 1959 and 1960. These destroyed the crops in some parts of China. There was so little food that many people went hungry.

A new leader brings about changes in farming and industry. When the failures of the Great Leap Forward became known, Mao stepped down as head of the government. Another Communist leader, Liu Shao-chi, took his place.

Under Liu, the communes were changed to make the farm workers happier and more willing to work hard. Each commune was divided into much smaller units called production teams. Each team was assigned a certain area of land to work on. At harvesttime, members of the production team were allowed to divide part of the team's earnings among themselves. Families were again given small plots of land to raise food for their own use. They were permitted to eat in their homes instead of in mess halls. Also, parents could spend more time with their children.

A number of changes were also made in industry at this time. For example, factory managers were told to increase production by offering extra money to the workers who were most efficient.

Mao opposed the changes made under Liu Shao-chi's leadership. He claimed that they encouraged people to be selfish and put their own interests first, instead of working for the good of the entire country. Mao also complained that government leaders were beginning to form a new "ruling class" like the one that had been overthrown when the Communists took control of China.

Although Mao had lost some of his power in the government, he held certain important advantages. He was still the chairman of the Communist Party and the most admired leader in China. In addition, he had the support of the Chinese army. It was controlled by Lin Piao, one of Mao's closest followers.

The Cultural Revolution sweeps through China. In 1965, Mao urged the Communist Party to start a campaign called the Cultural Revolution. According to Mao, China was starting to drift away from Communist ideas. Mao said the purpose of the Cultural Revolution would be to do away with errors and help China build a true Communist society.

There was great opposition to the Cultural Revolution among Communist Party leaders. So Mao began to work outside the Party organization to carry out his campaign. In 1966, he had Lin Piao form a huge new youth organization called the Red Guards. Giant rallies were held to stir up excitement among the young people who joined the Red Guards. These young people were urged to destroy the "Four Olds—old customs, old thinking, old habits, and old ideas."

In the summer of 1966, large groups of Red Guards marched through the streets of Peking. They put up huge posters criticizing Liu Shao-chi and other government officials. They also entered people's houses and took out old books and art objects. These articles were smashed, or burned in the streets, because they were symbols of the old way of life that had existed in China before the Communists took power.

Before long, all of China's schools were closed, and the Red Guards were sent throughout the country. The army arranged for their transportation and made sure that no one interfered with their activities.

The Red Guards set out to remove Mao's opponents from power. They did

this in various ways. For example, teachers and Communist officials who were suspected of opposing Mao were sometimes dragged from their houses and beaten. Sometimes they were forced to march through the streets wearing dunce caps. At public meetings, these persons were criticized and forced to confess their "crimes." Some were killed or forced to commit suicide. Others were sent to prison camps, where they spent years at hard labor.

During the Cultural Revolution, Mao succeeded in removing Liu Shao-chi as head of the government. Many other officials of the government and the Communist Party were also forced out of their jobs. In fact, so many jobs were left vacant that the government and the Party could no longer carry out all of their duties.

By this time, the Red Guards were completely out of control. Rival groups of Red Guards and angry citizens fought

The two photographs below show Red Guards holding demonstrations in Peking during the Cultural Revolution. In the picture at left, some Red Guards are changing the name on a street sign because the street's former name seemed "old-fashioned" to them. Many of the demonstrators are holding up booklets that contain the writings of Mao Tse-tung. What was the Cultural Revolution, and how did it come about? Do you think this was a good way to bring about change?

Mao Tse-tung, Lin Piao, and Chou En-lai (right to left) were three of the top leaders in China during the years after the Communists came to power. What positions did these men hold in the government or in the Communist Party? Who are the leaders of China at the present time?

each other in the streets. Even Mao, who had started the Cultural Revolution, was alarmed by the growing violence.

Peace and order are restored in China. The only organization that still had any real power in China was the army. In 1967, the army stepped in to restore order. Soldiers were stationed in farm communes, in factories, and in city neighborhoods. They arrested troublemakers and settled arguments. The schools were opened again, and the Red Guards were ordered to return to their classes. Some refused to go, however. As time passed, many of the Red Guards were sent to live and work in farm communes. There they were kept too busy to cause trouble.

It seemed likely that Lin Piao, the minister of defense, would take the place of Mao Tse-tung when Mao became too old to serve as China's leader. But in 1971 Lin was killed in a mysterious plane crash in a neighboring country, the Mongolian People's Republic. The Chinese government announced that Lin had been plotting to overthrow Mao and set up a military dictatorship.*

By the time of Lin's death, China was peaceful again. However, the effects of the Cultural Revolution were still being felt. During those years of disorder, industry and trade had come almost to a standstill. Careers had been ruined, and families had been separated. The Cultural Revolution had left China weaker and poorer than it had been before.

Two groups of leaders struggle for power. Although Mao Tse-tung was still China's top leader, he was now almost eighty years old. It would soon be time for someone to replace him. Gradually, a struggle for power developed between two groups of Communist leaders. These were the "radicals" and the "moderates." The radicals were led by Mao's wife Chiang Ching. They believed that the Cultural Revolution had been a good thing for China and that it should continue. The moderates felt that the Cultural Revolution had been a great mistake. They thought it was time for people to settle down and pay more attention to developing China's farming and industry.

The moderates were supported by Chou En-lai, China's second most powerful leader. Chou had been premier* of China since the Communists came to power in 1949. As time passed, Chou arranged to have moderate leaders named to key government posts. Among these people was a bold, clever leader named Teng Hsiao-ping. Teng had formerly been a high official in the Communist Party, but he had often disagreed with Mao's ideas. During the Cultural Revolution, he had been attacked by the Red Guards and removed from office.

The moderates take control of China's government. In 1976, several events of great importance took place in China. The first was the death of Chou En-lai. To replace Chou as premier, Mao appointed a little-known official named Hua Kuo-feng. Hua was probably chosen because he was acceptable to both the radicals and the moderates.

Mao himself died a few months later, and Hua Kuo-feng took his place as Communist Party chairman. The radicals had been hoping to take control of the government after Mao's death. However, their hopes were soon destroyed. In a surprise move, Chiang Ching and three other leading radicals were arrested and jailed on charges of plotting to overthrow the government. It was clear that the moderates had won their struggle for power in China.

Chiang Ching and her comrades, known as the "Gang of Four," were soon being blamed for all of China's troubles. Huge posters accusing them of various crimes appeared on the walls of buildings throughout China. Millions of people gathered for rallies in Peking and other cities to demand that the radicals be punished. Most Chinese were obviously glad to see the radicals overthrown. They were tired of the Cultural Revolution and the problems it had caused. They wanted greater freedom and a more peaceful life.

The "Gang of Four" remained in prison until 1981, when they were finally brought to trial. Chiang Ching was sentenced to death, but later the sentence was changed to life imprisonment. A number of other leading radicals were sentenced to long prison terms.

China's new leaders make plans to modernize the nation. Soon after coming to power, the moderates began making important changes in China's way of life. During Mao's last years, the government's main goal had been to create loyal followers of communism. People were forced to spend much of their time attending political meetings and studying Mao's ideas. Partly for this reason, little progress was made in farming, industry, and other fields.

Now the moderates announced a new goal—to make China into a modern industrial nation by the year 2000. To reach this goal, they realized, would take hard work and careful planning. China's new leaders were more practical than Mao had been. They were willing to try new ways of doing things, even if these ways did not always agree with Communist ideas. (See Chapter 13.)

In 1978, the new leaders started a major campaign to carry out their plans for China. The government began spending huge sums of money to build steel mills, chemical plants, and other factories. To modernize its industry, China needed many kinds of machinery and other goods it could not produce by itself. So it began buying large amounts of these goods from other nations. (See page 176.) Foreign companies were invited to help build new factories in China. The nation's schools began training more scientists and engineers for jobs in industry. Also, many young Chinese were sent to foreign countries to study.

China's people are given more freedom. The new leaders realized that they could not carry out their plans without the cooperation of the people. To win support, they began to allow people more freedom than they had enjoyed during the Cultural Revolution. For example, people were given more freedom to worship God as they chose. (See page 91.) They were also able to make speeches and put up wall posters criticizing the government and making suggestions for changes. Steps were taken to make sure that people accused of crimes received a fair trial.

China's artists, writers, and musicians were also granted more freedom than before. Chapter 11 explains how the arts in China have changed since the Cultural Revolution.

Teng Hsiao-ping becomes the top government leader. In the meantime, a new leader was rising to power in China. This was Teng Hsiao-ping. Even though Teng was only a vice-chairman of the Communist Party, he seemed to be making most of the important government decisions. He

A poster attacking Chiang Ching, the widow of Mao Tse-tung. Chiang Ching was a member of the famous "Gang of Four." What was the "Gang of Four," and why was it blamed for China's troubles? What important changes have taken place in China since the "Gang of Four" was overthrown in 1976?

also controlled the armed forces. Hua Kuo-feng, however, was losing power. In 1980 he was forced to resign as premier, and in 1981 he gave up his post as chairman of the Communist Party. Hua was replaced by two moderates who were followers of Teng. Zhao Ziyang† was named premier, and Hu Yaobang† became Communist Party chairman.

Under Teng's leadership, the Communist Party changed its attitude toward Mao Tse-tung. Formerly Mao had been treated almost as a god, who could do nothing wrong. Now he was strongly criticized for starting the Cultural Revolution and allowing the "Gang of Four" to have so much power. Mao was still honored for helping to bring communism to China. But many of his pictures and statues were removed from public buildings throughout the nation.

China continues to face serious problems. As time passed, China's new leaders discovered that their ambitious plans were not working out as well as they had hoped. Many of the projects that were supposed to develop China's industry had not been planned carefully enough. As a result, large sums of money had been wasted. Also, China's government did not have enough money to complete all the projects that had been started. It had to cancel some of these projects and postpone others.

†Pinyin spelling. See page 18.

Meanwhile, the moderates were facing opposition from two groups of people. On one side were the radicals, who still held important jobs in the Communist Party and the government. These people were unhappy with the changes that China's leaders were making. They hoped to regain power and start another Cultural Revolution.

On the other side were many Chinese who had been growing dissatisfied with communism. Some of them had suffered greatly during the Cultural Revolution. They had lost their faith in Communist ideas. Since Mao's death, the Chinese had been learning more about other countries from foreign visitors and from television broadcasts. They could see that other people enjoyed more freedom and a higher standard* of living than they did. Now some of them were asking why communism had failed to provide a better way of life.

China's leaders decided something must be done to keep their opponents from becoming too powerful. They took away some of the freedoms they had granted earlier. For example, people were forbidden to put up wall posters without the government's approval. A few people who criticized the government too strongly were given long prison terms. Gradually, some of the radical leaders were removed from their jobs in the Party and the government.

The Chinese people look to the future. In the last few years, China's leaders have made important changes in farming, industry, and trade. (See pages 102-103 and 139.) Today these changes are starting to bring results. China's output of farm products and manufactured goods has been growing steadily. Many Chinese are now enjoying a higher standard of living than they ever did before. Life in China is generally peaceful now.

Some people, however, are wondering whether this situation will continue. They point out that many Chinese are still opposed to the moderates' plans for China. Also, some of China's top leaders are quite elderly. When these leaders die or retire, there could be another struggle for power in China. If so, China's people are likely to face a very uncertain future.

China and the World

Since China became a Communist nation in 1949, important changes have taken place in its relations with other countries of the world. Let us explore some of these changes.

China and the United States. In 1949 China was a weak country that had suffered greatly from long years of war. The Chinese Communist leaders were suspicious of any country that they felt might be a threat to their independence. They were especially suspicious of the United States.

At that time, a struggle called the Cold War* was going on between the Communist nations and some of the non-Communist nations, including the United States. (See page 190.) Each side in this conflict felt that the other was trying to conquer the world.

Like many other countries, the United States did not recognize the Communists as the rightful rulers of China. Instead, it supported the Nationalist government that had been set up on the island of Taiwan. (See pages 179-181.) The United States government sent the

Nationalists large amounts of money and military aid. To prevent the spread of communism in Southeast Asia, the United States helped to establish an organization called SEATO.* In addition, it stationed large numbers of troops in countries close to China. These actions convinced the Chinese Communists that the United States wanted to drive them from power.

In 1950, troops from the Communist country of North Korea invaded the non-Communist country of South Korea. (See map on pages 20 and 21.) Our country sent troops to help the South Koreans. Later, China entered the war on North Korea's side. Although the two sides agreed to stop fighting in 1953, the Korean War* caused more ill feeling between China and the United States. The two countries also took opposite sides in the Vietnam War.*

China and the Soviet Union. When China first became a Communist nation, its closest ally was the Soviet Union. This country had been ruled by a Communist government for over thirty years, and it was accepted as the leader of communism around the world. The Soviet Union loaned large sums of money to China. It also sent a number of technical experts to help the Chinese develop their industry.

As time passed, however, the friendship between these two countries grew cooler. The Chinese claimed that the Soviet leaders were being disloyal to Communist ideas. In 1960 the Soviets stopped most of their aid to China and brought their experts home.

Representatives of China attending a meeting of the United Nations Security Council, at U N headquarters in New York City. Although the Communists took control of China in 1949, their government was not represented in the United Nations until 1971. Why was this so? (See pages 179-180.)

China tries to stand alone. During the 1960's, China had close ties with very few countries, either Communist or non-Communist. China's leaders felt that the nation should "stand on its own two feet" and not depend on any other country for help. So the Chinese carried on very little trade with other nations. Few foreign visitors came to China, and few Chinese traveled abroad.

In 1969 something happened that caused the Chinese leaders to change their minds. By this time, China and the Soviet Union were treating each other like enemies. Fighting broke out between Soviet and Chinese troops along the borders between the two nations. China's leaders feared that the Soviets were planning to invade them. Soon the fighting stopped. But the Chinese realized that they needed the support of other countries in case of further trouble with the Soviets.

A growing friendship with the non-Communist nations. In 1972 China's leaders did something that astonished the world. They invited the president of the United States, Richard Nixon, to visit China. During his visit, the two countries agreed to work toward closer relations. As time passed, other American leaders visited China and some Chinese leaders came to the United States. The two countries also began carrying on more trade with each other. In 1979 the United States officially recognized the Communist government in Peking as the rightful government of China.

China was also building closer ties with other non-Communist nations. For example, it signed a treaty with its former enemy, Japan. China also signed trade agreements with Japan and several nations in Europe, including Great Britain, France, and West Germany.

China's role in the world today. Presently, China and the United States are friendly toward one another. However, there are still a few serious disagreements. The most important one is over Taiwan. Since 1979, the United States no longer officially recognizes the Nationalist government. But it continues to trade with Taiwan, and it still supplies the Nationalist government with weapons to defend itself against a possible attack. This does not please the Communist leaders in Peking.

China has recently shown signs of becoming friendlier toward the Soviet Union. However, the Chinese remain deeply distrustful of Soviet plans. Huge numbers of Soviet troops are still stationed along the Chinese border. Also, the Soviet Union has been interfering in several Asian countries, such as Afghanistan, Vietnam, and Kampuchea. The Chinese leaders say this interference must stop before China and the Soviet Union can enjoy better relations.

In recent years, China has been trying to build closer ties with other developing nations in Asia and Africa. (See page 165.) These countries face many of the same problems that China does. China's leaders say that the developing nations should work together to solve their problems and to prevent interference from the world's two "superpowers" — the United States and the Soviet Union.

In the future, the United States and other nations will continue to watch with interest the changes that take place in China. What happens in this vast, heavily populated country is sure to have an important effect on the entire world.

The picture above shows China's top leader, Teng Hsiao-ping (left), and Communist Party secretary-general Hu Yaobang.† They are voting on a new constitution for China during a meeting of the National People's Congress in 1982. China's government is run by a small group of powerful leaders who allow very little opposition. What do we usually call this kind of government?

6 Government

China is a Communist dictatorship. The official name for China today is "People's Republic of China." This name might lead you to think that China has a government much like that of the United States. In our country, nearly all citizens have an opportunity to help choose the people who make and carry out the laws.

China's government is quite different, however. It is run by a small group of leaders who all belong to one

†Pinyin spelling. See page 18.

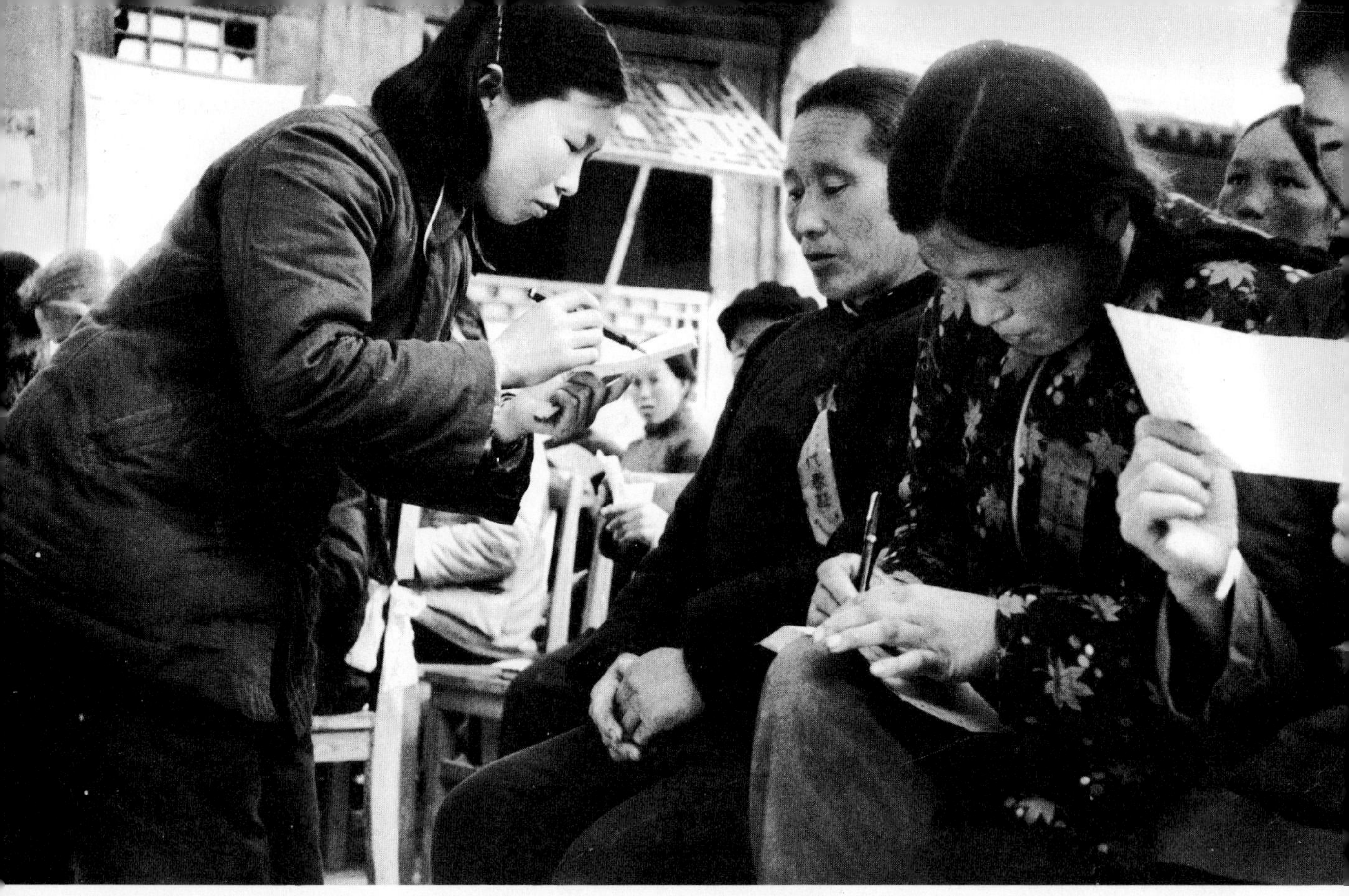

Voters in a farming village near Lanchou. How do elections in China differ from those in our country?

Elections in China

Chinese elections differ in certain ways from elections in the United States. In our country, citizens can vote directly for high government officials such as the president and members of Congress. In China, however, direct elections take place only at the lower levels of government. For example, people in the cities and rural areas vote directly for members of local lawmaking bodies called people's congresses. These bodies, in turn, choose delegates to the people's congress for each province. The provincial congresses then elect delegates to the National People's Congress. (See pages 79-80.)

Elections in China are supposed to be held at regular times, just as they are in the United States. For instance, the constitution says that a new National People's Congress is to be elected every five years. However, when Mao Tse-tung was China's leader, elections were not always held on schedule. In fact, there were no elections at all from 1964 to 1974. Today, elections are being held more regularly.

China's constitution states that all citizens the age of eighteen and over may vote. Elections are by secret ballot. However, voters in China cannot choose freely among candidates representing different points of view. Sometimes only one candidate is allowed to run for a particular office. At other times, there may be two or more candidates to choose from. But all candidates must be approved by the Communist Party before their names can appear on the ballot. In this way, the Communists make sure that all elected officials in China are people who will follow orders from the Party leaders.

political party—the Communist Party. The leaders of China were not chosen in free elections. What is more, they cannot be voted out of office if the majority of people become dissatisfied with their policies. China's government leaders have the power to make important decisions all by themselves. The rest of the people are expected to follow their orders. A country governed in this way is usually known as a dictatorship.

This does not necessarily mean that the Chinese leaders are unpopular in their country. But we cannot be sure of this, for China's people do not have a chance to express their feelings publicly through free elections.

China's people lack important freedoms. The people of China lack many freedoms that are taken for granted in the United States. For example, they are not free to speak or write whatever they please. Sometimes they can criticize the actions of government officials. But they must be careful not to express ideas that differ greatly from official Communist teachings. All of the books, magazines, and newspapers in China are published under the direction of government agencies. They are used to spread Communist propaganda.*

In China, freedom of religion is limited in certain ways. (See pages 90-91.) Many temples and churches were closed when the Communists came to power. Some of them have been reopened now, but they are closely controlled by the government. They cannot openly try to attract new followers.

People in China also lack certain economic* freedoms, such as the right to work at a job of one's own choice. The restrictions on economic freedoms are described more fully on pages 138-139.

Why the Communists have been able to stay in power. Why are the Chinese people willing to live under a dictatorship that allows them only a limited amount of freedom? Several facts about past and present-day China help to answer this question.

First, China's people have never had much experience with democracy. For thousands of years, China was ruled by powerful emperors. Anyone who disobeyed or criticized the emperor was likely to be punished severely. The Nationalists who ruled China earlier in this century also allowed the people little freedom. (See page 60.)

When the Communists came to power in 1949, they took strong measures to do away with all opposition. Many of their opponents were killed, put into prison, or driven out of China during the first few years of Communist rule.

Meanwhile, the Communists took a number of steps to improve the Chinese people's way of life. As a result, most Chinese were able to meet their needs for food, clothing, and shelter better than ever before. Today, many older Chinese support the Communist government because they remember the hardships they faced before the Communists came to power.

The Communists are also able to stay in power today because they use special methods of controlling China's people. These methods are described more fully on pages 186-188. They have been quite effective in producing citizens who are willing to obey the government's orders.

*See Glossary

A Problem To Solve
The picture above shows a government building in Peking. Ever since 1949, the government of China has been controlled by the Communist Party. Why have the Communists been able to stay in power for such a long time? In forming your hypotheses to solve this problem, you will need to consider facts about:
a. the history of China
b. achievements of the Communist government
c. methods of control used by the Communists

The National Government

China has a written constitution. Like the United States, China has a plan of government called a constitution. This document explains how China's government is supposed to be run. The present constitution of China was adopted in December of 1982.

The Communist Party of China runs the country's government. In China today, nearly all of the important jobs in the government are held by members of the Communist Party. A few other parties are allowed to exist, but they have very little power. They cannot oppose any of the Communists' main goals for China.

Communist Party officials known as cadres are found in factories, offices, schools, farming villages, and city neighborhoods throughout China. The cadres are supposed to encourage the rest of the people to give their loyal support to the government. They are also supposed to find out what people think about government policies.

Only about four out of every one hundred people in China are actually members of the Communist Party. Belonging to the Party is considered a great privilege, and members are chosen very carefully. They are expected to work hard to spread Communist ideas and to obey all orders given by their leaders. If they do not, they may lose their Party membership.

Every five years or so, the Communist Party holds a National Party Congress in Peking. Party officials from all parts of China attend this meeting. The National Party Congress helps to decide on policies for the Party to follow. It also chooses the members of a group called the Central Committee, which runs the Party between Congress sessions. At present, this committee has about 210 members. The Central Committee chooses about 25 of its top leaders to form a group called the Politburo. Most of the really important decisions in the Party are made by members of the Politburo.

The Central Committee also chooses the secretary-general, who is the highest official in the Chinese Communist Party. Formerly, the top Party official was called the chairman. But the chairman's post was abolished in 1982.

The National People's Congress is the chief lawmaking body. According to the constitution, the chief lawmaking body in China is the National People's Congress. It is made up of about 3,500 representatives from all parts of China. "Elections in China," on page 76, describes how these representatives are chosen. The National People's Congress meets in Peking for about two weeks every year.

The National People's Congress has never had much power. It is so large

Workers at an oil refinery near Harbin. Communist Party officials known as cadres are found in factories, offices, schools, farming villages, and city neighborhoods throughout China. What are their duties? If you lived in China, do you think you would like to be a cadre? Explain.

and it meets for such a short time that its members have no opportunity to really make any laws. In the past, they simply voted "yes" to laws that had been prepared beforehand by the Communist Party leaders.

A change may now be taking place, however. The National People's Congress elects a Standing Committee of about two hundred members to carry on its work when it is not in session. Under the new constitution, adopted in 1982, the Standing Committee has been given more power to make laws for China. It is possible that the Standing Committee may become a real law-making body, rather than just a "rubber stamp" for the Communist Party.

The National People's Congress elects a number of leading government officials. One of these is the president of China, who serves a five-year term. The office of president is mostly ceremonial. It was created by the constitution adopted in 1982. In June, 1983, Li Xiannian† became the first president elected under the new constitution.

The State Council carries out the laws. In the United States, the president and the cabinet* are responsible for carrying out the nation's laws. In China, this job is handled by the State Council. The State Council includes the heads of all main departments in the government. These departments deal with such matters as national defense, education, and public health. They employ thousands of people to carry on the everyday work of the government. The State Council is headed by the premier, who is elected by the National People's Congress. The premier is one of the most important government officials in China.

China is making changes in its system of courts. Like other countries, China has a system of courts to judge people accused of breaking the law. There are "people's courts" in cities and towns throughout China. The highest court in the land is the Supreme People's Court in Peking. It handles cases that are especially important, such as crimes committed by leading government officials.

In the past, it was very difficult for a person accused of a crime to receive a fair trial in China. The courts, like other government bodies, were controlled by the Communist Party. Often they were used to punish people suspected of opposing the Communists' goals. Few laws were written down, so people had no way of knowing if they were breaking the law. During the Cultural Revolution, innocent people were often arrested and sent to prison or even killed without any trial.

To try to keep this from happening again, China's new leaders have been making some important changes in the court system. More laws are being written down, so that people can know what they are. Most trials are held in public, and a person accused of a crime is allowed to have the help of a lawyer. Because of changes such as these, court trials in China are fairer than they were before. However, much remains to be done before China's court system is like that of democratic nations.

China has the world's largest army. About four and one-half million men and women serve in the People's Liberation Army, as China's armed forces are called. The People's Liberation Army defends the country against possible enemies. Sometimes it also carries out

†Pinyin spelling. See page 18.

The Great Hall of the People is located on Tien An Men Square in Peking. The National People's Congress meets in this building. Although the National People's Congress is supposed to be China's main lawmaking body, it has never had very much power. Why do you suppose this is so?

tasks that are usually performed by civilians* in the United States. For example, Chinese soldiers have been known to build highways and railroads, dig irrigation ditches, and even help farmers harvest their crops.

Local Governments

Provinces. As the map on page 82 shows, much of China is divided into provinces. There are twenty-one of these units, which are somewhat like states in our country. But the Chinese provinces do not have nearly as much power as our states have. In all important matters, they must follow the orders of

See page 194

China's government, like that of the United States, is made up of different branches. After reading this chapter, do research about the United States government in encyclopedias and other sources. Then, make a chart comparing the governments of the two countries showing:

(1) who is responsible for making the nation's laws
(2) who is responsible for carrying out the laws
(3) who is responsible for judging people accused of breaking the law

Write a brief essay to answer the following question:

Do you think that the different branches of government work the same way in China as they do in the United States?

the national government in Peking. Each province is governed by a lawmaking body called a "people's congress." The feature on page 76 explains how the members of these people's congresses are chosen.

Autonomous regions. There are five autonomous regions in China. (See map below.) These are areas containing large numbers of people who are not Han Chinese.* In Tibet, for example, more than nine tenths of the people are Tibetans.

The word "autonomous" means "self-governing." Supposedly, the autonomous regions were established so the minority* peoples of China could run their own affairs. Like other parts of China, however, these regions are closely controlled by the national government.

Municipalities.* China's three largest cities are not part of any province or

China is divided into twenty-one provinces, five autonomous regions, and three municipalities. What are provinces? How do they differ from our states? What does the word "autonomous" mean? Do you think this is a good word to describe regions such as Tibet and Inner Mongolia? Why? Why not? What three municipalities in China are not part of any province or autonomous region?

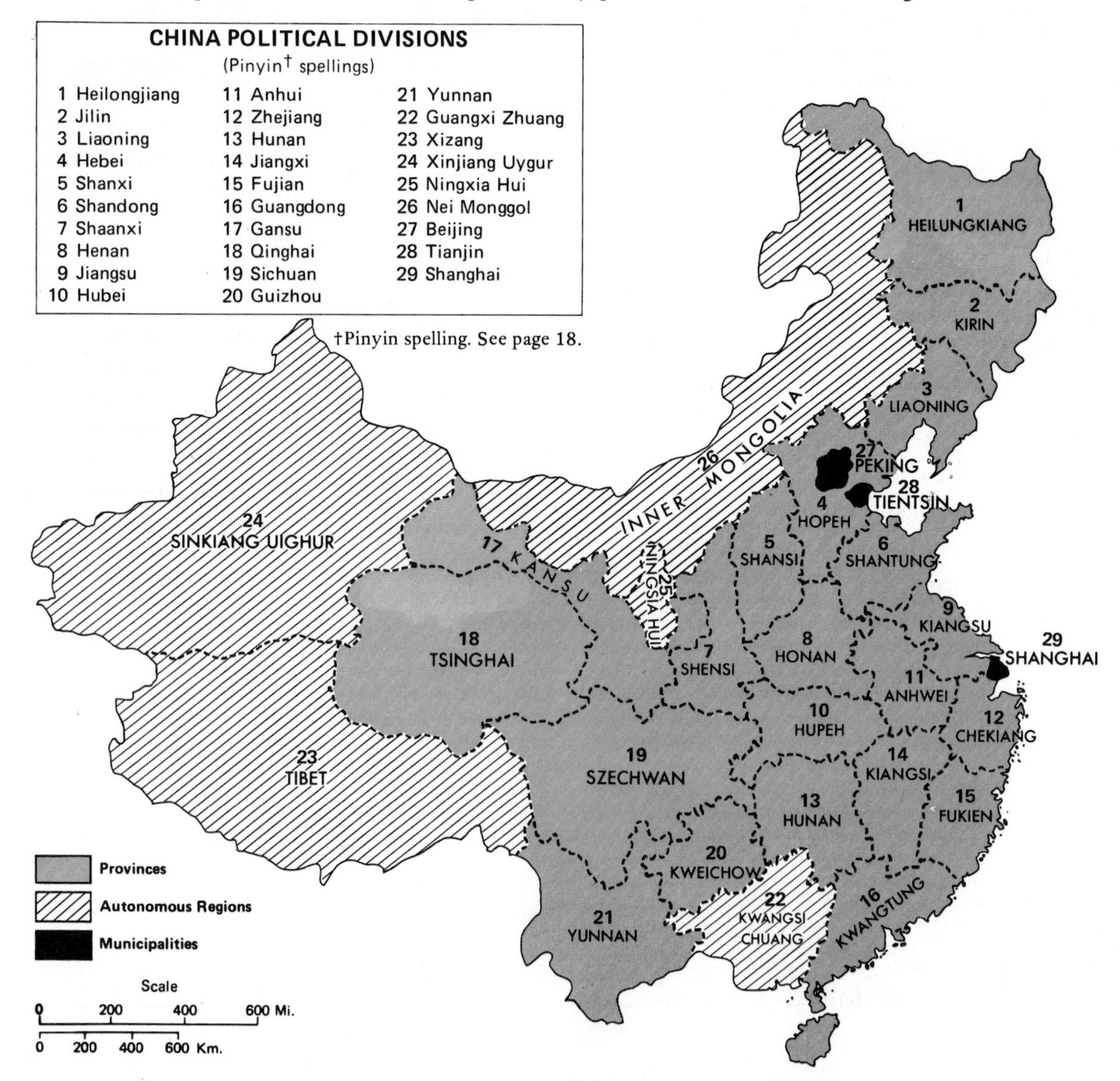

autonomous region. These are the municipalities of Shanghai, Peking, and Tientsin. They have their own governing bodies, which are responsible directly to the national government.

Other units of local government. Each province and autonomous region of China is divided into smaller units of government. Some of these are cities or large towns. They are governed by "people's congresses," whose members are elected directly by the people. (See page 76.) Rural areas are divided into counties and townships much like those in the United States. The Chinese counties and townships are also governed by people's congresses. In the farming villages of China, there are elected committees that take care of village affairs.

Be a Biographer

The people listed below played an important part in the history of China. Write a brief biography of one of these persons.

Confucius	Sun Yat-sen
Shih Huang Ti	Chiang Kai-shek
Kublai Khan	Mao Tse-tung
Empress Dowager Tzu Hsi	Chou En-lai

In addition to describing the person's life, your biography should include information about the ways in which he or she influenced the history of China. Some of the information you will need for your biography can be found in this book. Pages 201-203 provide helpful suggestions for finding additional information.

Make a Poster or Paint a Mural

The people who lived in China long ago made a number of important discoveries and inventions that have enriched the lives of people all over the world. Make a poster or a mural showing some of the contributions of early Chinese civilization. Write a caption to identify each discovery or invention. You may wish to refer to other sources to find additional information for this project. (See pages 201-203.)

Keep Up With Current Events

China is often in the news today. With your classmates, look for newspaper and magazine articles about China. Look especially for articles about China's government and about China's relations with other countries. Each person who brings in an article should read it to the class. Then the class as a whole should discuss the meaning of the news reported. You may wish to display the articles on a special bulletin board.Include pictures in your display whenever possible.

Make a Time Line

A time line can help you understand the history of China. In order to make your time line, you will need to use several yards of shelf paper or several sheets of poster board. You may work alone or with a group of your classmates. Each person in the group might take a different period of Chinese history and make a time line for that period. Then these different time lines can be combined to show China's long history. You will need to follow the steps suggested below in making your time line.

1. As you do research in this book and other sources about China's history, list the events you consider important. Include the year when each event occurred. (Be sure to indicate whether it is B.C. or A.D.)
2. Decide what intervals of time you will show on your time line, such as periods of one hundred years each. Mark these intervals with vertical lines on your time line. (See sample time line below.)
3. Record each event in its proper place on the time line.

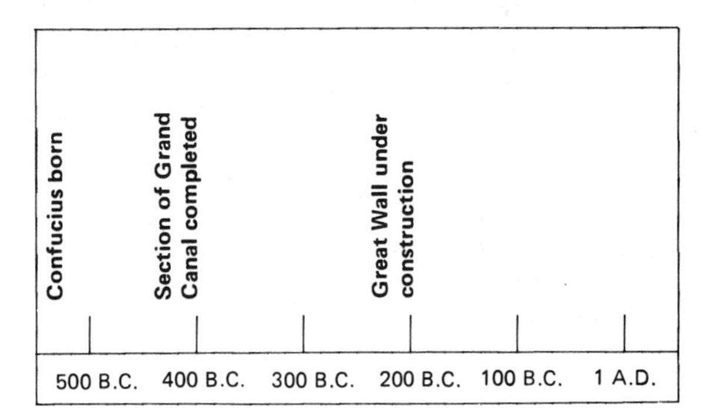

Meeting Needs

See pages 191-192

The photograph above shows a crowd of people on a street in the city of Canton, China. Examine this picture carefully. Do you think that these people have the same basic needs as you do? If so, what are these needs? Do you think most people in China today have a good opportunity to meet their basic needs? Why? Why not? The chapters in Part 3 and the feature on pages 191-192 provide information that will help you to answer these questions.

Part 3

People and Their Way of Life

Imagine that you are taking a trip through China. You know that when you return, your friends and relatives will ask you about China's people and their way of life. As you read the text and examine the pictures in Part 3, try to discover answers to questions you might be asked about your trip, such as the following:

- What are some of the different groups of people who live in China today?
- What parts of China have the most people? Why are these areas so densely populated?
- What would it be like to live in a farming community in China?
- What are some of China's important cities? Which did you think was the most interesting to visit, and why?
- How are schools in China like those in our country? How are they different?
- How do the arts and crafts of China today differ from those of the past?
- How do people in China spend their leisure time?

Chinese people in a park. Until recently, China's population was growing very rapidly. Why is the government taking steps to slow down the growth of population? How is it doing this?

7 People

China has the largest population of any country in the world. In 1982 the Chinese government took its first official census* in eighteen years. This census showed that China has a population of just over one billion. Nearly one fourth of all the people in the world live in China.

Why China's population is so large. In earlier times, most Chinese felt it was important to have many children. They wanted to make sure that there would be sons to care for them in their old age and to honor the spirits of their ancestors. (See page 49.) Although many children were born each year, large

*See Glossary

numbers of people died of hunger or disease. Also, millions of people were killed in wars that swept across China in the 1800's and early 1900's. So the population did not increase greatly from year to year.

About 1950, this situation changed. China was now at peace. Thanks to new medicines and better health care, fewer people were dying of disease. In addition, China's people had more food to eat. As a result, the population grew very rapidly. In some years, China gained at least twenty million people—more people than there are in the entire state of New York.

China's leaders have been trying to slow down population growth. At first, the Communist leaders were pleased with the increase in population. They believed that the more people China had, the stronger it would be. But as time passed, they began to realize that the growth of population was causing many problems. It was difficult to provide enough food, clothing, shelter, schools, and jobs for so many people.

Today China's government is taking strong measures to slow down the growth of population. Billboards and radio messages tell people it is patriotic to have fewer children. Families with only one child are given rewards such as higher wages and larger apartments.

Experts say that the government's program seems to be working in the cities. People there are having fewer children. As a result, China's population is growing more slowly than it was a few years ago. In rural areas,

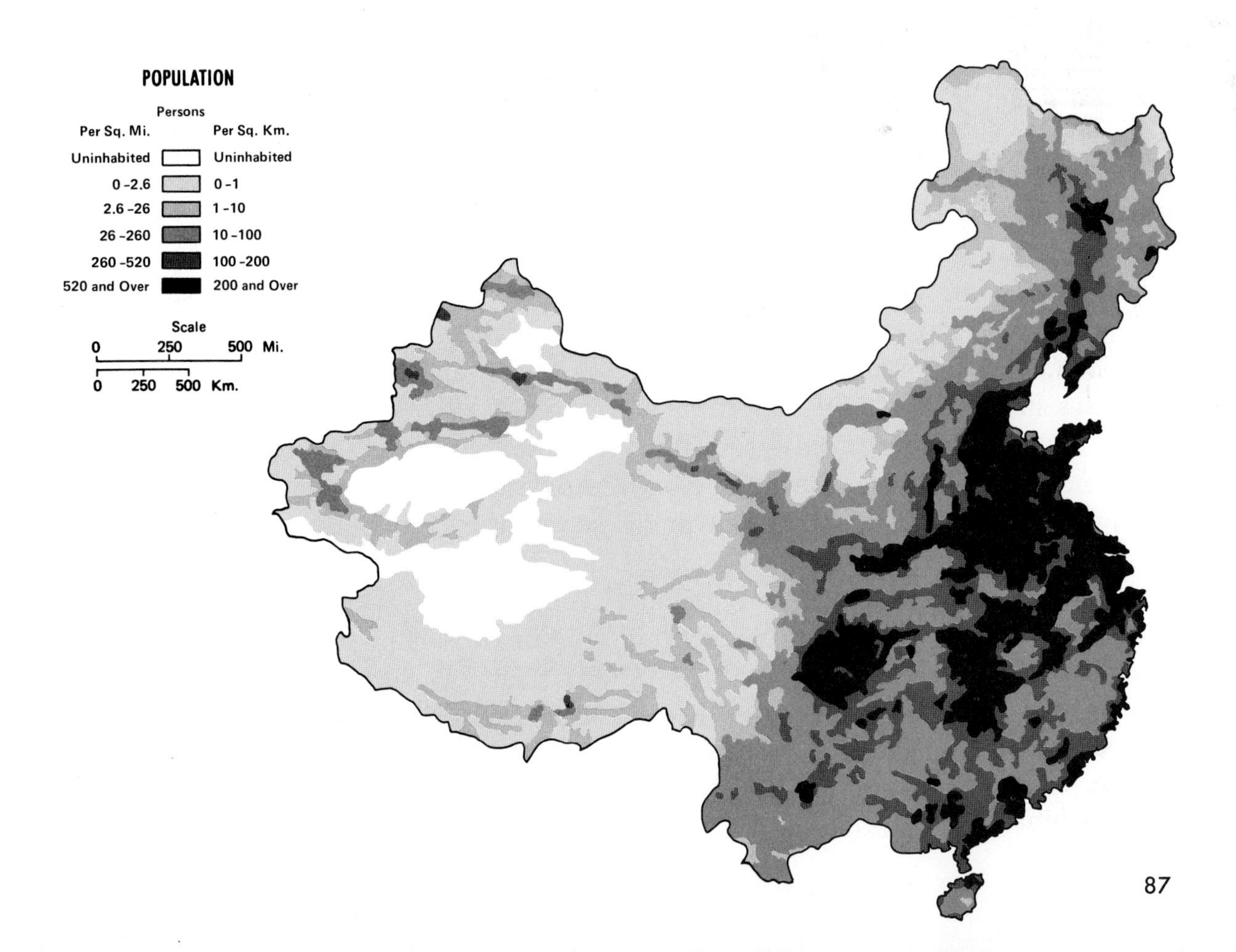

however, the program has been less successful. Many peasants still want to have as many sons as possible.

Some parts of China are very crowded, while others are almost empty. China is so large in size that if all its people were spread evenly throughout the country, no area would be very crowded. But this is not the case. Most parts of China are too dry or too mountainous to support many people. These areas are very thinly populated. The map on page 87 shows that nearly all of China's people live in the eastern part of the country. The most densely populated areas include the Yellow Plain, the Red Basin, the Yangtze River Plain, and the Canton Delta. For example, some parts of the Yangtze Plain have 2,500 persons or more on each square* mile of land.

Most of China's people live in farming villages. Since China is not yet an industrial country, most of its people still earn their living by farming. About eight out of every ten Chinese live in farming villages similar to the one described in Chapter 8. The rest of the people live in cities or large towns.

During the early 1900's, large numbers of Chinese moved from rural areas to cities in search of jobs. This migration* led to serious problems. There were not enough jobs for everyone, so many of the newcomers could not find any kind of work. Others had to work at low-paying jobs. Since the newcomers had little money, they were forced to live in crowded, dirty slums.

Today the Chinese government is trying to keep China's large cities from becoming even more overcrowded. People who live in rural areas are not allowed to move to the cities unless they have been assigned to jobs there by the government.

The Han Chinese

Most of China's people are alike in certain ways. About ninety-three out of every one hundred people in China belong to a group known as the Han Chinese. The people in this group generally have straight, black hair and dark eyes. Their upper eyelids have a fold that makes the eyes appear to be somewhat slanted. Usually their skin is tan or light brown in color.

The Han Chinese live mainly in North China and South China. (See map on page 25.) There are certain differences between the people of these two regions. The people of North China tend to be taller and heavier than those in the south. The southerners generally have darker skin. They are also more lively in their talk and gestures than the Han Chinese of North China.

The language used by the Han people of China is known simply as "Chinese." It is written in the same way by people throughout the country, although the spoken language differs greatly from place to place. The feature on pages 182-183 provides more information about the Chinese language.

The Han Chinese share a long history. People of the Han group have been living in what is now China for thousands of years. During this long period, the Han Chinese came to share many customs and points of view.

The Han Chinese placed great importance on family life. Usually a person

Culture

About ninety-three out of every one hundred people in China are Han Chinese. These people resemble one another in some of their physical features. (See the picture of a Han Chinese family at right.) The Han Chinese are also united by their written language, their history, and their culture. Social scientists use the word "culture" to mean all the customs and ways of living shared by a group of people. What were some of the main features of Han Chinese culture in earlier times? How did the Communists try to change this culture when they first came to power?

felt a stronger sense of loyalty to his or her family than to any other group of people. There were many rules that guided the behavior of family members toward one another. Some of these rules are described on page 48.

Among the Han Chinese in earlier times, women were considered much less important than men. A woman was expected to obey the men in her household at all times. She was not allowed to take part in government or in any other activities outside the home. The feature on pages 184-185 tells more about the traditional role of women in China.

In the past, most of the Han Chinese followed the teachings of the great thinker Confucius.* For example, they felt it was their duty to honor and obey all persons who were in positions of authority over them. Children should obey their parents, just as wives should obey their husbands. Peasants should obey the nobles, and everyone in China should obey the emperor.

The Han Chinese thought it was important to follow ancient rules and customs, such as ancestor* worship. Generally they believed that old ideas and ways of doing things were better than new ones. This is one reason why the

A Chinese scholar. Confucius believed people should study ancient writings to learn the right way to live. Why do you think the Communists were opposed to the teachings of Confucius?

Religion

In the past, the people of China could meet their need for religious faith in a number of different ways. Most Chinese followed a mixture of Confucianism, Taoism, and Buddhism. (See pages 49-50.)

Confucianism was not so much a religion as a set of rules for people to follow in their everyday lives. One of these rules was loyalty to parents and other ancestors. Ancestor* worship was an important part of Confucianism.

Taoism began in China about 2,500 years ago. At first Taoism was mainly a philosophy based upon the idea of living close to nature. Later it came to include such things as fortune-telling and magic.

Buddhism was brought from India about two thousand years ago. It became very popular in some parts of China. In the past, weddings and funerals were often conducted by Buddhist monks.

Like Buddhism, the religions of Islam* and Christianity were brought to China from other countries. They had fewer followers than the other religious faiths.

After the Communists gained control of China in 1949, they closed most places of worship. In addition, they began a

Han Chinese way of life remained much the same for centuries.

The Han Chinese way of life began to change in the late 1800's, as new ideas were brought to China from other countries. The Communists made further changes after they came to power in 1949. But even today, many Han Chinese still follow certain customs and ways of thinking that go back to earlier times.

Other Peoples of China

About seven out of every one hundred Chinese belong to other groups. China has about fifty-five groups of people besides the Han Chinese. The largest group is made up of the Chuang, who live mainly in South China. There are about twelve million Chuang. Other important minority* groups living in South China include the Yi and the Miao. The Manchus live in the northeastern part of China, which used to be known as Manchuria. The autonomous* region of Inner Mongolia is the home of the Mongols. Millions of Hui live in the Ningsia Hui autonomous region and nearby provinces. They are very much like the Han Chinese except that they

in China

propaganda campaign to discourage people from following any religion. This is because communism teaches that there is no God and that all religions are superstition.

The Communists were especially unfriendly to Christianity, because this religion had been brought by the foreigners who invaded China in the 1800's. Many Christian missionaries from Europe and the United States were killed, thrown into prison, or forced to leave the country. Taoism and Confucianism were also attacked by the Communists. These religions contained many ideas that did not fit in with the Communists' goals for China. However, Buddhism and Islam were treated somewhat more kindly. This was partly because China was trying to gain friends in neighboring Asian countries where the people are followers of these religions.

Since the death of Mao Tse-tung, China's government has allowed greater freedom of religion than before. A number of Christian churches, Moslem mosques, and Buddhist temples have been reopened. People are usually allowed to worship freely in these places. But they must not openly try to convert others to their beliefs.

A Buddhist temple in Peking. The Chinese Communists have been somewhat more friendly to Buddhism than to most of the other religions in their country. Why do you suppose this is so?

follow the religion of Islam. (See "Religion in China" above.) Other Moslem peoples, such as the Uighurs and the Kazaks, live in the Sinkiang Uighur autonomous region. The Tibetans make up still another minority group. They live mainly in the autonomous region of Tibet.

Although the minority peoples are few in number compared to the Han Chinese, they live in areas that are highly important to the nation. Most of these areas lie along China's borders with other countries, such as the Soviet Union. The Chinese government claims that it needs to control these areas in order to protect China from foreign invasion. Also, most of these areas are rich in minerals needed by modern industry.

Some of the minority peoples, such as the Manchus, have adopted the language and customs of the Han Chinese. Other minority peoples, such as the Mongols and the Tibetans, still speak their own languages. They also follow certain customs that are different from those of the Han Chinese. For example, some of the Mongols are shepherds who travel from place to place in search of pasture for their sheep.

China's government is trying to win the friendship of the minority peoples. In the past, the Han Chinese often looked down on members of minority groups. They tried to force these people to accept the Han Chinese language and customs. As a result, the Han Chinese and the minority groups did not always get along well with one another.

When the Communists came to power, they promised to respect the rights of the minority peoples. However, they did not always keep their promise. Supposedly the autonomous regions, such as Tibet and Inner Mongolia, were established to allow minority people to govern themselves. But most important government posts in the autonomous regions were held by Han Chinese. These officials made sure that the minority peoples followed orders from the national government. Some minority groups were forced to give up their customary way of living. For example, nomadic* herders such as the Mongols had to settle in permanent villages. In addi-

An army doctor in Sinkiang Uighur teaching medical skills to health workers. The minority peoples of China live mainly in border areas such as Sinkiang Uighur and Tibet. In the past, some of these peoples have rebelled against the Chinese government. Explain why.

tion, China's minority peoples were sometimes prevented from worshiping in their traditional ways. (See "Religion in China" on pages 90-91.)

As time passed, the Communist government began moving large numbers of Han Chinese into the autonomous regions. This was done partly to relieve crowding in eastern China. But it also helped the government keep closer control over the minority peoples. In some areas today, the Han Chinese now greatly outnumber the minority peoples who lived there in the first place.

Over the years, some minority groups rebelled against the government's efforts to change their way of living. For example, a serious revolt broke out in Tibet in the late 1950's. The Tibetans were angry because the Chinese government was trying to take away the power of their leader, the Dalai Lama.* In 1959 the Dalai Lama fled to India to avoid being taken prisoner by the Chinese. Soon afterward, Chinese troops succeeded in putting an end to the revolt. It is claimed that about 65,000 Tibetans died in the fighting.

In recent years, the Chinese government has been trying to improve its relations with the minority peoples. These groups have been given more freedom to worship in their traditional ways and to follow their old customs. Minority leaders are being trained to hold important government posts. In addition, the Chinese government is working to provide more jobs, more schools, and better health care in the autonomous regions. It is too soon to tell how successful these measures will be in winning the friendship of the minority peoples.

Life in Today's China

When the Communists first came to power in China, they started doing away with ideas and customs that they considered "old-fashioned." They tried to replace these with new ideas and ways of living based on Communist teachings. These efforts were more successful in some cases than they were in others. As a result, China's people now follow a mixture of old and new ways of living.

Family loyalty is still very important. The Communist leaders would like all people in China to feel a strong sense of loyalty to their nation and to the Communist Party. Under Mao Tse-tung, the Communists tried to weaken the traditional idea that the family is more important than any other group. For example, children were taught that they should not obey their parents if they thought their parents were not in agreement with Communist ideas.

In spite of these efforts, family ties are still very strong in China. Often parents, children, grandparents, and other relatives all live together in the same household. The grandparents may take care of the children while the parents are at work. Children are treated with great love and kindness. However, they are expected to obey and respect the older members of the family.

Some Chinese still follow their ancient customs. Over the years, the Communist leaders have tried to do away with ancestor worship and other old customs followed by the Han Chinese. They believe that these have no place in a Communist country. In the cities of China, the old customs have largely disappeared. But in the countryside, they are still followed by some of the peasants. On holidays, for example, many families still take food to their ancestors' graves.

Chinese women have more rights and opportunities than before. The treatment of women in China has changed greatly since the Communists came to power. Women now enjoy more rights and opportunities than ever before. However, they are still not treated as the equals of men. For example, there are very few women in high government posts. The feature on pages 184-185 tells more about the changing role of women in China.

People in China do not all have the same standard of living. One of the important teachings of communism is that all people should be equal in wealth. In other words, no one should be much richer or poorer than anyone else. Soon after the Communists came to power in China, most of the wealthy people had their property taken away. At the same time, the government tried to make sure that even the poorest people were able to meet their needs for food, clothing, and shelter.

Under Mao Tse-tung, the government tried to discourage people from living in a way that would make them seem richer than their neighbors. This desire to make everyone equal could be seen even in people's clothing. Both men and women wore baggy trousers and loose cotton shirts or jackets in plain colors. Most women did not wear jewelry or use makeup. They usually wore their hair short and straight, or in long braids.

Today, China's people have more freedom to live as they please. In the larger cities, people dress in a greater variety of styles and colors than they did before. Some women are starting to use makeup and to wear fashionable hairdos.

In spite of Communist teachings, some people in China are much better off than others. For example, city dwellers usually have easier and more enjoyable lives than peasants do. A skilled factory worker may earn twice as much money as an unskilled laborer. High officials in the government and the Communist Party earn more money than other people. They also enjoy a number of special privileges, such as the use of a car for transportation and a fine house to live in.

For most Chinese, life is easier than it used to be. Most people in China today have a better way of life than their parents or grandparents did. In earlier times, many Chinese

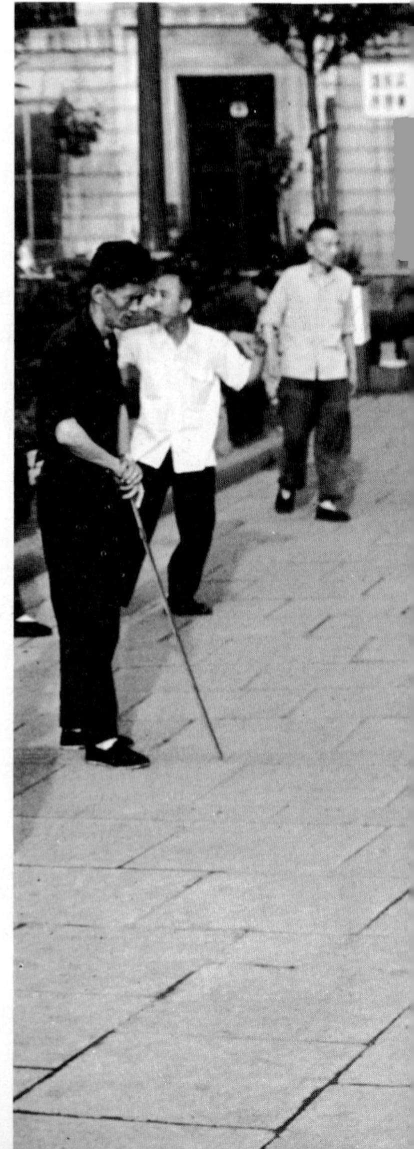

did not have enough food to maintain good health. Their clothing was poor, and they lacked decent housing. Sometimes millions of people died of hunger or disease. Today this is no longer true. Most Chinese are now able to meet their basic needs for food, clothing, and shelter.

China is still a very poor country, however. Many of the things that are part of everyday life in the United States are luxuries in China. For example, a Chinese family may have to wait up to two years to buy a bicycle or a sewing machine because these items are so scarce. Also, items such as these are very expensive for the average person. A black-and-white television set, for instance, may cost as much as a year's wages.

As you discovered earlier, the leaders of China are trying to provide a better life for their people. Progress is now being made toward this goal. But it will be many years before China has a standard of living like that of Japan, the United States, and other industrial nations.

This picture shows people doing *tai* chi chuan* exercises in Shanghai. *Tai chi chuan* is an ancient form of exercise that is still very popular in China. Although the Communists have tried to do away with some of the old customs, they approve of *tai chi chuan*. What do you suppose is the reason for this?

Fields and villages in the North China province of Hopeh. About four fifths of China's people live and work in farming villages. How does their way of life differ from that of farmers in our country? To answer this question, you may wish to do additional research in other sources.

8 Farming Villages

A visit to a farming village in North China. It is a warm day in June, and we are traveling through the province of Hopeh in North China. (See map on page 82.) Mr. Ho, a guide provided by the Chinese government, is accompanying us. The bumpy gravel road on which we are driving is lined with tall poplar trees. On both sides of the road are golden wheat fields and bright-green rows of corn, soybeans, and other crops. In the distance are steep hillsides covered with terraces on which more crops are being grown.

We pass several groups of men and women who are hard at work in the fields. Some are harvesting wheat. Others are hoeing corn or digging irrigation* ditches that will bring more water to the growing crops. In a few places, people are using small hand-guided tractors or other kinds of farm machinery. But most of the people we see are using simple tools such as hoes and shovels.

Every mile or two, we pass a small village almost hidden among the fields. Mr. Ho tells us that most of the people in China live in small farming villages like these.

A Chinese farmhouse. Our car is entering one of the villages now. We see several small houses grouped around a brick courtyard. The houses have tile roofs, and walls made of gray brick. Near each house is a tiny garden with rows of tomatoes, beans, and other vegetables. A few chickens are running loose around the courtyard. Nearby are some pens where hogs are kept.

As we stop in front of one of the houses, we are greeted by a smiling woman about fifty years old.

*See Glossary

A Problem To Solve
This picture shows some Chinese farmers threshing wheat. How is life changing today for the people in China's farming villages? In forming your hypotheses to solve this problem, you will need to consider changes in:

a. local government
b. the amount of freedom given to Chinese farmers
c. the standard* of living

Information in Chapter 5 will also be helpful in solving this problem.

See pages 198-200

This is Mrs. Chun. She and her husband live here with their son and his wife and two small grandchildren. A fifteen-year-old daughter and Mrs. Chun's elderly mother also live in this house. Every day except Sunday, Mrs. Chun's husband goes to work in the fields. The son and daughter-in-law go with him. Mrs. Chun and her mother stay at home and take care of the grandchildren. The teenaged daughter goes to a secondary school nearby.

Mrs. Chun invites us to come inside her house. While she prepares tea for us, we look around the room in which we are sitting. It is quite dark in here, for the windows are small. A single electric light bulb hangs from the ceiling.

This room is a combination living room, bedroom, and kitchen. On one side is a small stove in which charcoal is burned as fuel. This is where Mrs. Chun is preparing tea. Along another wall is a raised platform made of brick and cov-

Cooking a meal in a Chinese kitchen. The stove in this picture burns charcoal as fuel. What are some other furnishings that you might see if you were to visit a typical farmhouse in China?

ered with a bamboo mat. This is a *kang*, which serves as a bed. During the cold winter months, a small fire is built under the *kang* to keep the bed warm. The room also contains a wooden table, several chairs, a sewing machine, and a large chest for storage. A transistor radio stands on the table. Hanging on the wall are some photographs of the family and pictures of China's Communist leaders.

We learn that the only other room in this house is another bedroom. There is a loft above the ceiling, which is used for storing large clay jars full of grain.

This house has no running water. All of the water needed for cooking, washing, and other purposes must be carried in buckets from a well in the courtyard. There is an outdoor toilet nearby, which is used by several families.

How the villagers earn their living. As we sip our tea, Mr. Ho tells us how the people in this village earn their living. He says that they grow grain crops such as wheat and corn to sell. Each family farms a piece of land about two acres in size. It does not own this land, because in China all farmland belongs to the government. Instead, it rents the land for several years at a time.

In order to rent farmland, each family must sign a contract with the village production team. This is an organization made up of all the farmers in the village -about eighty people. In the contract, a family agrees to grow a certain amount of grain for the production team each year. The production team sells this grain to the government at a set price.

When a family produces more grain than the agreed amount, it can use the surplus in any way it pleases. For example, it may sell some of the extra grain to other villagers. Or it may take the grain to the nearby town of Lushan to sell at the market there. Thus, the more grain that a family produces, the more money it can earn.

In this village, each family is responsible for producing its own crops. But sometimes several families work together to carry out such tasks as planting and harvesting. Projects that will help all the villagers, such as digging irrigation ditches, are shared by everyone.

We ask Mr. Ho what the production team does with the money it gets from selling grain to the government. He says that the team pays the villagers for their grain. It also pays taxes to the government and buys needed supplies, such as fertilizer and farm machinery. For instance, the team has purchased several foot-powered threshing machines. (See picture on pages 140-141.) The villagers take turns using these machines to thresh their grain. Now the team is saving money to buy a large tractor. It will use this tractor to plow the villagers' fields before they plant their crops. At present, the team rents a tractor from the Red Star Agricultural Company in Lushan. (See pages 101-102.)

Mr. Ho asks us if we saw the vegetable gardens in the village. He says that each family is given a small plot of land in addition to the land it rents for growing grain. These private plots take up only 5 percent of the land around the village. But they give the villagers a place to grow vegetables and to raise a few chickens or pigs. Most villagers earn extra money by selling their vegetables or livestock at the market in Lushan.

Education and health care in the countryside. After thanking Mrs. Chun for her hospitality, we return to our car

Family members hoeing vegetables. In Chinese farming villages, each family is given a small plot of land on which to grow vegetables and to raise livestock such as chickens and pigs. Why do you suppose this is done? Chapter 5 also contains information that will be helpful to you.

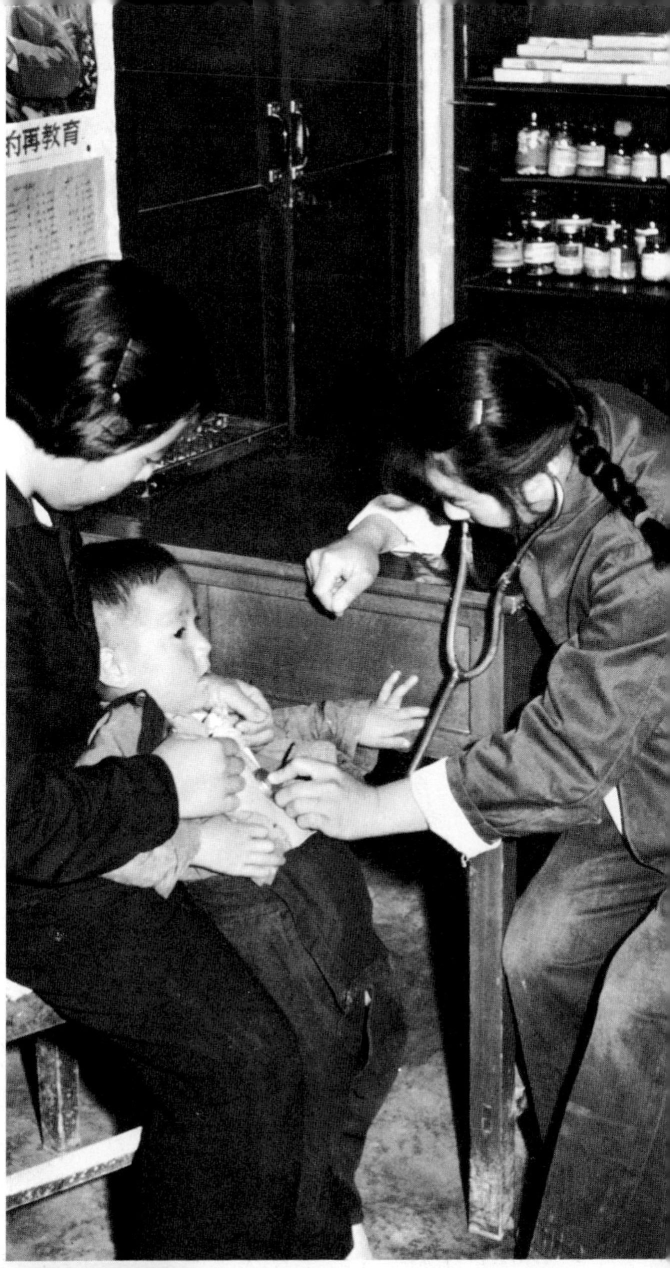

The picture above shows a "barefoot doctor" examining a young child in a Chinese clinic. What are barefoot doctors? What kind of training do these people receive? Today, barefoot doctors are employed in farming areas throughout China. Why do you suppose this is so?

Education

See pages 193-194

and leave the village. A short distance down the road, we pass a low brick building. This is an elementary school. In the past, there were no schools in this area. Most of the village children did not have an opportunity to learn to read and write. Today, nearly all the children attend elementary school, and some go on to secondary school. (See Chapter 10.)

Our car stops at another building, which we discover is a medical clinic. Here we see a girl about nineteen years old bandaging a cut on a man's hand. This girl, who received several months of training in a city hospital, is called a barefoot* doctor. She teaches the villagers how to prevent disease by observing rules of cleanliness and eating proper foods. She also treats simple injuries and illnesses. If people have more serious medical problems, they go to a hospital in Lushan. This hospital has beds for thirty patients.

A visit to the town of Lushan. Now we are approaching Lushan. The offices of the township government are located here. There are fifteen farming villages in this township, which covers an area seven miles (eleven km.) long and five miles (eight km.) wide.

Also in Lushan are the offices of the Red Star Agricultural Company. This is a collective* which is similar in some ways to business firms in the United States. The Red Star Company runs several stores where farmers can buy the supplies they need. We visit one of these stores in Lushan. Here we see people buying groceries, clothing, bicycles, and other items.

We learn that the Red Star Company also owns a dairy farm, a poultry farm, and a large apple orchard. It sells the milk, eggs, meat, and fruit produced on these farms to the government. Most of these products are then sold to people in China's cities.

Our last stop in Lushan is a small factory where workers are making electric light bulbs. Mr. Ho explains that this is one of several factories owned by the Red Star Company. These factories serve two purposes. They provide jobs for people who cannot earn a living by farming. They also supply the farmers with manufactured goods they need.

China's changing farm communes. As we leave Lushan, Mr. Ho tells us that great changes are taking place in China's countryside. Until recently, nearly all of China's farmland was divided into communes. (See pages 64-65.) These were like giant farms, covering many square miles in area. Each commune had its own government.

The commune leaders were usually very powerful. They could tell farmers what crops to grow, and what farming methods to use. They ran the schools, hospitals, stores, and factories in the commune. The villagers had little freedom to make decisions affecting their own lives.

In the communes, everyone was supposed to be equal in wealth. Most of the crops produced by the farmers were turned over to the commune government. A farmer who produced large amounts of crops was often no better off than one who produced very little. So farmers had little reason to work hard or to try new farming methods.

In the late 1970's, China's leaders began to make changes in the commune system. They knew that China could not make progress unless its farmers produced more crops and livestock. To reach this goal, they decided to give farmers more freedom and to reward the ones who were most productive.

Today, some of China's communes have been done away with. The ones that remain are gradually changing. Many of them no longer have any powers of government. These have been taken over by the townships. Schools and hospitals in the countryside are now often run by the township governments. In some rural areas, stores and factories are owned by collectives like the Red Star Company. Perhaps someday the communes will disappear entirely.

See pages 195-196

Farmers planting seed in Honan Province. In China most farm work is done by hand or with the help of animals. But today more and more farmers are using hand-guided tractors and other farm machines. How do you think this will change their way of living?

A changing way of life. Today, farm families in China have more freedom than they did in the past. Often they are allowed to choose what crops and livestock they will raise. They can also decide what farming methods to use. They can buy their own tractors and other farm machines. Once they have met their production quotas, any other crops and livestock they produce are theirs to use as they please. By selling these products, they can earn extra money to buy some of the things they need.

So far, the changes in China's system of farming seem to be quite successful. China's farmers are producing more crops and livestock than ever before. As a result, they are beginning to enjoy a higher standard* of living. Some of them are buying hand-guided tractors and other machines to make their farm work easier. They are also buying items such as washing machines, cameras, bicycles, and television sets. Even though most of the village farmers are still quite poor, they have hopes of a better future.

A view of Peking from Coal Hill. Peking is the capital and second largest city in China. Although most of China's people live in rural areas, there are more than thirty-five urban* areas with a population of over one million. Why do you suppose so many large cities have grown up in China?

9 Cities

As you have discovered, China is mainly a farming nation. Yet it also has some of the world's largest cities. In China today, there are more than thirty-five urban* areas with a population of more than one million.

Nearly all of China's cities are in the eastern part of the country. Many of these cities are more than two thousand years old. In some of them, ancient city walls with huge towers and gates can still be seen.

A tour of Peking. One of China's most beautiful cities is the capital, Peking. This city is located in the northern part of the Yellow Plain. (Compare maps on pages 21 and 25.) It is second only to Shanghai in population. More than nine million people live in Peking and the surrounding area.

To learn more about Peking, we are going to take a tour with our government guide Mr. Ho. We begin by climbing to the top of a tree-covered hill near

*See Glossary

the center of the city. From here, we can see some of the main avenues that extend through Peking. Most of these avenues are straight, and run either north and south or east and west. They were laid out by the great Mongol emperor Kublai Khan, who ruled China about seven hundred years ago. (See pages 46-47.) Peking was already very old when Kublai Khan came to power, but he rebuilt it and made it his capital city in China. Except for brief periods, it has been China's capital ever since.

Mr. Ho tells us that Peking is divided into two main parts, the Inner City and the Outer City. (See map on page 106.) The Outer City lies to the south. When the Manchus* ruled China, this was the part of Peking in which the Han* Chinese people lived. The Manchus lived in the Inner City.

One part of the Inner City is surrounded by a high red wall. This is the Imperial City. In earlier times, the government offices of the great Chinese Empire were located here. Today, the Communist leaders of China have their homes and offices in the Imperial City. The hill on which we are standing is in this part of Peking. It is called Coal Hill, and was built long ago of dirt that was removed to make three artificial lakes. These lakes stretch in a shimmering line through the western part of the Imperial City. Along their shores are beautiful old palaces and temples.

We leave Coal Hill and enter the Forbidden City, where China's emperors used to live. In those days, ordinary people were not allowed to come here, but now the Forbidden City is a public museum. As we walk through the Forbidden City, we see vast courtyards, beautiful gardens, and brilliantly colored palaces with yellow tile roofs.

Now we are approaching Tien An Men Square, which lies to the south of the Forbidden City. This is a huge open space used for political rallies and colorful parades. Near the middle of the square is a large, new building called the Mao Tse-tung Memorial Hall. It contains the tomb of China's famous leader. The enormous building that we see at one side of Tien An Men Square is the Great Hall of the People. The National People's Congress and other government bodies hold their meetings here.

A government car is waiting for us in Tien An Men Square. We get in the car and ride along one of the broad avenues that extend through Peking. Large stores and modern office buildings rise on both sides. The street is filled with people riding bicycles or pedicabs.* We are surprised to find very few cars here, although we do see a number of trucks and buses.

Now our car turns onto a side street. Leading into this street are many narrow, tree-lined alleys called *hutungs*.

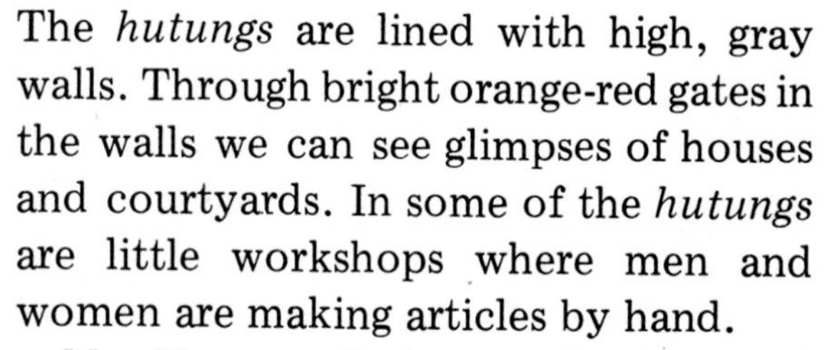

The *hutungs* are lined with high, gray walls. Through bright orange-red gates in the walls we can see glimpses of houses and courtyards. In some of the *hutungs* are little workshops where men and women are making articles by hand.

Mr. Ho says that our next stop will be at the Temple of Heaven. (See map below.) This is a cluster of religious buildings set in a beautiful park in Peking's Outer City. One of the buildings is the Hall of Annual Prayer for Good Crops. In times past, the rulers of China

Peking is divided into two main parts, the Inner City and the Outer City. Who lived in each part of the city during earlier times? The map below shows some of the places of interest in Peking. To the right is a picture showing one of Peking's main avenues. How does this street differ from an avenue in an American city like New York or Los Angeles?

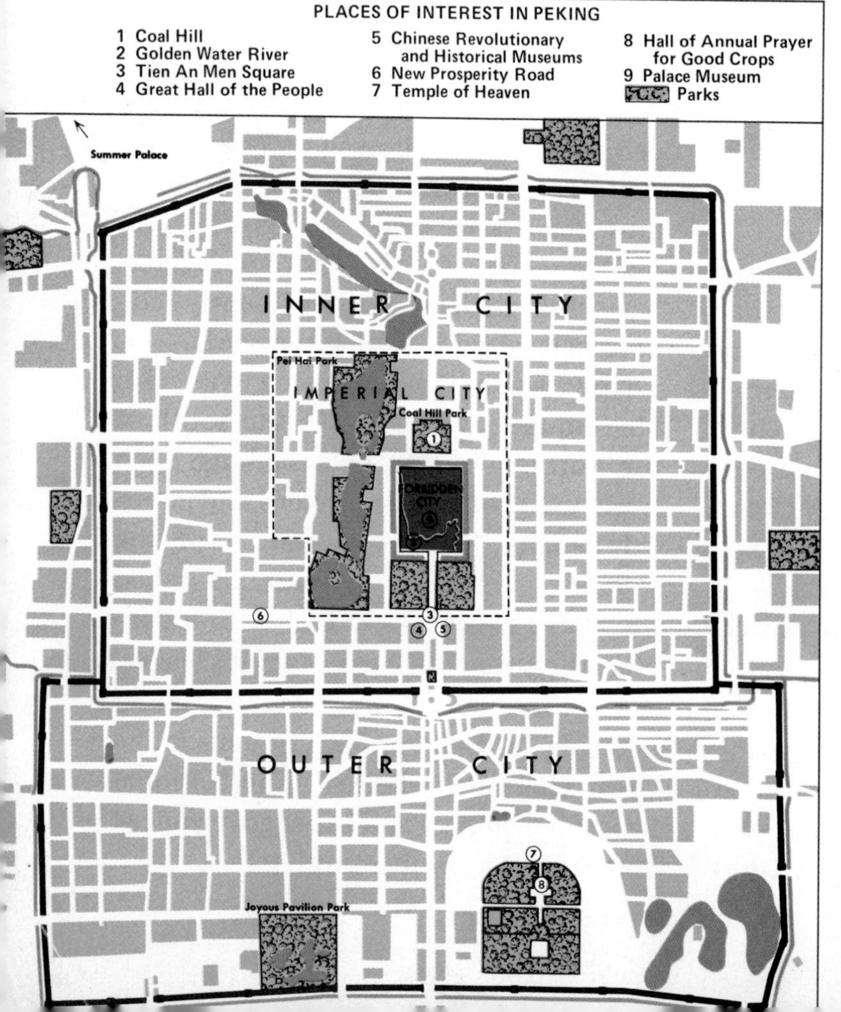

came here to offer sacrifices and ask the gods to give the farmers a good harvest.

When we leave the Temple of Heaven we ride eastward, toward the suburbs that stretch for miles around Peking. Many of the streets through which we ride are lined with trees. Mr. Ho says that the people of Peking have planted millions of trees in recent years. These trees have helped to cut down on the heavy yellow dust that swirls through the city whenever strong winds blow from the north.

We have reached Peking's eastern suburbs now. Many new factories have been built here. Since the Communists came to power, they have encouraged the growth of industry in the Peking area. Today, factories here produce a wide variety of goods, including steel, chemicals, textiles, locomotives, and farm machinery.

When we visit one of the industrial plants, we notice that the buildings are surrounded by fields of vegetables. These fields are tended by the factory

workers and their families. Nearby are brick apartment buildings where the workers and their families live.

Before leaving the Peking area, we drive several miles northwest of the city to visit the Summer Palace. Here we see a number of temples and pavilions* overlooking a beautiful lake. We also see many artificial hills and streams. In the late 1800's, Empress Dowager Tzu Hsi* spent vast sums of money on the buildings and gardens here. Today the Summer Palace is open to the public as a museum.

On our way back to the city, we pass the large campus of Peking University. This is one of more than thirty colleges, universities, and technical schools in the Peking area. Peking has the largest library in China, as well as many theaters and museums. We can understand why this city is usually considered the cultural center of China.

Shanghai. Now we fly southeastward to Shanghai, the largest city in China. About twelve million people make their homes in Shanghai and its suburbs. This enormous city spreads out along the banks of the Hwang Pu River, which flows into the mouth of the Yangtze River about fourteen miles north of here. Large, oceangoing ships travel to Shanghai by way of the Yangtze and the Hwang Pu.

Shanghai was a small, unimportant city until 1842, when China lost a war with Great Britain. (See page 56.) The British realized that Shanghai was in an excellent location to serve as a seaport for the densely populated Yangtze River Plain. They forced the Chinese to allow English traders to settle on the wastelands outside the city walls. Later, French, American, and Japanese traders also came to Shanghai. The foreigners built whole new sections of Shanghai, including homes, stores, factories, and office buildings. Thousands of Chinese poured into Shanghai in search of jobs. Most of them settled in the old part of the city. Shanghai soon became one of the busiest seaports in the world.

After the Communists took over China in 1949, most of the foreign traders and their families left Shanghai. Today, nearly all of the people in the city are native Chinese.

The morning after we arrive in Shanghai, we ride through the city. First we visit the old section, where we see narrow, twisting streets lined with houses and shops. Next we visit the part of Shanghai built by the foreign traders. Near the riverbank in this section is a wide avenue bordered by skyscrapers. These buildings are much like the skyscrapers that were built in the United States about fifty years ago. We also drive along Shanghai's main shopping street. Here we see store windows displaying a variety of goods. Shanghai is the most prosperous city in China, and the one that most resembles American cities.

When we drive along the Hwang Pu River, we notice that it is filled with ships of all sizes. Shanghai is China's most important seaport. From Shanghai, riverboats travel for hundreds of miles up the Yangtze.

We notice many factories in Shanghai, for this is China's leading industrial city. Some of the factories produce cotton or silk textiles. There are also large ship-

Migration

Apartment houses for workers in Shanghai. In the late 1800's and early 1900's, huge numbers of people from rural areas came to Shanghai and other Chinese cities in search of jobs. It was difficult to provide housing and other necessities for so many newcomers. Do research to find out whether cities in other countries have faced similar problems. How has the present government of China tried to solve the problems resulting from this great migration?

yards and steel mills here. Other products made in Shanghai include machinery, chemicals, fertilizers, and cement.

Many of the older factories in Shanghai are crowded into industrial areas that have no room for workers' housing. To provide homes for the people who work in these factories, new "workers' villages" have been built in outlying parts of the city.

We are approaching one of these workers' villages now. It includes a cluster of apartment buildings that house about 15,000 families. There are also shops, schools, medical clinics, and a park in the village.

We are invited to visit the Lin family, who live in an apartment building here. Both the mother and the father work in a factory several miles away. Their two small children are cared for in a nursery in the village.

There are only two rooms in the Lin family's apartment. Both rooms are

Shanghai is China's largest city. About twelve million people live in the Shanghai area. This view shows office buildings and apartments along Soochow Creek, which flows into the Hwang Pu River nearby. How did Shanghai's location help to make it an important trading and manufacturing city?

quite small, with whitewashed walls and cement floors. Although both rooms are used as bedrooms, the first room we enter is also used as a living and dining room. The furniture consists of a bed, a table, some chairs, a chest, and a sewing machine. Family pictures decorate the walls. This apartment has electric lights and a small sink with running water. The Lin family shares a kitchen and a bathroom with other families on the same floor of the building.

We join the family for supper at their favorite restaurant. It is a simple place with a bare wooden floor and plain tables and chairs. All the tables around us are full, and the people talk and laugh together good-naturedly as they eat. We order pork and noodles, which we eat with chopsticks. Much of the food served here is raised on farms in the Shanghai area.

Canton. Next we fly southwestward to Canton, which the Chinese people call Guangzhou.† The fertile delta on which this city lies is crossed by many rivers and canals. Canton stretches along the banks of the Pearl River, which empties into the South China Sea. (See map on page 21.) About seven and one-half million people live in Canton and its suburbs.

For many centuries, Canton was an important seaport. Traders from Southwest Asia* began coming here as early as A.D. 300. Later, people from Portugal and other European countries also came to Canton. In the late 1700's and early 1800's, Canton was the only Chinese port open to foreign trade. Today, modern oceangoing ships do not come to Canton, because the Pearl River is not deep enough for them at this point. These ships must dock at Whampoa, nine miles downstream, or at the British port of Hong Kong.*

Canton is still a major trading city, however. Twice a year it hosts a large trade fair, where new products that China offers for export are displayed. Thousands of business people from other countries come to Canton to view these products.

Canton is an important manufacturing city. Many of its factories are small workshops that produce craft articles such as jade carvings and gold jewelry. But Canton also has large sugar refineries and factories that make such products as machinery, chemicals, and paper.

The evening we arrive in Canton, we take a walk along the Pearl River. Here we see some little wooden houseboats like the ones shown in the picture above. These are called sampans. In the

†Pinyin spelling. See page 18.

past, thousands of Canton's people made their homes in boats like these because it was so expensive to buy land in the city. Then the government began to build housing on land for the sampan dwellers. Today, many of the houseboats that once crowded the Pearl River are gone.

As we walk back to our hotel, we notice that the streets are dimly lit and almost deserted. In China, people go to bed early and get up early in the morning. By 9:30 at night, restaurants and movie houses are generally closed.

Other cities of China. We are sorry that we cannot stay longer in China, because

Canton, which the Chinese people call Guangzhou, is an important seaport and manufacturing city. It lies along the Pearl River in the southern part of China. Canton's famous trade fair is held in the large building shown in the picture below. What is the purpose of this fair?

there are many other cities we would like to visit. Some of these are very old cities, with temples and palaces that were built hundreds of years ago. Others are modern industrial centers that have grown up during the past century.

Many of China's largest cities are located in the northeastern part of the country. (See map on pages 20 and 21.) For example, Tientsin lies in the fertile Yellow Plain, at the northern end of the Grand Canal. It is an important trading and manufacturing city. Shenyang* and Harbin are the largest cities on the Manchurian Plain. Factories in these cities process farm crops and minerals produced in the surrounding area. Port Arthur and Dairen are important seaports on the Yellow Sea. Together they make up the city of Luta.

Several large cities are located along the mighty Yangtze River. One of these is Nanking, whose name means "southern capital." It served as capital of China for a number of years while the Nationalists* were in control of the country. Today it is a busy river port and textile-manufacturing center. Farther upstream on the Yangtze is the important manufacturing city of Wuhan. Some of the largest steel mills in China are located here. The ancient city of Chungking lies in the fertile Red Basin. It, too, is a leading river port and manufacturing city.

Some of China's other cities would also be interesting to visit. Near Shanghai are the ancient cities of Soochow and Hangchow. Both of these cities are noted for their beautiful gardens, pagodas, and temples. The city of Sian is located on the same site as Changan, which was the capital of China under several of the early dynasties. Today Sian is an important trading center and textile-manufacturing city. The largest city in western China is Urumchi. This city lies in an oasis* on the northern slopes of the mountain range called Tien Shan. Many of the people in Urumchi are Uighurs, who follow the religion of Islam.* Lhasa, the main city in Tibet, lies in a valley more than eleven thousand feet above sea level. In Lhasa is a huge palace called the Potala. It was formerly the home of the Dalai Lama,* who used to be the ruler of Tibet.

The Potala is a huge palace that stands on a hill overlooking Lhasa, the ancient capital of Tibet. Who formerly lived in the Potala?

10 Education

A Chinese primary school. It is a cool, bright day in October, and we are on our way to visit a primary school in the city of Nanking. (See map on page 21.) A wall of gray brick surrounds the school. As we enter the gate, we see a group of low buildings with tile roofs. A neatly dressed young woman approaches us and speaks to us in English. This is Miss Wu, a teacher who has been asked to serve as our guide.

We enter one of the buildings and walk down a dark hallway to a classroom. There are about fifty students in

A Problem To Solve

The photograph at left shows a classroom in a Peking middle school. China's government is trying to provide enough schools for all young people in the country. Why do China's Communist leaders consider education so important? To solve this problem, you will need to consider facts about the following:

a. ways of earning a living in China today
b. changes in China's customs and religion
c. China's form of government

Chapters 6, 7, and 16 of this book contain additional information that will be helpful to you.

See pages 198-200

this room, seated on wooden benches behind plain wooden desks. The classroom is quiet and orderly. On the walls are several brightly colored posters, with messages written in large Chinese symbols.

This is a mathematics class, and one of the students is preparing to work a problem on an abacus.* The teacher says, "In the old days, farmer Chang had to give his landlord two thirds of his crop. If farmer Chang produced fifteen hundred catties* of rice in a year, how much would he have to give the landlord?" After the student has solved the problem, the teacher tells the class what a hard life the farmers had before the Communists took over China. She says that life is much better for farm workers today.

In the next classroom we enter, the children are learning English. They are memorizing a poem that praises the heroic deeds of the Chinese Communist soldiers during the Long March. (See page 59.)

Miss Wu tells us that the school we are visiting is quite typical of primary schools all over China today. She says that children begin primary school when they are six or seven years old. They have classes six days a week, with a month's vacation in the summer and another month in the winter. The younger students spend a great deal of time learning to read and write Chinese, because this is a very difficult language. (See pages 182-183.) They also have classes in mathematics, science, art, music, physical education, and politics. The older children also study English or some other foreign language.

Now we go to another building and enter a workshop. Here the teacher is showing some children how to file grooves in pieces of metal that will be made into bus steps. All the children spend several hours a week in this

*See Glossary

workshop, doing useful tasks. In addition, the older students spend two weeks every year working in a factory or on a farm. This helps to teach them to respect people who work with their hands.

A Chinese secondary school. After children attend primary school for five or six years, they are ready for secondary school. In China, secondary schools are called "middle schools." Let's visit a middle school in Nanking. More than two thousand students attend classes in this large, four-story building.

We are met at the door by Mr. Fan, the principal of the middle school. He tells us that students here attend classes six days a week and study a number of different subjects. Among these are Chinese language and literature, mathematics, chemistry, physics, art, history, and politics. Some foreign languages are also taught. On the school grounds are small factories where students make such articles as radio parts and wooden chairs. Students also spend about one month a year working in a factory or on a farm.

Higher education in China. Mr. Fan tells us that students attend this middle school for five years. After they graduate, most of them will go to work at jobs assigned by the government. These jobs are usually in factories, on farms, or in the army. If they wish, these people can continue their education by taking spare-time classes in subjects such as bookkeeping or the repair of farm machinery.

A small number of graduates from the middle school have an opportunity to attend colleges and universities. There are about 675 colleges and universities in China today. Some of them offer courses in many different subjects. Others train students for a particular field of work, such as agriculture, engineering, medicine, or teaching. Students usually spend about five years in college. After graduation, they, too, must work at jobs assigned to them by the government.

Education in earlier times. Through the centuries, education has always been considered very important in China. In the past, however, only a few families could afford to send their children to school. A small group of educated people held all the important positions in government. They thought that they were better than the great majority of people, who earned their living by working with their hands.

After China became a republic, the Nationalists* made great efforts to improve education. During the 1920's, new schools and universities were established in China. Many classes were also set up where adults could learn to read and write. In spite of these efforts, most people in China were still unable to obtain much education. Before 1949, only two out of every ten Chinese knew how to read and write.

After the Communists came to power, they, too, tried to provide more opportunities for education. Spare-time classes were organized for peasants and factory workers. Many new schools were built in villages throughout China. The government also established new colleges and universities to train students for careers in science and other fields.

The Communists also changed the way that schools in China were run. Students were required to spend many hours each

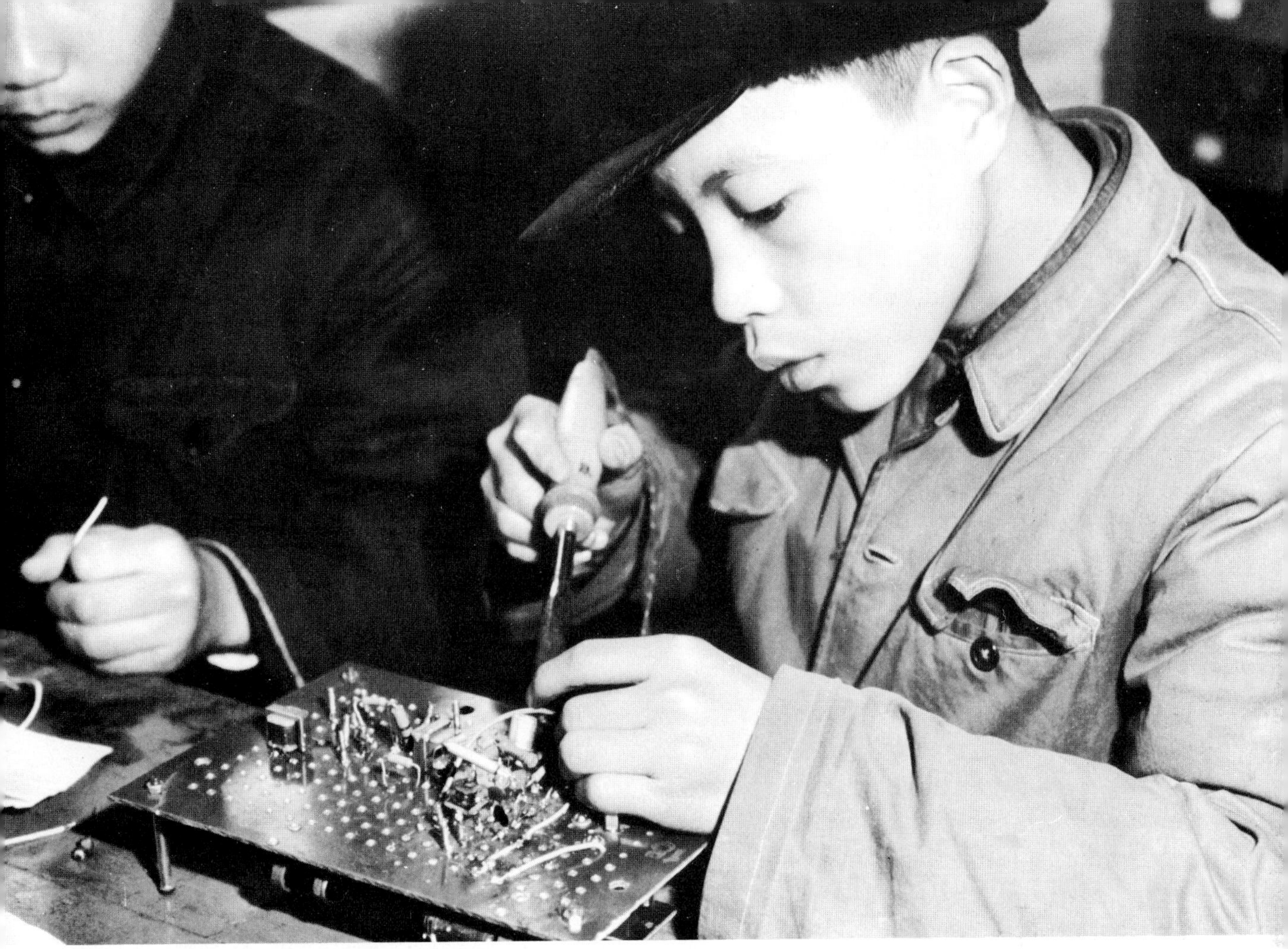

Learning to repair a radio. Students in China usually spend part of their time in factories or workshops, learning to do useful tasks. What do you suppose are some of the reasons for this?

week learning about communism. They also had to spend part of their time working on farms or in factories.

Why Mao was dissatisfied with education in China. Even these changes did not satisfy China's leader Mao Tse-tung. In the early 1960's, he began to criticize Chinese schools. Mao complained that some teachers were not trying hard enough to inspire their students with loyalty toward communism. He also said that students were being forced to learn many things that would be of little value to them when they began working at full-time jobs.

At that time, most colleges and universities in China required young people to pass examinations in order to be admitted as students. Usually the children of well-educated government officials found it easier to pass the examinations than the children of peasants and factory workers. In Mao's view, this was wrong. He said that the schools were helping to create a new "ruling class" in China instead of providing equal opportunities for everyone.

The Cultural Revolution brought great changes in education. In 1966, Mao issued an important statement describing some of the changes that he wanted to make in education. This was near the beginning of the Cultural Revolution. (See pages 66-68.) As the Cultural

Revolution spread through China, all schools and universities were closed.

When the schools finally opened again, many changes had been made. Students no longer had to spend as many years in school as they did before. For example, primary school was shortened from six to five years. Students were required to spend much of their time outside the classroom, working in factories or on farms. They also had to spend more time studying Communist ideas.

Nearly all examinations were done away with. As a result, colleges and universities had to use a new method of selecting students. Most farm communes, army units, and large factories were allowed to choose a certain number of persons to attend colleges and universities. These were people who had worked at full-time jobs for at least two or three years after graduating from middle school. They had to be recommended by their fellow workers. Also, they had to have political views that were approved by the Communist leaders.

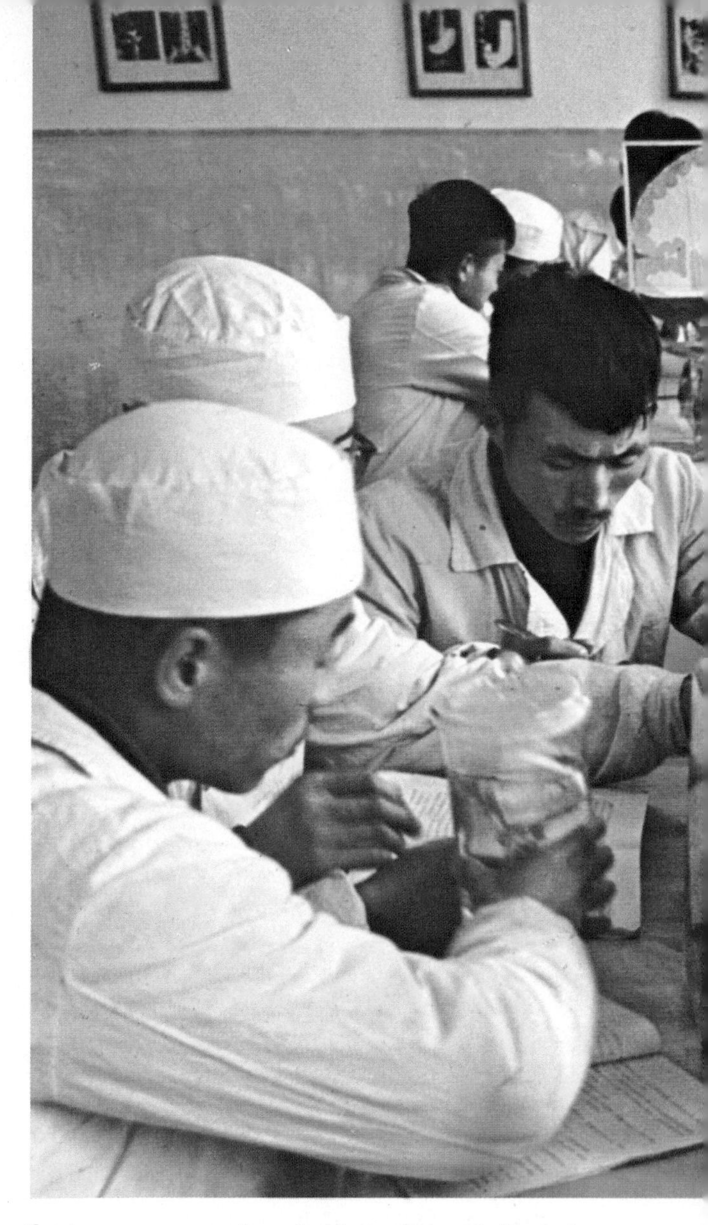

Chinese education has changed again since Mao's death. Mao Tse-tung died in 1976. (See page 69.) Before long, the new leaders of China were strongly criticizing the changes that had been made during the Cultural Revolution. They said that these changes had made it impossible for many bright young Chinese to get a good education.

As you know, China's new leaders want their country to become a modern industrial nation. They realize that this goal cannot be accomplished without a large supply of scientists, engineers, and other well-educated people. To improve education, the Chinese government has done away with many of the changes that were made during the Cultural Revolution.

Today, students in China spend less time working with their hands and studying Communist ideas. This gives them more time to learn subjects such as mathematics and science. Students are again required to pass difficult examinations in order to enter Chinese colleges and universities. It is no longer necessary for young people to work at full-time jobs for two or three years before going to college. Instead, they can enter college as soon as they graduate from middle school.

Medical students in the city of Harbin. What changes took place in Chinese colleges and universities during the Cultural Revolution? What changes have been made since that time?

The government has also tried to improve education by establishing "key schools" throughout China. There are key primary and middle schools as well as key colleges and universities. Only the best students may attend key schools, which are provided with better teachers and more modern equipment than other schools.

In the past, only a few Chinese young people were allowed to travel abroad to study. Today, thousands of students are attending colleges and universities in foreign countries, including the United States.

China still faces great problems in providing education for its people. Since the Communists came to power in 1949, China has made much progress in education. The government claims that at least eight out of every ten Chinese adults can now read and write. Many serious problems remain, however. The opportunities for a good education are much fewer in rural areas than in the cities. Rural communities often do not have enough money to build schools or to buy the necessary equipment. There is a severe shortage of trained teachers. Also, many rural children drop out of primary school after a few years in order to help their families earn a living.

China also faces problems in higher education. It cannot build buildings or train professors fast enough to serve all the young people who are qualified to attend college. Today about one million students attend Chinese colleges and universities. This is a very small number for such a large country. Many more people will need to have a college education if China is to become a modern industrial nation.

Activities outside of school. Much education in China takes place outside the classroom. Often parents and teachers meet to plan special projects for children to work on after school and during vacations. The Communist Party has two main youth organizations, the Young Pioneers of China and the Communist Youth League. These organizations also plan spare-time activities for young people. For example, a student may spend part of his or her time planting trees or writing plays about political subjects. Like classes in school, these activities are supposed to help China's young people become loyal followers of communism.

Elementary school students visiting the Forbidden City in Peking. In China much education takes place outside the classroom. Parents and teachers plan various activities for children after school and during vacations. Do you think this is a good idea? Why? Why not?

11 Arts and Crafts

For thousands of years, people in China have been creating beautiful works of art. Today, Chinese paintings and sculptures are displayed in many of the world's leading museums. Poems and stories written by Chinese authors have been translated into a number of different languages. Pottery and other handicraft articles made in China are sold in stores around the world.

Traditional Arts and Crafts

Painting. One of the most important arts in ancient China was painting. Some paintings showed fierce dragons and other imaginary creatures. Others were of Chinese lords and ladies, or of holy people honored by the Buddhist* religion. But most of the paintings showed scenes from the Chinese countryside, including mountains, lakes, and forests. Chinese artists loved the beauty of the out-of-doors, and felt they could live more happily by being close to nature.

Imagine that it is the year 1200 and an old, white-haired artist is preparing to paint a landscape. He travels to a beautiful spot where he can see steep, rugged mountains and a flowing stream. Hour after hour passes while he studies the view and decides what to put into his picture. Now the artist goes home. In his quiet garden he spends more time thinking about what he has seen and the picture he plans to paint.

Finally the artist is ready to begin. He takes out a soft brush and some ink

*See Glossary

A mountain landscape. In ancient times, Chinese artists often painted scenes from nature. What do you suppose was the reason for this?

made of soot from burned wood. He also places a long strip of silk cloth on a table. With swift, sure strokes he begins to paint mountains and a stream on the cloth.

Paintings like the one described here were mounted on scrolls, which could be rolled up and stored away. Some of the loveliest Chinese picture scrolls are of birds, flowers, or bamboo. Just as four-leaf clovers make us think of good luck, certain birds and flowers make the Chinese think of special things. For example, a peach tree is the symbol of long life. Chrysanthemums stand for autumn, and plum blossoms for winter. Chinese artists of earlier times used these symbols to help their paintings give a message. Even today, some Chinese artists paint in this traditional manner.

Most picture scrolls are decorated with rows of Chinese word symbols. (Chinese writing is described on pages 182-183.) Chinese artists use the same careful brushstrokes to write words as they do to paint pictures. The art of making these decorative word symbols is known as calligraphy.

Architecture. In the past, architects in China were careful to design their buildings to fit into the landscape around them. Often, small pavilions* were built on hillsides that looked out across a scenic view. An especially lovely spot might be marked with a gateway.

Some of the most beautiful architecture in China is found in old temples and palaces. Many of these buildings have tile roofs that turn up at the corners. Walls and pillars are sometimes painted in bright colors. Tall, graceful towers called pagodas were built by the Chinese people to honor the religious leader Buddha. Many of these pagodas are still standing today.

Sculpture. When we tour an old Chinese temple, we see another form of traditional art. We enter a shadowy room and walk past a row of red pillars until we come to a huge statue of Buddha. There are many religious statues similar to this one in China. Some are made of stone and stand in dim caves. (See picture on pages 50-51.) Chinese artists also created many exciting sculptures of lions, elephants, and other animals.

Opera. Another form of art that has been enjoyed in China for centuries is opera.* In a traditional Chinese

The Hall of Perfect Harmony is one of many beautiful palaces in Peking's Forbidden City. (See page 105.) Long ago, the Manchu emperors of China held official ceremonies in this building. Architecture is one of several forms of art that have been enjoyed by China's people for hundreds of years. Other important arts include painting, sculpture, literature, and music. How can the various arts of China help us understand the history of this country?

opera, the actors tell a story by singing and performing dances. They also make dramatic gestures, such as wiping away make-believe tears to show sorrow. The actors wear heavy makeup, and elaborate costumes of rich, rustling silk. Until recently, there were no women performers in traditional Chinese operas. Men played both men's and women's roles.

The orchestra has an important part in the traditional Chinese opera. When something exciting happens, the musicians beat drums and clash noisy gongs and cymbals. To set the mood for quieter scenes, they play Chinese flutes and stringed instruments. Chinese music sounds unusual to most Americans. One reason is that all instruments play the same note instead of blending in harmony.

Literature. The most famous collection of writings in the Chinese language is called the Confucian Classics. These writings were gathered together by followers of the great teacher Confucius more than two thousand years ago. Some parts of the Confucian Classics tell about the ancient history of China. Others contain wise sayings or poems.

The kind of literature that the Chinese have loved best through the years is poetry. Two of China's greatest poets were Li Po and Tu Fu, who lived during the T'ang dynasty, about twelve hundred years ago. Let's read a few lines of a poem by Li Po:

> We leave the blue mountains behind us
> and the moon follows after us.
> Our sleeves grow heavy with dew.
> We turn to see how far we have come,
> But the country is swallowed up in a
> white mist.

Novels are another kind of literature that has long been popular in China. One of the most famous novels is *Dream of the Red Chamber*. This sad love story was written during the 1700's.

Crafts. To learn about traditional Chinese crafts, we visit a shop in the city of Peking. Here we see several shelves filled with little statues. These are mostly copies of statues that were created by Chinese artists hundreds of years ago. Some of them have been carved from ivory. Others are made of a very hard stone called jade, which comes in white, green, red, and other colors. On other shelves are boxes, bowls, and jewelry carved from the same materials.

Next we look at bowls and vases made of porcelain.* Many have designs painted on them. Others are quite plain. Their graceful shapes and glowing colors do not need any decoration to make them beautiful. Long ago, the Chinese became the first people to discover the art of making fine porcelain. For this reason, porcelain is usually called "china" in the United States.

Now the shopkeeper shows us a roll of shiny, peach-colored silk. It is embroidered with delicate pictures of plum blossoms. Chinese craft workers have been making beautiful cloth like this for thousands of years.

Last we look at some vases, boxes, and furniture made of wood that has been painted with many layers of lacquer.* These objects feel as smooth as satin when we touch them. Like the other articles we have seen, these pieces of lacquer ware were made by hand. Much skill and patience were needed to produce these beautiful objects.

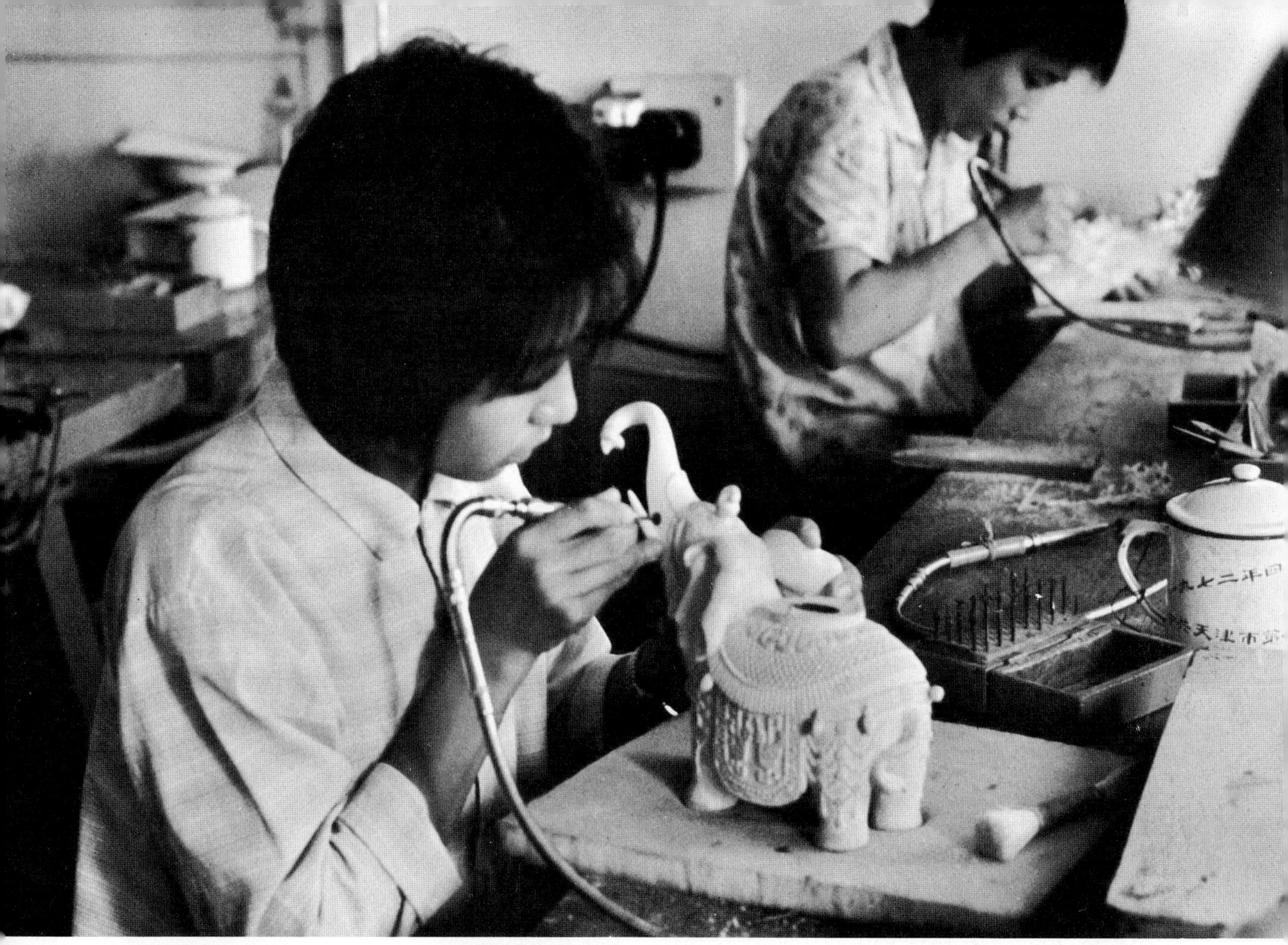

Carving a statue of an elephant from ivory. Craft workers in China still produce carvings, lacquer ware, and other traditional art objects. Most of these objects are exported or sold to foreign tourists, to help the government pay for the goods it buys from other countries.

Chinese Art Under Communism

The Communist leaders who took control of China in 1949 had mixed feelings about their country's traditional arts. They were proud that China had produced some of the world's oldest and finest art. But they also felt that some of these art works were "old-fashioned" and out of place in a Communist country. In the Communists' view, a work of art should do more than simply give people pleasure. It should help persuade them that communism is the best way of life. So Chinese artists were encouraged to add a propaganda message to their works whenever they could. For example, an artist painting a mountain landscape might include a new power plant to show that China was making great progress under communism.

How the Cultural Revolution affected China's arts. The Cultural Revolution started by Mao Tse-tung in 1966 caused great harm to the arts in China. (See pages 66-68.) During this time of unrest, the Red Guards damaged or destroyed many traditional works of art. In addition, they severely punished Chinese artists whose works did not show enough "loyalty" to Mao's ideas. As a result, many artists stopped creating any new works at all.

During and after the Cultural Revolution, the person with the most influence on China's arts was Mao's wife Chiang Ching. (See page 69.) She insisted that all "old" forms of art must be replaced with "new" forms praising communism and the leadership of Chairman Mao. For example, traditional Chinese opera was banned throughout the country. It was replaced with eight new "model operas" approved by Chiang Ching. These were long and boring propaganda pieces that featured brave Communist heroes fighting evil landlords or foreigners. For several years, these were the only operas that could be shown in Chinese theaters or on television.

During the time of Chiang Ching's influence, the people of China had little contact with the arts of the Western nations. Most books by Western authors were banned in China. People could not listen to music by Western composers such as Mozart and Beethoven. Western paintings and sculptures were not displayed in Chinese art museums.

A time of greater freedom for China's artists. In 1976 Mao Tse-tung died, and Chiang Ching lost her power in China. Since that time, artists in China have been given much more freedom than before. For example, painters and sculptors are once again producing works of art in the traditional styles. Authors can write about other subjects besides the greatness of Mao. Traditional Chinese operas are being performed again, and they are attracting larger crowds than ever. People are no longer limited to the eight "model operas" when they watch television or go to the theater. They can see a wide variety of new ballets, operas, plays, and musical programs. Some of the historic palaces and temples that were damaged during the Cultural Revolution have been restored by the government and reopened to the public.

Since the fall of Chiang Ching, the people of China are able to enjoy Western art as well as their own. People can read the works of Western authors in books and magazines, and Western plays

are being performed on the stage. Western artists are showing their works in Chinese galleries. Western classical music can be heard on radio and television throughout China. Also, a number of Western musicians have toured China, playing to large and enthusiastic audiences.

The arts in China are still under government control. Even today, however, artists in China do not have total freedom to express their own ideas. They must be careful not to create works of art that would displease the present leaders of China's government. For example, an author might be praised for writing a book that criticized the "Gang of Four" or some event in China's past. But if the same author wrote a book criticizing China's present leaders, he or she would probably be in trouble. Just as in earlier times, the arts are expected to support the Communist Party and its goals for China.

A scene from a modern Chinese opera called *Battle in the Plains.* In the years following the Cultural Revolution, the Chinese government allowed only eight "model operas" to be performed in theaters or on television. What changes took place after the death of Mao Tse-tung in 1976?

The picture above shows a group of Peking factory workers playing volleyball. China's people enjoy some of the same sports that are played by people in the United States and other nations.

12 Sports and Recreation

Sports. Young people in China enjoy some of the same sports that are played by people in other parts of the world. Basketball, volleyball, and table tennis are especially popular. Chinese players have won several world championships in table tennis.

Most sports activities in China are carried on by organizations that are under the control of the Communist Party, such as the Communist Youth League. The government encourages people to take part in sports in order to improve their physical fitness. However, it does

In the picture at right, above, a young gymnast is practicing on a balance beam. China's government encourages people to take part in many kinds of sports. Why do you suppose it does this?

not encourage boxing and other sports that require body contact. Instead, it favors such sports as gymnastics, track, and swimming. Some activities, such as marching, are intended to train people for military duty. In the larger cities, the government has built huge athletic stadiums and swimming pools. It has also built children's "palaces" that contain facilities for various sports.

Festivals. In the past, China's people held a number of festivals to celebrate holidays throughout the year. The most important was the New Year's Festival, which marked the beginning of the year in the Chinese lunar* calendar. The New Year's Festival did not come at exactly the same time every year. The start of the festival might fall on any date from January 20 to February 20.

*See Glossary

Many of the customs followed during the New Year's Festival were connected with ancestor* worship. (See page 49.) People offered food and wine to the spirits of their ancestors at this time. They also made offerings to the kitchen* god and decorated their homes with signs wishing long life and happiness.

Another holiday connected with ancestor worship was *Ching Ming*, whose name means "pure brightness." *Ching Ming* usually fell in April. During this holiday, families visited the local cemetery to tidy up the graves of their ancestors. Then they would have a picnic.

When the Communists came to power, they did away with some of the old festivals and changed others to fit in more closely with their ideas. For example, the New Year's Festival was renamed the Spring Festival. The Communists tried to discourage many of the old customs connected with ancestor worship. However, they were not entirely successful. Even today, many Chinese still make offerings to the kitchen god, and visit the graves of their ancestors during *Ching Ming*.

To see how festivals are celebrated in China today, let's visit the city of Hangchow a few days before the Spring Festival. Already people are making preparations for the holidays. They are buying colorful pictures of Communist heroes which they will use to decorate their homes. Members of organizations such as the Communist Youth League are practicing plays to put on during the holidays. The stores are crowded with shoppers. People have been saving money all year long to buy new clothes and special foods for the Spring Festival.

At last it is time for the festival to begin. Throughout the city, people are enjoying family reunions and exchanging presents. Theaters and movie houses are crowded with people watching special performances. In one section of the city, a fair is being held. Here people are buying colorful kites and masks, as well as candy and long sticks of sugar-coated berries.

In addition to celebrating old festivals, China's people also observe several newer holidays. National Day marks the founding of the People's Republic

See pages 191-192

Dancers at a May Day celebration in Peking. In China and other Communist countries, May Day is a special holiday to honor working people. The Communist leaders of China have done away with some of China's traditional festivals and changed others to fit in more closely with their ideas. But festivals are still an important part of life in China. How do festivals and other celebrations help people to meet their social needs?

of China. It comes on October 1. Two other important holidays are May Day, on the first of May, and Army Day, on the first of August. Communist countries throughout the world celebrate May Day as a holiday to honor working people. Army Day honors the military forces of China. All of these new holidays are celebrated with colorful parades and demonstrations.

Other leisure-time activities. When we walk through a Chinese city on a Sunday afternoon, we see some other activities that people enjoy in their leisure time. The sidewalks are crowded with people. Some are going shopping. Others are waiting in line to buy theater or movie tickets. Still others are entering teahouses, where they will sip a cup of tea and chat with their friends.

We have come to a park now. Here we see many people strolling around or sitting in the sunshine. Several people are performing the graceful movements of *tai* chi chuan*. This is an ancient Chinese form of exercise, which includes certain skills of self-defense. (See picture on pages 94-95.) We notice a group of teen-aged girls enjoying a game of cards. Two men are playing the Chinese version of chess, which is quite different from the game we know. Western-style chess is also popular in China. Some of the children we see are shooting marbles. Other children are kicking shuttlecocks* to see who can keep them in the air the longest.

In one corner of the park, a large group of children are gathered around a storyteller. The children look intently at the brightly colored pictures she holds up to illustrate her stories. Some of these stories are tales of adventure. Others show how Communist young people are supposed to behave. Even during their leisure time, people are expected to be thinking about the Communists' goals for China.

Playing a game of Chinese chess. This game is quite different from the kind of chess that is played in the United States. What are some other leisure-time activities that are popular in China?

Visit a Chinese Restaurant

From the yellow pages of your local telephone directory, find out whether there is a restaurant in your community that serves Chinese food. If so, have one member of your class (or your teacher) telephone to make arrangements for your class to visit the restaurant. If the restaurant prepares take-out orders, you might prefer to order a variety of Chinese foods to sample in class. In either case, have a committee find out from the manager or the owner of the restaurant how the food you are eating was prepared. Some members of your class may wish to try eating with chopsticks.

Use Your Imagination

Perhaps there is a museum in your area that has an exhibit of Chinese arts and crafts. If so, visit the museum with other members of your class. Then draw a picture or write a poem or a paragraph expressing your feelings about what you have seen.

Conduct an Interview

Work together with another student to prepare a taped conversation between an American visitor to a Chinese primary school and one of the teachers at the school. In your conversation, discuss the following topics:

1. what the school looks like
2. how many years a student attends this school
3. what subjects the students study
4. the size of a typical class
5. what work experiences the students have
6. what attitudes the students are expected to develop at school
7. what types of schools some of the students might attend in the future
8. the problems China faces in providing education for its vast population

Chapter 10 contains information that will help you prepare this conversation. When you have finished your tape, play it for the class.

Make a Travel Poster

Choose one of China's important cities, such as Peking, Shanghai, or Canton. Make a poster that would encourage a traveler to visit this city. Your poster might include pictures, a map, and information about the city. Share your poster with your classmates. This book contains some of the information you will need. The suggestions on pages 201-203, in the Skills Manual, will help you locate additional information.

Sharpen Your Writing Skills

Imagine that you live in a farming village in China. Write a letter to a friend in the United States describing your life in the village. Tell about such things as:

(a) the kind of work your family does
(b) the place where you live
(c) the kinds of food you eat
(d) the school you attend
(e) the medical care available to you
(f) where you buy the things you need
(g) how you enjoy your life in the village

Chapter 8 provides much of the information you need for writing your letter. You may wish to locate additional information in other sources.

Learn More About Tai Chi Chuan

The ancient Chinese form of exercise known as *tai chi chuan*, or simply *tai chi*, is good for improving physical fitness. Perhaps you know someone who is familiar with the basic exercises in *tai chi*, such as "Grasp the Bird's Tail" and "Wave Hands Like a Cloud." If so, invite him or her to demonstrate these exercises to the class. Otherwise, try to find a book about *tai chi* in your school or community library. Practice doing some of the exercises, on your own or as part of a group. Then put on a demonstration of *tai chi* for the rest of the class, explaining the different movements.

Part 4

Earning a Living

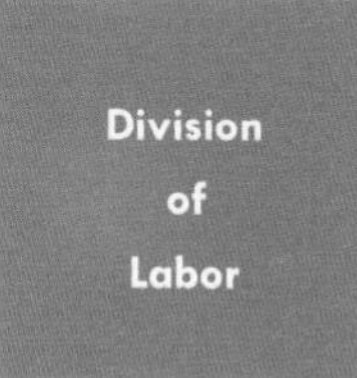

See page 196

Farm workers in Kwangsi Chuang planting rice seedlings in a flooded field. (See map on page 82.) The strangely shaped hills in the background are a famous sight in this part of South China. About four fifths of the people in China earn their living by farming. The others work in a variety of occupations, such as manufacturing, mining, trade, and government. Dividing up the work of a community among people who do different jobs is called division of labor. How does division of labor help people to meet their basic needs?

13 China's Economic System

In every country, there has to be a system for producing goods and services and distributing these to people who need them. In other words, every country must have an economic system.

Since China is a Communist country, it has an economic system based on Communist teachings. (See pages 189-190.) China's economic system is like that of the United States in some ways, but in other ways it is very different.

Who owns farmlands, factories, and other means of production? In China, just as in our country, people are allowed to own property for their personal use. For instance, they can own furniture, dishes, and articles of clothing. But an individual person cannot own farmland, buildings, and certain other kinds of property needed for producing goods. These are owned by the government or by collectives.* The government also owns China's coal mines, oil wells, forests, and other natural resources.

In the United States, most factories are owned by individuals or by business corporations. This is not true in China. There the national government runs some of the largest factories, such as steel mills, textile mills, and electric power plants. Many of the smaller factories are owned by provinces, cities, or collectives.

Who controls the distribution of goods and services? In China the government is in charge of distributing goods and services to people throughout the country. For example, it controls almost all of the transportation facilities, such as railroads, airlines, and shipping companies. It also operates all of the banks in China. Most of the wholesale* trade in China is carried on by government-owned companies. The government also owns some retail* businesses, such as large department stores. Many other stores are owned by collectives such as the Red Star Agricultural Company described in Chapter 8.

*See Glossary

How are prices and wages determined? In the United States, the prices of most goods and services are set by the people who sell them. Usually these prices are based on the amount that customers are willing to pay for a particular item. In China, the prices that are charged for many kinds of goods and services are set by the government.

People in China obtain the goods and services they need in about the same way Americans do. They work to earn money, which they use to buy the things they need. Workers in factories

Freedom

The picture below shows people making iron in backyard blast furnaces during the "Great Leap Forward." This was a campaign started by the Chinese government in 1958. Its goal was to make China into a modern industrial nation as rapidly as possible. How successful was the Great Leap Forward? (See Chapter 5.) Do you think the results of the Great Leap Forward were affected by the amount of freedom given to people in China at that time? Explain. Do you think people who do not have very much freedom can produce as many goods and services as people who have a large amount of freedom? Why? Why not?

and offices are paid regular wages, which vary according to their skill and experience. These wages are usually controlled by the government. Chinese farmers do not receive regular wages. Instead, they earn money by selling the crops and livestock they raise. (See pages 99-100.)

How does China's economic system affect the lives of the people? Since the Communists took control of China in 1949, there has been a gradual rise in the standard* of living. Today, most of the Chinese people are supplied with better food, clothing, shelter, and medical care than they were in earlier times. However, China is not yet a "developed" nation. (See map on page 165.) The standard of living there is much lower than it is in countries such as the United States and Canada. People in China lack many kinds of goods and services that are part of everyday life in our country.

In addition, the Chinese lack a number of economic freedoms that are enjoyed by people in the capitalist* nations. For example, most Chinese men and women are not free to work at jobs of their own choosing. Their jobs are assigned to them by government of-

Billboards in China. The woman on the right is wearing shoes like the ones being advertised on the billboard. Since the death of Mao Tse-tung in 1976, there have been important changes in China's economic system. What are some of these changes, and why do you think they were made?

ficials. In order to change jobs, they must have the government's permission. People cannot form their own labor unions to seek higher wages or better working conditions. There are labor unions in China, but these are controlled by the Communist Party. Their main purpose is to persuade the workers to carry out the Communists' goals.

In the United States and other capitalist countries, people can spend the money they earn on a wide variety of goods and services. In China, the government has much more power to decide what goods and services will be produced. Therefore, the Chinese people have less freedom of choice.

What changes are being made in China's economic system? The present leaders of China came to power in the late 1970's. At that time, they found many things wrong with the country's economic system. China's farming and industry had made little real progress since the 1950's. Many Chinese were forced to work at jobs they did not enjoy. Also, they saw little chance of raising their standard of living. It is not surprising that they took little interest in their jobs and did not work very hard. The government-owned factories were not required to make a profit, so there was no reason for them to find better and cheaper ways of producing goods. As a result, they were often wasteful and inefficient. Also, China's industry was not growing fast enough to provide jobs for the growing population.

To help solve these problems, China's leaders have been making a number of changes in the economic system. For example, factories now give extra pay to workers who do an especially good job. Factories are expected to operate at a profit. This means that they must cut costs and produce goods that people are willing to buy. Chinese farmers now have more freedom to decide how they will produce and sell their crops. (See Chapter 8.)

In Chinese cities today, some workers are being allowed to go into business for themselves. Among these people are cooks, tailors, and workers who do household repairs. There are also merchants who sell goods in the streets. City workers are being encouraged to join collectives instead of seeking jobs in government-owned factories and offices. These collectives are run in much the same way as private businesses in the United States. The members of the collectives can decide for themselves what goods to produce. They can also decide what price they will charge for these goods, as long as they stay within limits set by the government. After paying taxes and other expenses, they share the remaining profits.

As you have seen, the Communist leaders are trying to make China into a great industrial nation. To reach this goal, they have been inviting foreign companies to build factories and offices in China. These companies are free to carry on business in much the same way they do in their homelands.

All of these changes might make it seem that China is becoming a capitalist nation. However, the Chinese leaders have no plans to do away with communism. They are merely trying to make their economic system work better than it has in the past.

Harvesting rice. Rice is one of China's main farm crops. The picture above shows farmers harvesting rice in a field near Canton. Some of these farmers are using small, foot-powered machines to thresh* rice. In the picture at far right, a farmer is threshing rice by hand. The map shows that South China is the country's main rice-growing area. Why do you suppose this is so?

14 Farming

China's farms must produce enough food for more than a billion people. Although China has developed much industry in recent years, it is still mainly a farming country. About eighty out of one hundred people in China make their living by farming. In comparison, only about two out of one hundred people in the United States are farmers.

China's output of farm products is among the largest in the world. China produces more rice, tobacco, chickens, and hogs than any other country. It is also a leading producer of corn, wheat, tea, cotton, silk, soybeans, peanuts, potatoes, and sheep.

In spite of its huge farm output, China still has great difficulty producing enough food to meet its needs. Most of the land in this vast country is too dry or too mountainous for farming. Only about one tenth of China's land area is

*See Glossary

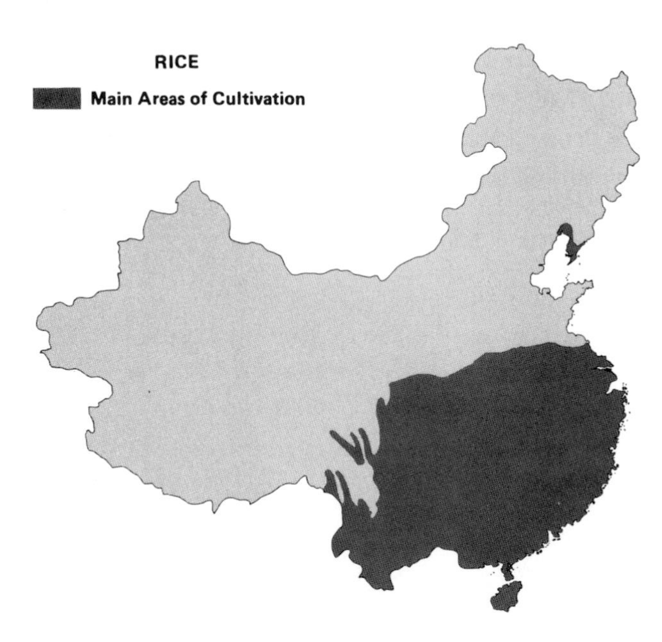
RICE
Main Areas of Cultivation

suitable for growing crops. China not only has less farmland than the United States, but it has more than four times as many people to feed. Even in places where the land is fertile, Chinese farmers sometimes find it difficult to produce good crops. There are often severe droughts or floods in North China. In South China, crops are sometimes destroyed by floods or typhoons. Insects and disease are a threat to crops in many parts of the country.

There is another reason why Chinese farmers have difficulty producing enough food. They lack modern methods and equipment. For example, there are not enough factories in China to produce all the modern farm machinery and chemical fertilizers that the country needs. Most Chinese farmers still use hoes, sickles, and other simple tools. They tend their fields by hand or with the help of farm animals such as oxen, horses, and donkeys. The most common types of fertilizer used in China today are natural substances such as animal manure, human wastes, and garbage.

Chinese farmers make good use of their land. To make up for these handicaps, farmers in China try to use their precious land as carefully as possible. Crops are grown on every acre of fertile land. Even steep hills are used for farming. Level fields have been created on these slopes by building giant steps called terraces, like the ones shown in the picture on page 144.

Some farmers in China also make good use of their land by growing two or more crops in the same field during a single year. This practice is especially common in parts of South China where the weather is warm nearly all year long. For instance, some farmers are able to grow two crops of rice between spring and fall. After harvesting their second rice crop they plant wheat. It will be ripe and ready to harvest the following spring.

Long ago, the Chinese learned that more food can be produced on an acre of land if it is used for growing crops rather than for raising animals. Today there is very little pastureland in the country, except in thinly populated Outer China. In more densely populated areas, the only kinds of livestock that are raised in large quantities are hogs, chickens, and ducks. These animals do not need pasture to graze in. They can live on waste materials such as corncobs and table scraps.

Sheepherders in Inner Mongolia. This picture shows herders dipping their sheep in a chemical solution to kill lice and other insect pests. The raising of sheep, cattle, and other animals is an important occupation in thinly populated areas of Outer China. Why is raising livestock more important than growing crops in these areas?

Terraces like these in Kansu Province make it possible to grow crops even on steep hillsides. In what other ways have China's people changed the land to make it better for farming?

Through the centuries, the Chinese have changed the land in various ways to better control their supply of water. Earthen walls called dikes have been built along the banks of rivers to protect surrounding farmlands from floods. Canals have been dug to bring water to farmlands that receive little rainfall, or to carry away water from fields that are flooded.

Since the Communists came to power, large numbers of people have been put to work building dams in different parts of China. When there is too much rain, excess water is stored in lakes behind the dams so it will not cause the rivers to flood the land. In times of little rainfall, this water is used for irrigation.

New forests have been planted on many bare hillsides in China. The roots and fallen leaves of the trees hold rainwater in the soil and keep it from rushing down the hillsides. This helps to prevent floods and to keep good soil from being washed away.

China's leaders have been placing great importance on farming. During the early years of Communist rule, little money was spent to improve farming. The new leaders felt it was more important to develop industry. Also, they believed they could solve many of China's farm problems simply by establishing huge communes. (See pages 64-65.) The Communist leaders felt it would be easier to introduce modern machinery and farming methods in the communes than on the small farms that had been owned by the peasants.

As time passed, China's leaders came to feel it was a mistake to put industry ahead of farming. For one thing, a series of poor harvests caused a serious food shortage in China. To feed its people, China's government had to import large amounts of grain from foreign countries.

China's leaders also discovered that to develop more industry, farm production would have to be increased. One of the main ways China could earn money for building factories was by exporting farm products. In addition, many factories in China depended on farms for raw materials. This was especially true of textile factories, which produced one of China's main exports, cotton cloth.

In the last twenty years, the Chinese government has been giving more attention to farming. For example, it has spent large sums of money to import fertilizers and farm machinery. It has also built a number of factories in China for making these products. Recently, it has made important changes in China's system of farming. (See pages 102-103.) For all of these reasons, China's farm production has been increasing rapidly. But it will have to increase even more in the future to meet the needs of China's growing population.

Plowing with a tractor in Shensi Province. The government of China has been making a greater effort to improve farming than it did in earlier years. What are some of the reasons for this?

Farm Products of China's Three Regions

If you traveled through China, you would not see the same kinds of crops and livestock in all sections of the country. Farmers in each section raise products that are suited to the land and climate of their area. Let us see what farming is like in each of China's three main regions. (See map on page 25.)

Farming in South China. Nearly everywhere in South China, the main farm crop is rice. This crop grows very well where summers are long and hot, and rainfall is plentiful. Rice plants yield a large amount of grain for each acre of land. For this reason, rice is a good crop to grow in densely populated areas where the amount of good farmland is limited.

Rice plants stand in several inches of water while they are growing. Chinese farmers plant the rice seeds in small plots of ground called seedbeds, which are later flooded with water. The young rice plants grow in the seedbeds for about a month. Then they are moved to larger fields that are also flooded.

When the plants are fully grown, the water is drained off the fields and the crop is harvested. Only land that is flat can be flooded evenly. Therefore, rice is usually grown either on level lowlands or on hillside terraces.

Rice is not the only kind of grain produced in South China. Large amounts of corn and wheat are grown in hilly areas where the land cannot be flooded for producing rice. Also, many rice farmers grow wheat or barley in their fields during the cooler winter months.

Tea is another important crop in South China, especially in the South Yangtze Hills. (See map on page 25.) The tea bushes grow well in the warm, humid climate of this area. They can be grown on steep hillsides that are not suitable for raising other kinds of crops. Since the Chinese people drink large amounts of tea, only a small part of the crop is exported to foreign countries.

The level, fertile Yangtze Plain is an important cotton-growing area. Large amounts of cotton raised in this area are used by Chinese textile factories in making cloth.

Mulberry bushes are also raised on the Yangtze Plain, as well as in other parts of South China. The leaves of the mulberry bushes are used to feed silkworms. These tiny worms eat continuously for about five weeks, until they begin to spin their cocoons. At that time, a glue-like fluid comes from a hole in the lower lip of each silkworm. This fluid hardens into silk thread when it touches the air.

Picking tea leaves in the province of Chekiang. Although China is one of the world's leading tea producers, it sells only a small part of its tea crop to other countries. Why is this so?

The worm waves its head back and forth to wind the thread around itself and form a cocoon. Silk cocoons are soaked in hot water and unwound. Then the thread is sent to textile factories, where it is woven into silk cloth.

Farmers in South China produce large amounts of vegetables and fruits. Sweet potatoes are raised on sandy and stony hillsides where many other kinds of crops will not grow. They are an important food in South China. Other vegetables raised in this part of China include beans, peas, and cabbages. Along China's southern coast farmers grow pineapples, oranges, and other warm-weather crops.

Several other kinds of farm crops are important in South China. Large quantities of tobacco are grown in the fertile Red Basin. The Red Basin also has many orchards of tung trees, which are native to this area. Tung nuts contain a quick-drying oil that is used in making paint and other products. Rapeseeds* and peanuts are grown throughout South China. Both crops produce oil that is used for cooking and other purposes. There are large fields of sugarcane in the Canton Delta, where the rich soil and warm, humid climate are well suited to growing this crop.

Farming in North China. Farming north of the high Chin Ling Shan* is quite different from farming in South China. (See map on page 25.) The climate in most of this region is too cool and dry for rice and other warm-weather crops to grow well. Because summers are shorter here, most farmers harvest only one crop from their fields in a single year instead of two or three.

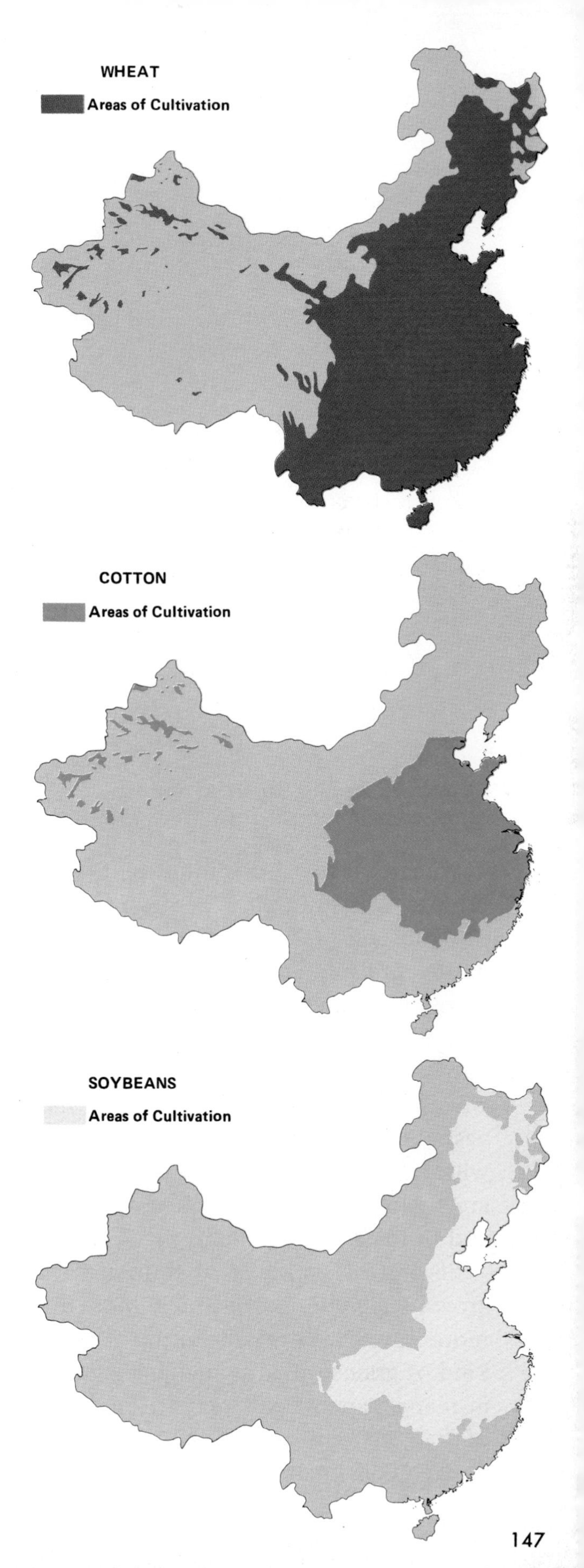

A villager tending ducks in Liaoning Province. In the densely populated parts of China, the most common kinds of livestock are chickens, ducks, and hogs. How would you explain this?

Wheat is the most important grain crop in North China. Where winters are not too cold, farmers plant their wheat in the fall and harvest it the following spring. Wheat grown in this way is called winter wheat. In places where winters are very cold, such as Inner Mongolia, wheat is planted in the spring and harvested in the fall. This is known as spring wheat. The main wheat-growing areas are the Yellow Plain, the Loess Plateau, and the Manchurian Plain.

Several other kinds of grain are also grown widely in North China. More and more farmers here are raising corn. A kind of grain known as kaoliang is grown in many parts of this region. The seeds of kaoliang are ground into flour and used to make pancakes or mush. Millet* is another important grain crop in North China. It can be grown where the climate is too dry or the soil is too poor for growing other kinds of grain.

Many farmers in North China raise soybeans, which are native to this part of the world. Soybeans are grown in the same areas as corn, but they stand dryness and cold weather better than corn does. China's main soybean-growing area is the Manchurian Plain.

A number of other crops are grown on farms in North China. Cotton is an important crop in parts of the Yellow Plain where the growing season is at least two hundred days long. Many farmers on the Yellow Plain also grow tobacco or peanuts. Large numbers of silkworms are raised in the province of Shantung.

(See map on page 82.) Sugar beets are an important crop in the far northeastern part of China, where summer days are long but cool. Orchards in North China produce apples, peaches, and other kinds of fruit. Farms supply cabbages, potatoes, and other fresh vegetables to people in nearby cities.

On the Manchurian Plain, farming is somewhat different than it is in other sections of North China. Much of the land here is not densely populated. There are a number of large state* farms in this area. These are owned by the national government, which hires workers to tend the crops. On the state farms, much of the work is done with tractors, combines, and other modern farm machines.

Farming in Outer China. On the Mongolian Plateau in Outer China, there is usually too little rain for crops to grow. But the vast grasslands here are suitable for grazing livestock. People on the Mongolian Plateau raise large herds of cattle, sheep, and horses.

Much of the land in Sinkiang Uighur is too dry or too rugged for farming. However, at the foot of the mountain ranges in this region are a number of oases.* Farmers here use water from mountain streams to irrigate their fields. Grain, cotton, and various kinds of fruit, such as grapes and melons, are grown in the oases. Herds of sheep are raised for their wool on mountain pastures in Sinkiang Uighur.

Among the snowcapped mountains of Tibet are a few grassy plateau areas where herders pasture flocks of sheep and goats. Barley, peas, and other crops are grown in the valleys that cut across the southern part of Tibet.

The Chinese government has been developing new farmlands in the vast, nearly empty region of Outer China. Over the years, millions of workers have been sent from the crowded eastern part of the country to work on farms here. New irrigation projects have been started to provide more water for growing crops.

As you have seen, farming differs greatly from one part of China to another. But there is one important way in which farmers throughout this huge country are alike. They must all work very hard, for they have the most important job in China. If they cannot produce enough crops, many people will go hungry. Also, China will not have the farm products it needs to export in order to buy goods from other countries.

15 Natural Resources

China is well supplied with many of the natural resources needed by modern industry. Within the borders of this vast country are rich deposits of coal, petroleum, iron ore, and other minerals. A number of these deposits have been discovered only recently, and are not yet being mined. Other natural resources of China include waterpower, forests, and fisheries.

Minerals

Coal. One of the most important minerals found in China is coal. The people of China use coal in a number of ways. For example, coal is burned as a fuel in power plants that produce electricity. It is also used in homes for cooking and heating. Factories use coal as a raw material in making many different products, including iron and steel, fertilizer, and plastics.

There are deposits of coal in every province of China. But the largest coal mines are in North China. (See map on page 25.) In some places, the coal is removed by digging tunnels deep under the earth. In other places, power shovels scoop the coal from huge open pits. One of the largest open-pit coal mines in the world is located at Fushun, in the province of Liaoning.

Most of the coal mined in China today is the bituminous* type. China's bituminous coal is generally poor in quality. Before it can be used, it must be cleaned to remove various waste materials. China has a few deposits of high-quality bituminous coal, which is suitable for making coke.* Coke is an important raw material used in the manufacture of iron and steel.

China's coal-mining industry faces serious problems. Some of the deposits of good-quality coal are located far from any large industrial cities. More railroads must be built to carry the coal to places where it can be used. In China there is a shortage of wood for making pitprops, which are long pieces of timber used to keep the roofs of mine tunnels from caving in. Although modern machines are used in some of the larger coal mines, China also has many small mines that still use old-fashioned methods. In

*See Glossary

Using Natural Resources

See page 195

Making steel in Taiyuan. China has many natural resources needed by modern industry. For example, large deposits of iron ore and coal provide the main raw materials needed for manufacturing iron and steel. What are some products made from iron and steel? How would the lives of people in China be different if these metals were not available? Make a chart listing the different mineral resources of China and telling how each is used.

some places, for example, the coal is mined with picks and hauled to the surface in baskets tied to ropes. Then it is carried away on the backs of mules.

In spite of problems such as these, China ranks as the world's third largest coal producer. Only the Soviet Union and the United States produce more coal each year than China does.

Petroleum. Before the 1950's, many experts believed that there were no large deposits of petroleum in China. Then the Chinese government began sending teams of scientists to various parts of the country to explore for oil. Large oil fields were discovered in the deserts and grasslands of northwestern China. But these oil fields were far from the areas where most of China's people live. It was difficult and costly to transport the oil to the places where it was needed.

In the 1960's, new oil fields were discovered in more densely populated parts of China. The largest of these was the Taching field, near the city of Harbin. (See map on page 21.) It now produces about half of China's oil output. Other large oil fields are located on the Yellow Plain, near the Gulf of PoHai. Since these fields were discovered, China's oil

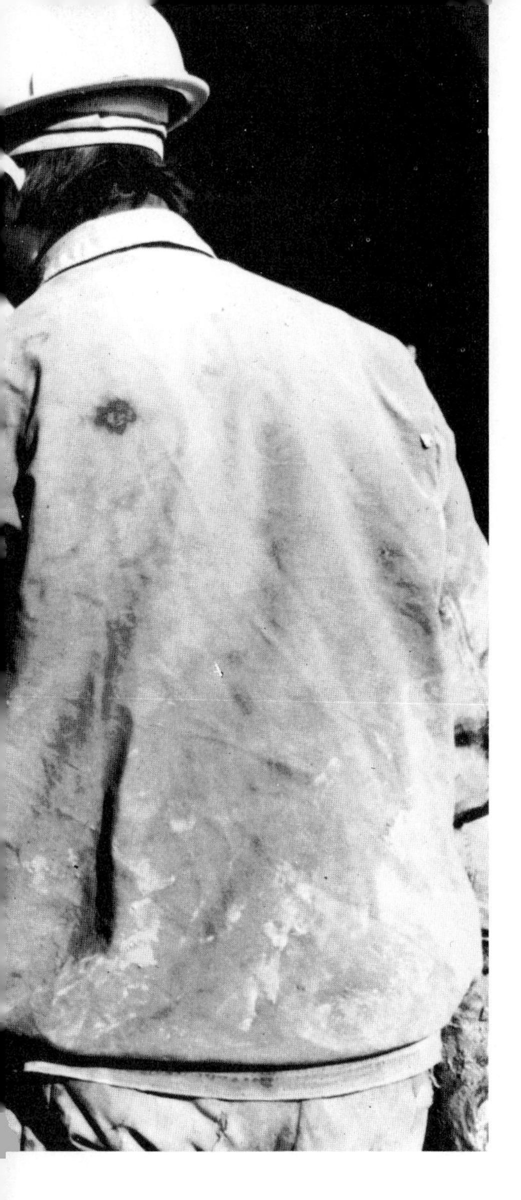

A Problem To Solve

The picture above shows workers drilling for oil at the Taching field in northeastern China. This field now produces about half of China's oil output. Oil deposits play an important part in China's plans for becoming a great industrial nation. Why is this so? You may wish to consider facts about:

a. the number and size of China's oil deposits.
b. China's need for energy to run machines in factories.
c. China's need to buy machinery and other goods from foreign nations.

See pages 198-200

production has been increasing rapidly. Today China ranks among the top ten oil-producing nations. It not only meets its own needs but it even exports some oil to Japan and other countries.

In the future, China may produce even more oil. Scientists believe that huge oil deposits lie beneath the shallow waters of the Pacific Ocean, just off China's coast. China's leaders are anxious to make use of these deposits, for two main reasons. As industry grows, China will need new sources of energy to run machines in factories. Also, by selling oil to other countries China can earn money to buy machinery and other foreign goods it needs.

At present, China is unable to develop the underwater oil deposits by itself. It does not have enough trained workers or modern oil-drilling equipment. So it has been seeking help from oil companies in the United States and other Western nations. These companies will search for oil deposits and drill wells in China's offshore areas. In return, they will receive a share of the profits.

Metal ores. The most important raw material needed for making iron and steel is iron ore. China ranks among the top five producers of this mineral. Most of the iron ore mined in China today comes from deposits in the northern and northeastern parts of the country. These deposits are close to the coal mines that supply another important raw material for steelmaking. However, much of the iron ore produced in northern and northeastern China is poor in quality. There are deposits of better-grade iron ore in central and southern China.

To make high-quality steel, iron must be combined with small amounts of certain other metals. One of these is tungsten. China is the world's leading producer of tungsten. (See map on page 154.) It is also well supplied with two other metals used in steelmaking—manganese and molybdenum.

Mines in China produce several other metals that are useful in manufacturing. For example, China leads the world in the production of antimony. This metal is often added to lead to make it harder and stronger. Alloys* of lead and antimony are used in

making automobile batteries, printing type, and other products. There are rich deposits of tin in South China. Lead and zinc are mined in some areas, and deposits of aluminum ore are scattered throughout the country. China is also well supplied with mercury. Although there are copper deposits in China, most of them are so deep in the earth that they are very expensive to mine.

Other minerals. In addition to fuels and metal ores, China has deposits of several other minerals. It produces more salt than any other country except the United States. Much of China's salt is produced near the seacoast. Seawater is allowed to flow into huge, shallow ponds where it evaporates in the sunlight, leaving salt and other minerals behind. The salt is used mainly for food. China is also one of the world's leading producers of asbestos.* It has deposits of phosphate rock, which is used mainly for fertilizer. China also produces kaolin, a type of clay needed for making fine porcelain.

Waterpower

In China, many rivers flow from the highlands down to the ocean. By building dams and power plants, it is possible to use a number of these swiftly flowing rivers to produce electricity. Some experts claim that China's supply of waterpower is larger than that of any other country.

During recent years, the Chinese government has been building a number of dams and power plants on rivers in China. One of the largest of these is the San-Men Gorge plant on the Yellow River. At the present time, however, China is still using only a small part of its total supply of waterpower. Most of China's electricity is produced in steam power plants that burn coal or other fuels.

There are several reasons why the Chinese have not developed more of their waterpower resources. First, many of the places where dams and hydroelectric* plants could be built are in rugged, mountainous areas—far from the places where most of China's people live. Also, these plants are more expensive to build than steam power plants. Finally, China is well supplied with coal and oil to use as fuel in steam power plants.

Forests

Forests cover less than one tenth of China's land area. In ancient times, the country's forests were much larger. But

Building a dam on a river near Hangchow. China has many rivers that could be harnessed to produce hydroelectricity. However, only a small amount of waterpower is now being used. Why?

Lumbering on the slopes of the Tien Shan. China has only a few natural forests, and these are located in remote and mountainous parts of the country. What are the reasons for this?

as the centuries passed, most of the forests in the densely populated parts of China were cut down. This was partly because people needed as much land as possible for farming. Also, many people used wood as a fuel to heat their houses and cook their food. Today wood is very scarce and expensive in the populated areas of China.

The few natural forests that remain in China are located in remote or mountainous parts of the country. For example, forests of evergreen trees grow on the mountains that lie to the east of the Manchurian Plain. (See page 25.) Both evergreen and deciduous* trees grow on the slopes of many rugged hills and mountains in southern China. Wood from China's forests is used mainly for lumber, pitprops for mines, and railroad ties. Small amounts are used in making paper, furniture, and other products.

In some parts of southern China, there are forests of bamboo. This is a treelike plant with long, hollow stems that are very strong and flexible. People use bamboo to build houses and to make furniture and other articles. The tender shoots of the bamboo plant are used for food.

The government of China is trying to protect the country's forests and to establish new forests wherever possible. Belts of trees have been planted along the edges of deserts and grasslands in the northern part of China. These trees help to shelter farmlands from strong winds and blowing sand. People in rural areas are being encouraged to start seedbeds* of new trees and to plant trees on bare hillsides that are too steep for farming.

Fisheries

China ranks among the leading fishing nations of the world. Many different kinds of fish live in the waters off China's seacoast. Fish are an important source of food in China, especially since most people cannot afford to eat very much meat.

Most of China's fishing ports are located along the southeastern coast. Here there are many deep, sheltered bays that provide good harbors for fishing boats. Also, the forests that grow on steep hillsides nearby provide wood for shipbuilding. Large sailing vessels known as junks travel from these ports to fishing grounds in the Yellow Sea and the South China Sea. (See map on page 21.) These junks serve as the homes of the fishing crew and their families. Most of them are equipped with modern machinery for catching and processing fish.

Freshwater fishing is also important in China. The lakes and rivers are well supplied with catfish, carp, and other kinds of fish. In many farming areas there are ponds where fish are raised for food. People also raise fish on flooded fields used for growing rice.

Chinese fishermen at work. China is one of the world's leading fishing nations. Most of the country's fishing ports are located along the southeastern coast. What are some reasons for this?

Inside a textile mill in Hangchow. During recent years, the people of China have been making a great effort to develop more industry in their country. What are some of the reasons for this?

16 Industry

For a country so large and so rich in natural resources, China does not have a great deal of industry. Less than ten out of every one hundred workers in China are employed in manufacturing. There are not enough factories and modern machines to produce all the goods that China's people want or need. Many goods are still produced with simple tools that are powered by the muscles of human beings or animals such as horses and oxen.

The people of China have been making a great effort to develop more industry in their country. They would like to have a higher standard* of living, and they know that this cannot be accomplished without using modern machinery to produce a variety of manufactured goods. Also, they want China to be powerful enough to defend itself from possible enemies and to play an important part in world affairs. To achieve this goal, factories in China must produce large quantities of weapons and other military equipment.

Why industry was slow to develop in China. The history of China helps to explain why this country does not have more industry. During the late 1700's, people in western Europe began to make great changes in the way goods were produced. We call these changes the Industrial Revolution. (See page 164.) Although the Industrial Revolution soon spread to North America and other parts of the world, it had little effect in the distant land of China. The people who ruled China at that time were satisfied with their traditional way of life. They saw no need to borrow new inventions and ideas from other countries.

About the middle of the 1800's, business people from Great Britain, the United States, and other Western nations began coming to China. They built a number of small factories in port cities such as Shanghai

*See Glossary

and Canton. In the rest of China, there were hardly any factories at all.

Little new industry developed in China until the 1930's. Then, Japan seized control of a large area in northeastern China called Manchuria. This area was rich in coal, iron ore, and other resources needed by modern industry. The Japanese built a number of factories in Manchuria to produce supplies for their military forces.

World War II* caused great damage to many of the factories in China. Other factories were destroyed or shut down during the war between the Nationalists and the Communists. By the time the Communists came to power in 1949, China was producing only a very small quantity of manufactured goods.

China's industry has grown rapidly in recent years. China's leaders were anxious to make their country into a modern industrial nation. At first they had help from another Communist country, the Soviet Union. The Soviet government loaned money to China for building new factories. It also sent many engineers and technicians* to help the Chinese develop their industry.

In 1953, the Chinese government made a plan listing the goals China should reach during the next five years. This was known as the First Five-Year Plan. It gave special importance to heavy

See pages 195-196

A Problem To Solve

The picture at left shows a welder in a Shanghai truck factory. On the opposite page is a picture of a tractor plant near Loyang. China does not have enough factories and modern machines to produce all the goods that its people want or need. Why has it been difficult to establish modern industry in China? To solve this problem, consider how the growth of industry has been affected by:

a. China's history
b. transportation facilities in China
c. education in China
d. the availability of money and equipment needed to start new factories

Other chapters in this book provide additional information that will be helpful in solving this problem.

See pages 198-200

industries such as steelmaking and the manufacture of machinery. More money was spent on developing these industries than on producing modern farm equipment or supplying consumer* goods such as clothing and furniture. While the First Five-Year Plan was in effect, China's industry grew rapidly.

In 1958, the Communist leaders of China started the "Great Leap Forward." (See pages 64-65.) One of the main goals of this campaign was to make China into a modern industrial nation as quickly as possible. For a time, there was a large increase in the production of manufactured goods. But it soon became clear that the Great Leap Forward was not working out as the Chinese leaders had expected. This campaign was brought to an end in the early 1960's.

Meanwhile, China was no longer on friendly terms with the Soviet Union. (See page 73.) In 1960 the Soviets stopped lending money to China and ordered their engineers and technicians to return home. Since the Chinese Communists came to power, they had been depending heavily on Soviet help in building new factories. Without this help, many industrial projects in China had to be postponed or given up entirely.

The Chinese continued to work toward their goal of developing modern industry. But they now went about this task in a different way. First of all, they began to place more importance on producing consumer goods. They also tried to increase the production of tractors, water pumps, and other machines needed by farmers. The Chinese decided they would no longer depend on any other country to help them build and run their factories. Instead, they would try to develop new industry by themselves.

Since that time, China has made considerable progress in manufacturing. Its output of manufactured goods is now larger than that of any other Asian country except Japan. However, it is important to remember that China is still one of the world's "developing" countries. (See map on page 165.) It has far less industry than developed nations such as the United States.

Where is China's industry located? When the Communists gained power in China, nearly all of the country's factories were located in a few large cities. Most of these cities were on or near the seacoast. The Communist leaders announced that they would try to distribute industry more evenly throughout the country. In case of war, they said, China's factories would be safer from foreign attack. And each part of the country would be able to meet its own needs for manufactured goods.

In the years that followed, the Chinese government built many factories in cities far inland, such as Wuhan, Sian,

A woodworking plant near Shanghai. Although many factories have been built in cities far inland, China's leading industrial centers are on or near the seacoast. Why is this so?

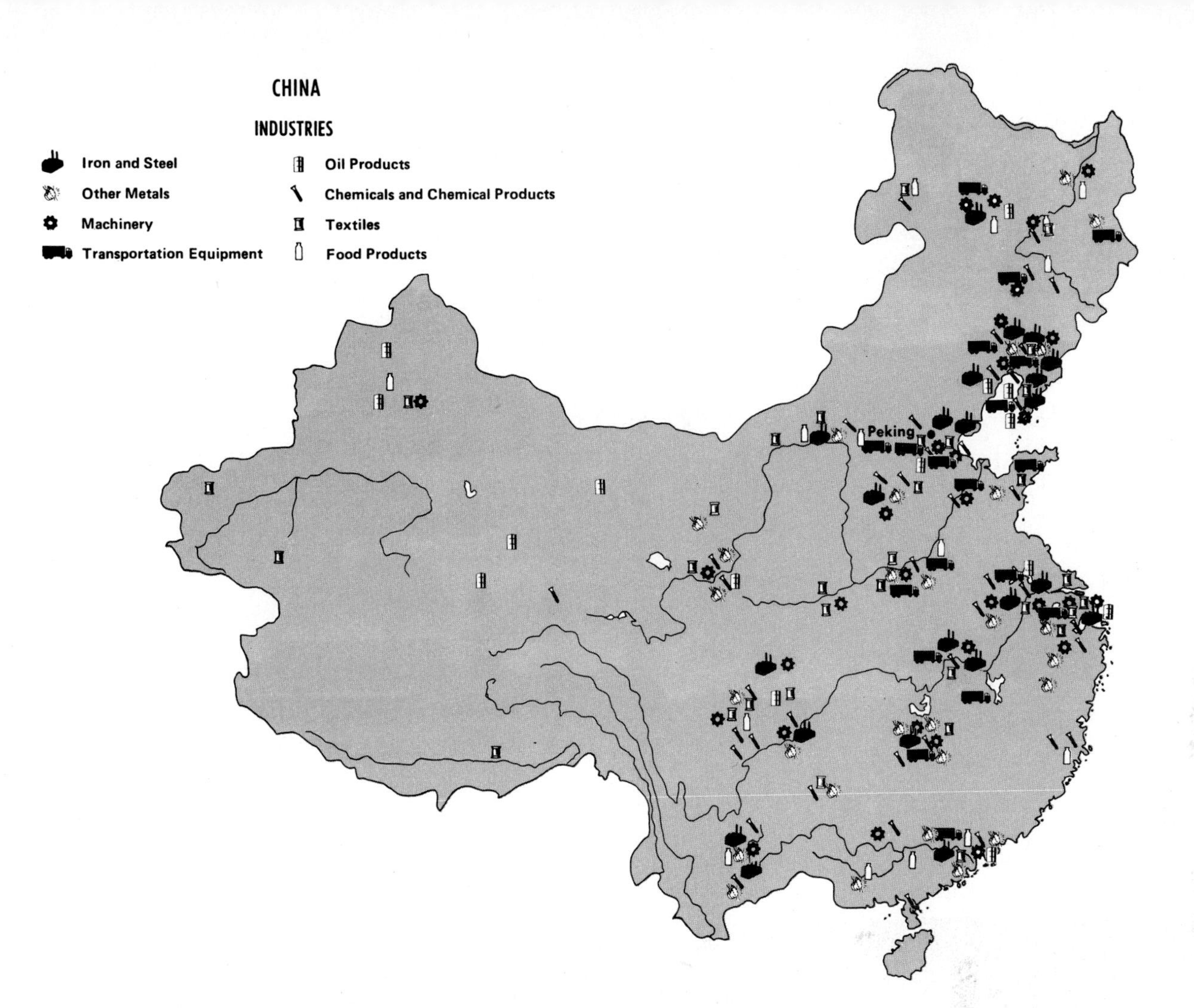

and Lanchou. (See map on pages 20-21.) As a result, these cities grew rapidly in population. Even today, however, China's main industrial centers are on or near the seacoast. (See map above.) These areas have a larger supply of trained managers and skilled workers. Because they are more densely populated, there are more customers for manufactured goods. Also, transportation is better near the seacoast. Goods from foreign countries can be brought to China's seaports by ship, and other goods can be carried away.

Products of Industry

Iron and steel. One of the most important kinds of modern industry is the manufacture of iron and steel. These metals are used as raw materials in making many kinds of products.

China's iron and steel industry has grown very rapidly during the last twenty-five years. Many small iron and steel plants have been built in cities and towns throughout the country. These plants produce iron and steel for making farm implements and other tools. But most of the high-quality steel made in China is produced in large, modern plants. These are located mainly in the northeastern part of the country. As Chapter 15 explains, there are large deposits of iron ore and coal in this area.

The city of Anshan in northeastern China is one of the largest steelmaking

Cotton-spinning machines in an early factory. The Industrial Revolution that began in England in the 1700's included three main developments. What were these developments? How did they help industry grow?

The Industrial Revolution

New ways of producing goods were developed. People in many parts of the world still live much as their ancestors did hundreds or even thousands of years ago. We in America, however, as well as people in certain other parts of the world, are living in ways that are very different from those of our ancestors. One main respect in which our lives differ from theirs is the way we produce goods.

During the seventeenth century, most goods were produced by people in their own homes or on farms. Work was performed mainly by the muscle power of human beings or animals, although a few simple tools and machines were in general use. Wind and waterpower were used for certain work, such as grinding grain.

Beginning about the middle of the eighteenth century, three important developments occurred in the way goods were produced. First, many new machines were invented to help people make things more quickly and easily. Second, steam and other new sources of power came into use. Third, factories were built to house the new machines. Together these three main developments, which all began in England, are known as the Industrial Revolution.

The Industrial Revolution spreads. The new ways of producing goods soon spread from England to other parts of the world. The United States, Belgium, France, and Germany were among the first countries to adopt the new methods.

The Industrial Revolution has continued to spread. Today, it is in different stages in different countries. In much of the world, industry is just beginning to develop. (See map on page 165.) Most parts of Europe and North America are already highly industrialized.

Industrialization changes people's lives in several ways. For one thing, the standard* of living is generally higher in nations that have experienced the Industrial Revolution. Also, more of the people in such nations live in cities. The people in industrialized nations carry on more foreign trade than those who live in countries with little industry. They depend on people in many parts of the world for raw materials. They also depend on people in foreign countries to buy the goods and services that they produce.

*See Glossary

centers in the world. Another important iron and steel center is the city of Wuhan, in South China. It is located near a large deposit of high-quality iron ore. There are also large steel mills in the cities of Shanghai, Peking, Paotou, and Chungking.

Other metals. Factories in China produce several useful metals in addition to iron and steel. Large aluminum plants are located in Fushun, Lanchou, and a number of other Chinese cities. China also has factories that produce lead, zinc, copper, and tin. Usually, such factories are located near mines that supply the ores needed to produce these metals.

Machinery. Much of the iron and steel produced in China today is used in making various kinds of machinery. China has been trying to increase its production of machines used in farming, such as tractors, combines, and water pumps. It also produces large numbers of machine tools. These are machines that cut, grind, and shape metal. Some factories in China make bearings.*

China produces large amounts of electrical and electronic* equipment. For example, a number of factories make generators, motors, and other kinds of electrical machinery. China's production of household appliances such as refrigerators and washing machines is still quite small. Most Chinese families do not have any of these appliances in their homes. However, a growing number of families own radios or television sets. The production of these articles has increased greatly during recent years. Some factories in China produce computers and other kinds of complicated electronic machinery.

China is not yet highly industrialized. Countries like China, where the Industrial Revolution has not as yet had great effect, are generally known as developing nations. Most people in these countries earn their living by farming. The world's most highly industrialized countries are called developed nations. In the partly developed nations, the Industrial Revolution is well under way.

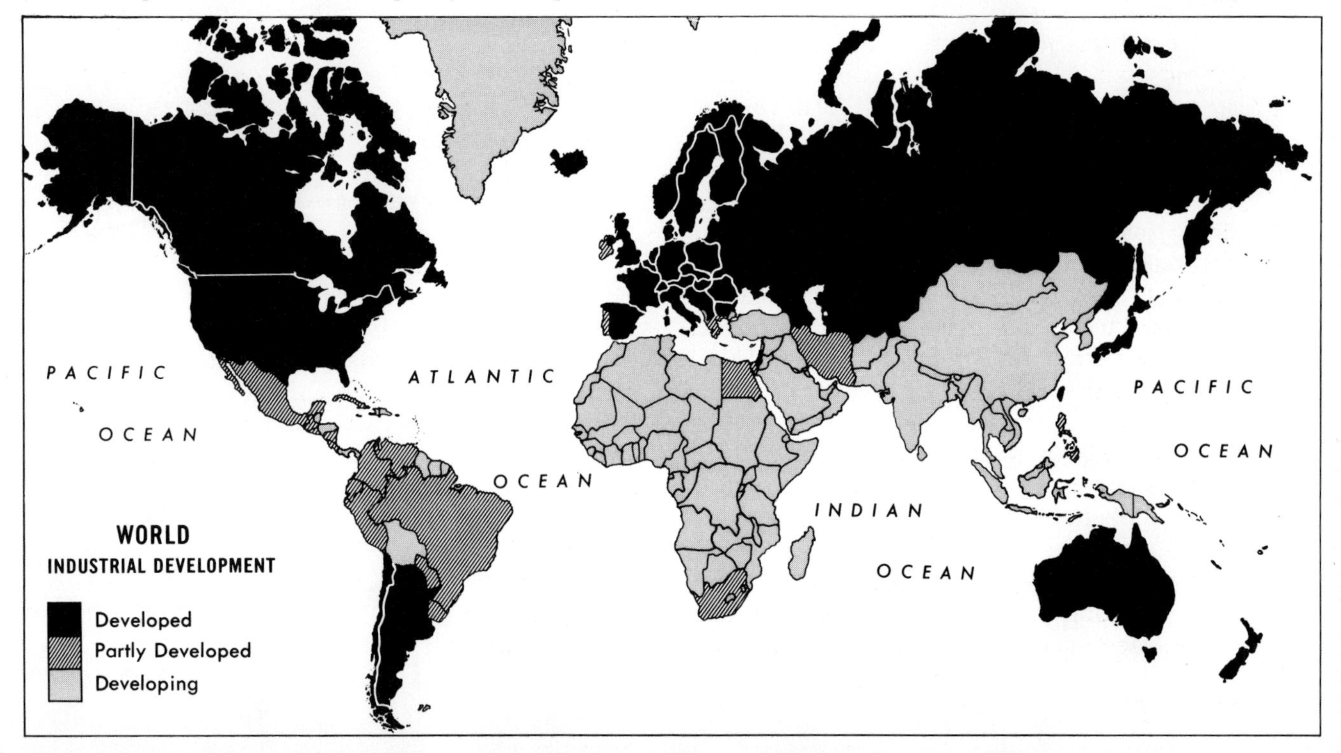

Transportation equipment. Several kinds of equipment for transporting people and goods are made in China today. For example, there are shipyards in Shanghai, Luta, and other Chinese seaports. All kinds of vessels, from fishing boats to huge oceangoing freighters, are constructed here. Factories in North China produce trucks, buses, locomotives, and railroad cars. There are also automobile factories in China, but they produce only a small number of cars each year. Most of the cars in China are owned by government agencies. They are used mainly for transporting government officials or foreign visitors.

For many people in China, bicycles are the most important means of transportation. Chinese factories produce millions of bicycles every year.

Weapons. One of the main industries in China today is the manufacture of weapons. Factories here turn out large quantities of guns, tanks, airplanes, guided missiles, and other military

The first nuclear* reactor in China was built during the 1950's with the help of experts from the Soviet Union. Do you think the Soviets would be likely to help the Chinese on such a project today? Why? Why not? Chapter 5 provides information that should help you answer this question.

equipment. China's leaders claim that this is necessary to protect the country in case of foreign attack.

Over the years, China has made much progress in developing nuclear* energy and carrying on space flights. In 1964 the Chinese exploded their first atomic bomb in the deserts of Sinkiang Uighur. A hydrogen bomb was exploded in the same area three years later. Since that time, the Chinese have tested other nuclear devices and developed missiles that can hit targets thousands of miles away. They have also launched several space satellites into orbit around the earth.

Petroleum products. As you discovered in Chapter 15, China has rich deposits of petroleum. The Chinese have built a number of oil refineries to make use of this valuable resource. Some of these refineries are located near the oil fields where crude* oil is taken from the ground. Others are in major cities such as Peking, Nanking, and Shanghai. In these refineries, the crude oil is changed into gasoline, fuel oil, and other useful products.

Chemicals and chemical products. China's mines and oil wells provide the raw materials needed to make many different chemicals. Some factories in China produce basic chemicals such as sulfuric acid and soda ash. Other plants use these chemicals in manufacturing a variety of products, including fertilizers, medicines, and plastics. Basic chemicals are also used to produce synthetic* fibers for making cloth.

Perhaps the most important chemical product in China today is fertilizer. Large amounts of fertilizer are needed to help farmers produce better crops. To meet this need, fertilizer plants have been built in cities and towns throughout the nation.

Textiles. Another important industry in China is the manufacture of textiles. This industry supplies the cloth that is needed to make clothing for China's huge population. Also, large amounts of cloth are exported to other countries. (See page 176.)

Cotton is the main kind of fiber used in China's textile mills. As you discovered in Chapter 14, this crop is grown on the Yangtze Plain and in other fertile farming areas of China. Many cotton mills are located in or near the city of Shanghai. There are also mills in Sian, Peking, Tientsin, and a number of other cities. For centuries, the production of silk textiles has been an important industry in China. Today large amounts of silk cloth are produced each year for export. Hangchow is a leading city for silk manufacturing. Woolen cloth is now being manufactured in the northwest part of China as well as in other areas.

Cotton, silk, and wool are all made from natural fibers produced on farms. China is not always able to produce enough of these natural fibers to supply its textile mills. For this reason, the Chinese sometimes import large amounts of cotton from the United States and other countries. In addition, they have been increasing their production of synthetic fibers such as nylon and Dacron.

Food products. In a nation with more than one billion people, it is not surprising that food processing is a major industry. China has many small factories that process grains such as rice and wheat to make flour and other products. There are also factories that make

A small steel plant in the province of Szechwan. China is not yet able to produce all of the equipment needed to establish new manufacturing plants. How is it trying to solve this problem?

products such as cooking oil from soybeans. Some of the factories in South China process tea grown on the hillsides nearby. In this part of China there are also canneries that process pineapples and other kinds of fruits. Fish canneries are located in a number of ports along China's seacoast. There are dairies and meat-packing plants in Inner Mongolia and other livestock-raising areas.

Sugar is another important food product manufactured in China. Some sugar refineries are located in Canton and other cities of South China, near the places where sugarcane is raised. Other refineries are near the sugar beet fields in the far northeastern part of the country.

Other products. China produces many other types of goods besides those that

have been mentioned. For example, there are large cement plants in a number of Chinese cities. They produce cement to use in constructing highways, bridges, dams, and buildings. Other construction materials manufactured in China include bricks, tile, and lumber. Chinese factories also produce a variety of consumer goods, including furniture, shoes, clocks, dishes, paper, and bicycles.

Problems of Industry

Today, China's leaders face several problems in their efforts to develop more industry. For one thing, the country is not yet able to produce all the different kinds of machines and equipment needed to establish new manufacturing plants. China is trying to solve this problem by buying some of the necessary equipment from other countries. (See "China's Foreign Trade," page 176.) However, such equipment is usually very expensive. Sometimes China has had to postpone new industrial projects because it did not have the money to pay for them.

Often the Chinese make up for the shortage of modern machines by using their large supply of workers. If you were to travel in China, you would see large groups of people using hand tools such as picks and shovels to build dams, and to do other kinds of projects. In the United States, many of these same jobs would be done by machines.

China faces other serious problems in its efforts to develop industry. For example, it does not have enough trained engineers and factory managers. Chinese schools have been trying to develop new programs to train people for these jobs.

Another problem is the lack of good transportation in China. There are not enough good roads and railroads. As a result, it is often difficult to bring raw materials to factories and to send manufactured goods to the people who will use them. Chapter 17 tells what China is doing to improve its transportation system.

A Chinese passenger train on the route between Hong Kong and Canton. Railroads are an important means of transporting freight and passengers in China. What improvements have been made in railroad transportation during recent years?

17 Transportation and Communication

A Problem To Solve

Through the years, the leaders of China's government have made a great effort to improve railroads, highways, and other transportation routes within the country. Why do the Chinese leaders place so much importance on good transportation? To solve this problem, you will need to consider how transportation affects:

a. the supply of food and other goods
b. farming and manufacturing
c. the unity of the nation

See pages 198-200

China is trying to develop a modern system of transportation. Like other countries, China needs ways of transporting goods and people from place to place. But providing good transportation has always been a difficult problem in this country. In the first place, China is very large. Also, the land features and climate in many areas make it hard to build roads and railroads. There are

many high, rugged mountains and deep canyons that act as barriers to transportation. In the deserts of northwestern China, blowing sand often covers highways and railroad tracks. In places where there is more rainfall, roads are sometimes destroyed by floods or washed away during severe storms.

When the Chinese Communists came to power in 1949, the country's transportation system was very poor. Most of the roads and railroads in eastern China had been damaged severely during World War II* and the years of warfare that followed. In some parts of China, the only transportation routes were narrow dirt trails and waterways. Airline transportation hardly existed.

The lack of modern transportation caused serious problems in China. If crops failed in one part of the country it was difficult to bring in food from other areas. As a result, people sometimes starved to death. Factories could not be started in remote parts of the country, because there was no way to bring in machines and raw materials or to send out manufactured goods. Also, the national government found it hard to keep control of areas that lacked good transportation routes. Troops and military supplies could not be transported easily to such places.

To solve these problems, China's Communist leaders made the development of a good transportation system one of their chief goals. As the following pages will show, much progress has been made toward achieving this goal. But China still does not have enough good highways, railroads, and airlines.

Railroads. In China, the most important way of transporting freight is by railroad. Trains are also used to carry large numbers of passengers from one city to another.

When the Communists came to power, they gave the railroads first place in their plans for improving China's transportation system. Groups of soldiers, prisoners, and farm workers were assigned to repair the railroads that had been damaged by war. In addition, more than 11,000 miles (17,500 km.) of new

*See Glossary

railroads were built. Much of this construction took place in parts of central and northwestern China where there had been no railroads before. The national government was responsible for building the main railroads. Small railroads leading to these main routes were constructed by work teams from China's communes.

Today, China has about 32,000 miles (51,000 km.) of railroads. This figure is not very high compared with the more than 152,000 miles (245,000 km.) of railroads in the United States. However, China's railroads form a network that reaches all parts of the country except Tibet. (See railroad map on page 174.) Railroads also connect China with several neighboring countries, including the Mongolian People's Republic, North Korea, the Soviet Union, and Vietnam.

Train travel in China is dependable and fairly pleasant. Even though most of the trains are quite old, they are spotlessly clean. Passengers may eat their meals in a dining car or buy food at stations along the way. While they are traveling, they listen to music, news, and

A street in Peking. There are very few automobiles in China, although trucks and buses are quite common. What would it be like to live in a country where hardly any families owned cars? Can you think of any problems that might be avoided by not having many cars on the roads? Explain.

See page 196

The picture at right shows a Chinese farmer driving an oxcart. Such carts are still widely used in China to transport farm products and other goods. In every country, people have to exchange goods and services with one another in order to meet their needs. Would it be possible to carry on much exchange without having some form of transportation? Explain your answer.

political programs broadcast over loudspeakers or radios on the train.

Roads. Many new roads have been built in China during recent years. Some of the most important of these roads are in remote parts of the country, such as Tibet and the western part of Sinkiang Uighur. (Compare map on page 82 with highway map on page 174.) Formerly it had been difficult to reach these areas from eastern China. In addition to main highways, many miles of local roads have been constructed in China. Most of these roads have been built by people in rural areas to make it easier to transport farm products.

By our standards, most of the roads in China are poor. Only a few thousand miles of roads are paved with asphalt or concrete. The rest are either dirt roads or roads that have been surfaced with loose material such as gravel. China's road builders generally use simple equipment. For example, they haul dirt in baskets or wheelbarrows, and they use shovels to make the surface of the roads smooth.

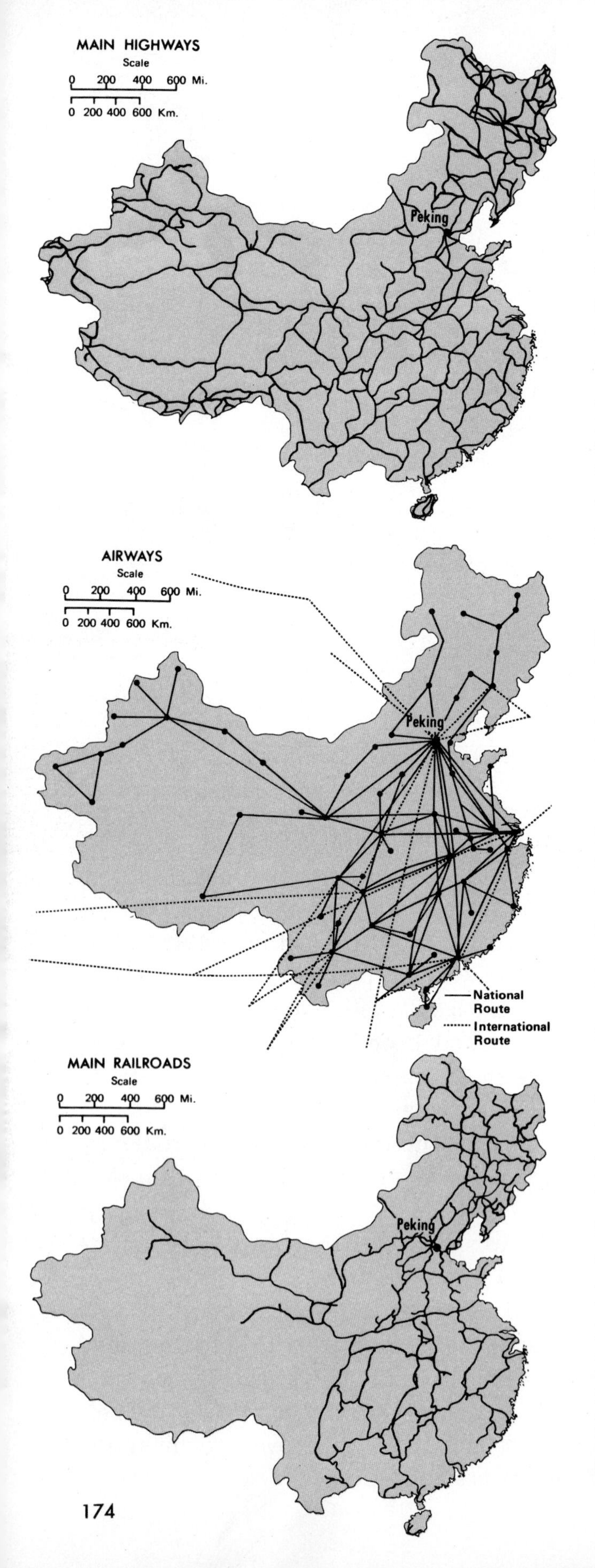

Traffic on China's roads is light. Automobiles are seldom seen, for there are hardly any privately owned passenger cars in China. Trucks and buses are more common. They are usually owned by government agencies. Bicycles are a very important means of transportation in the cities. Small three-wheeled vehicles called pedicabs* are also popular. Carts pulled by oxen, horses, or other animals are widely used in China. In many parts of the country, people still travel on foot from place to place.

Waterways. Since very early times, the Chinese have traveled and transported goods by boat. Water travel is especially useful in central and southern China, where there are a number of large rivers. By far the most important inland waterway in China is the great Yangtze River. (See map on pages 20-21.) Boats can travel for about 50,000 miles (80,000 km.) on the Yangtze and its many tributaries. Rivers in North China are much less important as transportation routes. For example, some parts of the Yellow River are too shallow for navigation during much of the year.

In addition to rivers, there are many canals in China. These canals were built to allow small boats to travel from one part of the country to another. Perhaps the most interesting is the Grand Canal.* One section of this famous waterway was built nearly 2,500 years ago. For a long time, the Grand Canal was not kept in good repair. In recent years, however, part of the canal has been improved and made larger. Today, this part is used by barges that weigh as much as five hundred tons.

Many kinds of boats travel on China's water highways. Some are modern motor vessels. Others are sampans or junks, which have been used in China for centuries. The sampan is a small, flat-bottomed boat moved by two short oars. The junk is a type of sailing ship. (See picture on pages 24-25.)

China also has a large fleet of oceangoing ships. Some of these ships carry goods to and from foreign countries, while others travel between cities along China's coast. Recently the Chinese have been adding more ships to their fleet to take care of their growing foreign trade. (See page 176.) Also, the ports where ships load and unload their cargoes are being improved and made larger. China's leading ocean ports are located in or near the cities of Luta, Tientsin, Tsingtao, Shanghai, and Canton.

Airways. When the Communists came to power, China did not have any regular air transportation service. The government bought airplanes from the Soviet Union and set up new airline routes. Later, the Chinese began to manufacture their own airplanes and also to buy planes from Western countries such as Great Britain.

Airplanes now make flights to more than eighty Chinese cities. In addition, there are airline routes connecting China with a number of foreign countries, including the Soviet Union, Japan, Burma, Pakistan, France, and the United States.

In most countries, the fastest way to travel a long distance is by airplane, but this is not always true in China. Airplanes there are not allowed to fly unless the weather is almost perfect.

Continued on page 177.

A ship in Tientsin harbor. The Chinese have been improving their ports and building new ships. Why have they been doing this?

China's Foreign Trade

Like other nations of the world, China cannot meet its needs all by itself. It must trade with other countries to obtain some of the goods its people need and want.

Important changes have taken place in China's foreign trade since the Communists came to power there. From about 1950 to 1960, China traded mainly with the Soviet Union and other Communist countries in eastern Europe. At that time, the Cold War* was at its height. A number of Western countries, including the United States, would not allow their citizens to carry on any trade with Communist China.

By 1960 a quarrel had developed between China and the Soviet Union. (See page 73.) China's trade with the Soviet Union and other Communist nations dropped sharply. Meanwhile, some of the Western countries began to do away with their restrictions on trade with China.

In the early 1960's, poor harvests led to a serious shortage of food in China. The Chinese government had to buy large amounts of wheat from non-Communist countries such as Canada and Australia. It also began to import fertilizer and other items needed to increase food production. However, the Communist leaders wanted China to depend on foreign countries as little as possible. So for years, China carried on much less foreign trade than other nations its size.

This policy changed after the death of Mao Tse-tung in 1976. The new leaders who took Mao's place started a campaign to develop more industry in China. To reach their goal, they had to import large amounts of machinery and other equipment from the developed* nations. They signed trade agreements with Japan, the United States, and several countries in western Europe. Since that time, China's foreign trade has been growing very rapidly. China now trades with more than 170 countries and territories all over the world.

Among China's main exports are cotton and silk textiles and cotton clothing. China also exports minerals such as oil and tungsten, and food products such as rice, tea, and fish. Its main imports are manufactured goods. These include machinery, iron and steel, chemicals, and jet airplanes. In addition, China imports large amounts of farm crops such as wheat, corn, and soybeans.

Today China carries on more trade with its island neighbor, Japan, than with any other country. This small, crowded nation is poor in natural resources, but it has developed many important industries. Japan sells China a wide variety of manufactured goods. In return, China supplies Japan with food and with raw materials, such as oil and coal.

China has several other important trading partners. One is the British territory of Hong Kong,* which lies along China's coast. Others include the United States, Canada, and Australia. China also carries on much trade with European countries such as West Germany, France, and Great Britain. Only about one tenth of its trade is with other Communist nations.

The Chinese would like to purchase more goods from foreign nations than they are buying now. However, they lack the money. So far, they have not been able to sell enough of their own products abroad to pay for all the imports they want. Sometimes they have borrowed the money they needed from foreign banks, but the Chinese leaders do not like to go into debt.

To solve this problem, the Chinese are trying to increase their exports to other countries. For example, they are working to attract more customers by providing better goods at a lower cost. Also, they are searching for new deposits of oil and other minerals. By selling these minerals abroad, China can earn some of the money it needs to pay for its imports.

*See Glossary

Language

See page 193

The picture at right was taken inside a post office in Shanghai. China has very good postal service. There are about 50,000 post offices scattered throughout the country. What are some other methods used by people in China to send messages from one place to another? Do you think it is important for every country to have rapid, dependable means of communication? Give reasons for your answer.

Sometimes passengers may be delayed two or three days waiting for skies to clear. For this reason, people often go by train if they want to reach a place on a certain day.

Communications. In China, just as in other countries, there are several ways of sending messages from one place to another. China has very good postal service. At the present time, few Chinese have telephones of their own. However, most government offices and places of business have telephone service. All the important cities in China are connected by telegraph. In China, the postal, telephone, and telegraph services are all run by the government.

The government of China also controls all the means of spreading information to large masses of people, such as newspapers, radio, and television. One of the most important newspapers in China is the *People's Daily*, the official paper of the Chinese Communist Party. Another is the *Liberation Army Daily*, which is the army's official paper. There are hundreds of other daily and weekly newspapers in China. Most of these print the same news as the two official papers.

There are more than 150 radio stations in China. All of them are organized into a single broadcasting system with headquarters in Peking. Many people in China own inexpensive transistor radios. In addition, radio programs are broadcast over loudspeakers in factories, offices, and other public places.

Until recently, television service in China was very limited. Few families owned television sets, and programs were broadcast for only a few hours each day. Today, this is changing rapidly. Factories in China are producing millions of television sets each year. Even though these sets are expensive, more and more families are buying them. There are television stations in all of the major cities in China.

A change is also taking place in the kinds of programs that are broadcast. Formerly, Chinese television programs were devoted mainly to Communist propaganda.* But now people can watch a variety of shows, including news reports, comedies, movies, soap operas, and sports programs. There are even ads for commercial products.

Hold a Discussion

With your class or a group of classmates, hold a discussion on the following topic:

In what ways is transportation in China different from transportation in the United States and in what ways is it similar?

To prepare for your discussion, do research in this book and other sources. The pictures in Chapter 17 will be helpful. In your discussion, consider the following kinds of transportation in China and in the United States:

a. railroad travel
b. travel on highways and streets
c. water transportation
d. air travel

The suggestions on pages 201-207 will help you to locate additional sources of information and to hold a good discussion.

Make Discoveries About Iron and Steel

Write a brief report on the manufacture of iron and steel. In your report, include the following information:

a. the three main raw materials needed for making iron and steel
b. how iron is made in a blast furnace
c. how steel differs from iron
d. the different kinds of furnaces used for making steel
e. the metals added to make special kinds of steel, such as stainless steel
f. some of the important products made from steel

Chapter 16 in this book provides some of the information you will need for your report. Pages 201-206 provide helpful suggestions for locating additional sources of information and for writing a good report. Share your completed report with your classmates.

Make an Agriculture Map

On a large sheet of poster board, draw a map of China. Do research in this book and other sources to discover what crops and farm animals are raised in China. List these crops and animals, together with the regions or parts of China where they are important. Then make a sketch or find a picture of each of these crops and farm animals. To find out where your pictures should be pasted on your map, refer to your list of regions. The maps on pages 25, 141, and 147 provide information that will be helpful to you in carrying out this project.

Taiwan

About one hundred miles off the Pacific coast of China is the island of Taiwan, or Formosa.* (See map at right.) In the past, Taiwan was governed as part of China. Today it has a separate government. Let us discover how this came about.

Land and climate. The island of Taiwan extends for about 240 miles from north to south and 90 miles from east to west. Rugged, forested mountains make up two thirds of the island. The highest of these peaks rises more than 13,000 feet above sea level. Most of western Taiwan is a low coastal plain, with gently rolling hills and level land that is good for farming.

Taiwan's climate is hot and humid in the summer and mild in the winter. Rainfall is heavy during most of the year. In the summer months, fierce storms called typhoons sometimes damage houses and crops.

History. As early as the sixth century A.D., small numbers of Chinese people from the mainland began coming to Taiwan. At that time the island was already occupied by brown-skinned people who are known today as the aborigines.* In the late 1600's, the Manchu rulers of China conquered Taiwan and made it part of their empire. Soon many Chinese settlers from the mainland were coming to Taiwan to live.

In 1895, Japan defeated China in a war and took control of Taiwan. The Japanese built schools, highways, and railroads on the island. They also developed farming and industry. But they treated Taiwan's people harshly and tried to force them to give up Chinese culture. After Japan was defeated in World War II,* Taiwan again became part of China.

In 1949, the Communist forces of Mao Tse-tung gained control of the Chinese mainland. (See pages 60-61.) Chiang Kai-shek, the leader of the Nationalists,* fled to Taiwan with about two million of his followers. The newcomers were greatly

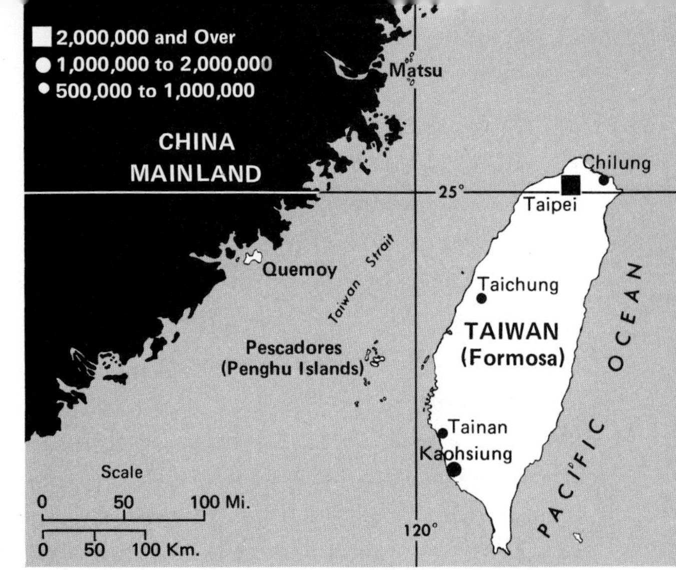

The island of Taiwan lies about one hundred miles off the Chinese mainland. The government of Taiwan controls not only this island but also a number of smaller islands, including Quemoy, Matsu, and the Pescadores.

outnumbered by the native people of Taiwan. Nevertheless, they took over the government by force and refused to allow any opposition. The Nationalists believed that they were still the rightful rulers of all China, so they established the "Republic of China" on Taiwan. They began making plans to return to the mainland and overthrow the Communist government there.

At that time, the United States and other Western countries were deeply concerned about the threat of communism. (See page 72.) The United States refused to recognize the Communist government as the rightful government of China. In 1954 our government signed a treaty with the Nationalist government, promising to defend Taiwan in case of a military attack from the Chinese mainland. The United States began sending advisors, weapons, and large amounts of money to Taiwan. With American help, the island soon became quite prosperous.

Largely because of American efforts, the Nationalist government was allowed to represent China in the United Nations.* The Communist government in Peking was not represented in the UN at all. As time passed, however, a growing number of nations

*See Glossary

came to feel that this was wrong. In 1971, the General Assembly of the UN voted to expel the Nationalists and admit Communist China instead.

Meanwhile, the United States and Communist China were becoming more friendly toward each other. In 1979 the United States finally recognized the Communist government as the lawful government of China. A year later, it ended its defense treaty with Taiwan. However, the United States continued to supply the Nationalist government with weapons to defend itself against a possible attack.

In recent years, the Chinese Communist leaders have been trying to persuade Taiwan to become part of China again. They have promised that Taiwan's people will be allowed to keep their present way of life without interference from Peking. So far, the Nationalist government has strongly rejected this offer. Many people believe that Taiwan will someday be reunited with China. But no one knows when or how this might come about.

Government. Chiang Kai-shek was president of the Republic of China on Taiwan until his death in 1975. Today his son Chiang Ching-kuo serves as president. The chief lawmaking body of Taiwan is called the Legislative Yuan.

Taiwan's government is still controlled by the Nationalist Party, which allows little opposition. Freedom of speech and freedom of the press are limited in various ways. Most of the important government jobs are held by people who came from the mainland in 1949. But the native people of Taiwan are now trying to gain a larger voice in the government.

People and their way of life. Taiwan is the home of about eighteen and one-half million people. Nearly all of these people are crowded into the lowlands along the western coast.

About fifteen million people on Taiwan are Chinese whose ancestors came here from the mainland provinces of Fukien and Kwangtung during the 1700's and 1800's. Most of the others are Chinese Nationalists

A street in Taipei, the capital and largest city of Taiwan. Compare the photograph below with the pictures of Peking, Shanghai, and Canton on pages 106-107, 110-111, 112, and 172-173. What differences do you notice? Why do you suppose Taiwan has been so prosperous in recent years?

who came to Taiwan in 1949, or their children. There are still about 200,000 aborigines on Taiwan. Most of them live on reservations in the mountains.

The official language of Taiwan is a form of Mandarin Chinese. (See pages 182-183.) But many people also speak other Chinese dialects, depending on what part of China their ancestors came from. Taiwan's people are free to worship as they please. The majority of them follow a mixture of Confucianism, Taoism, and Buddhism.

Since the Nationalists came to Taiwan, they have been making a considerable effort to improve education. Today about nine tenths of the people can read and write. Taiwan has about 2,400 primary schools, 1,000 secondary schools,and 100 colleges and universities.

The capital and largest city of Taiwan is Taipei, near the northern tip of the island. It has a population of about 2,225,000. Kaohsiung (pop. 1,063,000), the second largest city in Taiwan, is an important seaport and manufacturing center.

Earning a living. About 3 out of every 10 workers on Taiwan earn their living by farming. After the Nationalists moved here in 1949, the government bought land from wealthy landowners and distributed it to peasant families. As a result, most families now have farms of their own. These farms are generally very small, but they are highly productive. Farmers on Taiwan use large amounts of chemical fertilizers. Many of them have small tractors to do such jobs as plowing and cultivating.

When the Japanese controlled Taiwan, they encouraged farmers to grow crops for export. Among these were sugarcane, bananas, pineapples, tea, and citronella* grass. Today all of these crops are still grown on the island. But more attention is now being given to raising food crops for Taiwan's people. The leading food crop is rice. Taiwan's production of rice per acre is one of the highest in the world. Other food crops include sweet potatoes, peanuts, soybeans, wheat, and oranges. Hogs and poultry are the main kinds of livestock.

Taiwan is not rich in minerals, but small amounts of coal, sulfur, copper, and gold are mined on the island. There are also wells that produce oil and natural gas. Salt is obtained from seawater along the western coast. The dense forests that cover the mountains of Taiwan provide wood for lumber, paper, and other products. Dams and power plants have been built on a number of swiftly flowing rivers. They produce electricity for homes and factories. Fishing boats from Taiwan sail the waters of the Pacific Ocean and bring back catches of tuna, sardines, and other fish.

Ever since the early 1950's, industry has been growing rapidly on Taiwan. Today about 4 out of every 10 workers on the island earn their living in factories.

Taiwan produces many different kinds of manufactured goods. For example, there are factories that make cloth from cotton, wool, flax, or synthetic* fibers. Other factories make clothing. Sugar refineries and pineapple canneries make use of farm crops grown here. Several chemical plants have been built to produce fertilizer for Taiwan's farms. Iron, steel, aluminum, and cement are all manufactured on Taiwan. So, too, are jet airplanes and helicopters for Taiwan's air force. A leading industry is the manufacture of electronic devices such as transistors and television sets.

The people of Taiwan earn large sums of money by selling goods to other countries. Among the island's main exports are textiles, electrical machinery, sugar, bananas, canned pineapples, and plywood. Most of these exports go to the United States, Japan, Hong Kong, and West Germany.

Trade and manufacturing have helped to make Taiwan very prosperous. Today Japan and Singapore are the only countries in eastern Asia that have a higher standard of living.

The Chinese Language

More people speak the Chinese language than any other language in the world. The number of Chinese-speaking persons is larger than the number who speak English, French, Spanish, and German combined.

The spoken language. The Chinese language is not spoken the same way in all parts of China. More than two thirds of the people use a form of the language known in English as Mandarin. This dialect* is spoken throughout North China and in some parts of South China.

In addition to Mandarin, there are several other important Chinese dialects. These are spoken mainly in certain parts of South China. Some of them differ from one another and from Mandarin as much as English differs from German. For example, the word for "no" is pronounced "bu" in Mandarin and "baht" in the dialect used around Canton.

If you listen to any Chinese dialect being spoken, you will notice that the speaker's voice goes up and down, almost as if he or she were singing. This is because Chinese is what we call a tonal language. Most words in Chinese have only one syllable. Of course, no language can have enough different syllables to stand for all the ideas that need to be expressed. For this reason, the same syllable is spoken in different tones in order to express different ideas. For example, the syllable *li* spoken like a question in a high voice may mean "monkey." When spoken in a low voice it may mean "plum." Sometimes one syllable has dozens of meanings. It must be used in a complete sentence before a listener can be sure which meaning is the correct one.

The written language. The Chinese way of writing words is quite different from our own. In our country, we use an alphabet made up of twenty-six different letters. Each letter represents a certain sound or sounds. These letters can be combined to form written words that represent the sounds we make when we speak the words. By using only these twenty-six symbols, we can write all the words in our language.

The Chinese, on the other hand, use a separate symbol or group of symbols for each word in their language. For example, the symbol 人 means "person," 再见 means "good-bye," and 看 means "to read." These symbols are called characters.

Unlike words written with an alphabet, Chinese characters do not depend on sounds for their meaning. Instead, they stand for things or ideas. For example, the word for "morning" may be pronounced one way in Mandarin and a different way in another Chinese dialect, but the symbol 上午 always represents the idea of morning. Chinese characters are somewhat like numerals in mathematics. The numeral "3" means the same to people in the United States, France, and Germany, even though Americans say "three," French people say "*trois*," and Germans say "*drei*."

A written language like Chinese, which uses characters to represent ideas rather than sounds, has certain advantages. Because the written characters mean the same thing to everyone, Han Chinese who speak different dialects can communicate by writing even if they cannot understand one another's speech. Also, Chinese writing is considered more beautiful than most other forms of writing. Chinese paintings are often decorated with rows of gracefully written characters.

There are also some disadvantages to a written language like Chinese. Since a different character or group of characters is used for every word in the language, people must learn many characters in order to read and write. For example, it is necessary to know more than three thousand characters in order to read a newspaper well. Also, learning to write the complicated Chinese characters with a pen or brush is a slow and painstaking task. These facts help to explain why most Chinese in earlier times never learned to read and write.

*See Glossary

Changes in the language. In the present century, China's leaders have been trying to make it easier for people to communicate with one another. The Nationalists* decided that all Chinese should learn the Mandarin dialect as it is spoken in Peking. Today, this is the official language of China. It is called *putonghua*, which means "common speech." People who grow up speaking a different dialect learn *putonghua* also, because it is taught in all the schools.

Since the Communists came to power, they have been experimenting with ways to make the Chinese language easier to read and write. In the 1950's, a committee set up by the Communists developed simpler versions of about eight hundred commonly used characters. For instance, 当 took the place of 當噹 . These simplified characters are now used in books, newspapers, and other publications.

The committee in charge of revising the language also developed a new Chinese alphabet with letters that stand for sounds. This alphabet is called Pinyin, which means "spell-sound." It uses the same twenty-six letters as our alphabet. However, the letters do not always represent the same sounds as they do in English. For example, the letter "q" represents the sound of "ch." Pinyin is now being used along with traditional Chinese characters on street signs and in other public places. (See picture on pages 66-67.)

Pinyin has some disadvantages. People who speak in different dialects cannot communicate by writing Pinyin, as they can when they use traditional Chinese characters. Also, with Pinyin there is no easy way to represent the different tones used in spoken Chinese. For these reasons, China's leaders are being cautious about giving up the present system of writing.

A writing class in a Nanking elementary school. Learning to write Chinese is very difficult, because a different symbol or group of symbols is used for every word in the language. But changing to an alphabet like ours would also present problems to the Chinese. Explain.

The Changing Role of Women in China

How were Chinese women treated in the past? One of the greatest changes that has taken place in China during this century has been in the treatment of women. In earlier times, women were considered less important than men. They often suffered great hardships because of their low position. For example, in poor families a girl might be sold or traded to someone else for money or food. She became a servant of the person who bought her. In times of famine,* girl babies were sometimes put to death.

In the traditional Chinese family, males always held a higher position than females. Older women ranked higher than younger women. Young girls held the lowest position of all. They had to respect and obey everyone else in the household, including younger brothers.

In old China, people did not usually choose their own husbands and wives. Marriages were arranged by the parents. Often a girl would be promised to a young man when she was still very small. She would be sent to live as a servant in her future husband's household until she was old enough to marry.

After a girl was married, she had to obey her husband and his parents without question. Otherwise, she might be beaten. Often a young bride was treated very harshly by her mother-in-law and other members of the family until she gave birth to a son

*See Glossary

Mothers and children in the city of Changchun. During the day, these women work in an automobile plant while their children are cared for in a nursery nearby. After work, they all ride home in a factory bus. How has the life of Chinese women changed since the beginning of this century?

to carry on the family name. If she had no sons, her husband could take a second wife. A woman who lived long enough might eventually become the oldest female in the family. Then she would have considerable power in running the household, and could treat her daughters-in-law in the same way she had been treated.

Chinese women lacked many rights and opportunities enjoyed by men. For example, they could not take part in government or in other activities outside the home. Few women ever went to school. A woman could not divorce her husband, no matter how badly he treated her. If her husband died, she was not allowed to marry again. Women had no possessions of their own. All property was owned by the men of the family.

The custom of foot-binding made women in China even more dependent on men. When a girl was very young, her feet were wrapped tightly in strips of cloth to keep them small. The constant pressure of the tight bindings made her toes turn under and broke the arches of her feet. This process was very painful, and it left the girl partly crippled for the rest of her life. But most girls endured it because a woman with normal feet was considered ugly, and it was difficult to find a husband for her.

How did Chinese women gain more freedom? Early in the 1900's, educated people in China began to question the customs that gave women a lower position than men. The custom of foot-binding was gradually given up. Schools for girls were established, and some women began to take jobs outside their homes. Then, in 1930, the Nationalist* government passed the Kinship Relations Law. This law gave more rights to women and to younger members of families. The law was not strictly enforced, however. Only a small number of women–mainly those in the cities–benefited from it.

In 1950, after the Communists came to power in China, a new law called the Marriage Law was passed. Under this law, men and women in China were given all the same rights. These included the right to seek a job outside the home, to own property, and to get a divorce. In case of death or divorce, either partner had the right to marry someone else. Parents were no longer supposed to arrange marriages for their children, and girls could no longer be traded or sold.

The Marriage Law of 1950 was strongly enforced by the government. Officials were sent to villages throughout China to make sure that all women knew about their rights. Today the position of women in China is similar to that of women in the United States and other Western countries.

Shaping Public Opinion in China

The government leaders of China would like every person in the country to be a loyal follower of communism. To achieve this goal, they try to control the everyday lives of China's people in a number of different ways. Let us examine these methods of control more closely.

Newspapers and other means of communication. First of all, China's leaders control nearly all means of communicating information to the people. All newspapers, magazines, and books in China are published under the direction of government agencies. Also, the government controls the radio and television stations and the motion-picture studios.

In China, the main purpose of newspapers and other means of communication is not to entertain people or to give them facts. It is to persuade them to support the government. For example, a newspaper will carry articles praising the Communist leaders and criticizing people who oppose them.

If you were to travel through China, you would see many large, colorful posters and billboards. These carry messages urging people to support the government and to work hard to meet the Communists' goals. For example, a poster in a farming village might show a group of smiling workers carrying bundles of wheat. The caption might say, "Let's all work together to produce a record crop of wheat this year!"

On your trip through China, you would often hear messages and lively band music coming from loudspeakers in trains, hotel lobbies, and department stores. The government wants to make sure that its propaganda* programs are heard by everyone in China—even people who do not own radios or television sets. For this reason, it has set up loudspeakers in public places throughout the country.

Study groups. The Communist leaders also use other methods to influence people's thinking. For example, small study groups have been organized in factories, farming villages, schools, and city neighborhoods throughout China. Nearly every adult is expected to belong to one or more of these groups.

The study groups usually meet at least once a week, after work or in the eve-

*See Glossary

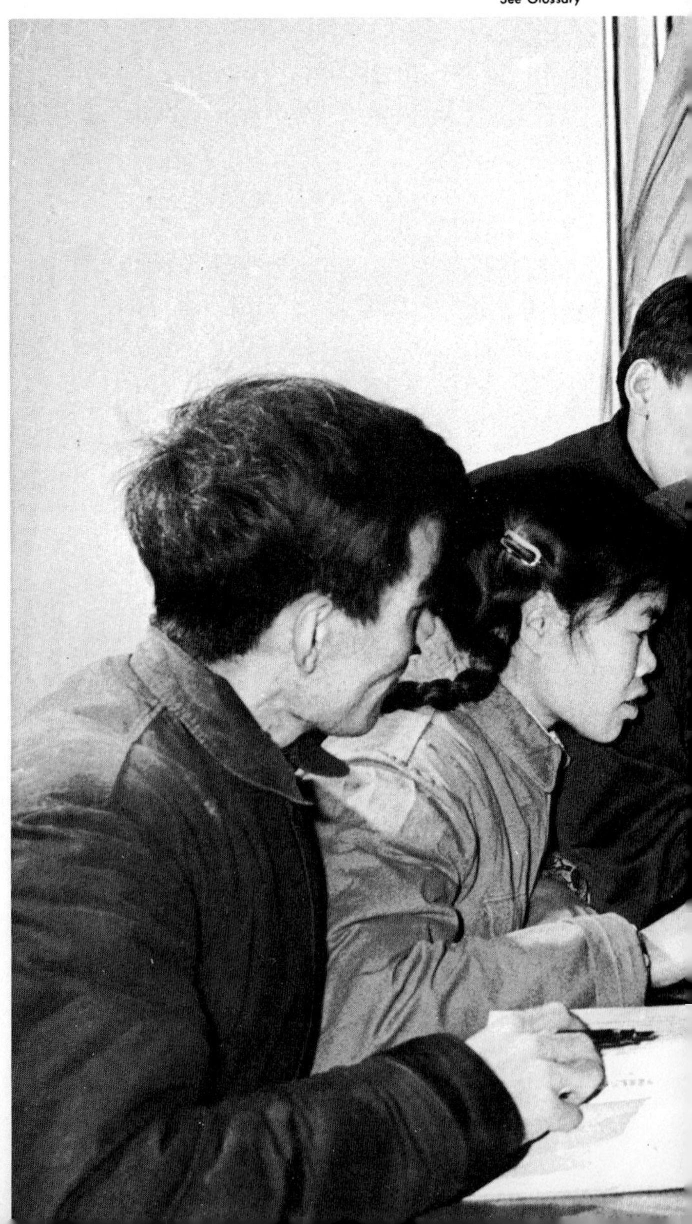

nings. Members of each group study the writings of Communist leaders, as well as articles from Chinese newspapers. Then they discuss what they have read. Sometimes they are encouraged to confess their faults, such as being lazy or making careless mistakes at work. They are also expected to criticize the faults of other members and urge them to do better in the future.

The study groups are led by people who have shown a strong loyalty toward communism. They encourage the members of the study groups to give their views of

See pages 193-194

A study group. Small study groups like the one pictured below have been organized in factories, farming villages, schools, and city neighborhoods throughout China. What is their purpose? Would you say that the study groups are a way of educating China's people? Does every country have a need for education? Explain your answers. How does education in China differ from education in a democratic nation like the United States?

Communist teachings and how these can be applied in everyday life. The purpose of these discussions is to persuade everyone to support the Communist leaders' goals for China.

Prisons and labor camps. All of these methods have been quite successful in persuading citizens to follow the Communists' orders. But there are still many people in China who act in ways that are not approved by government leaders. Some of these are people who commit crimes such as robbery or murder. Others are not really criminals at all. They are people who say or do things that displease the Communists, such as questioning whether communism is the best form of government.

Although some of these people are put in prison, a much larger number are sent to labor camps. There they spend much of their time doing hard physical labor. For example, they may dig irrigation ditches or carry heavy rocks for building highways. Often they are not given enough food to maintain good health. In their spare time, they are required to study the writings of Communist leaders. Communist officials meet with them regularly to point out their faults and to urge them to change their way of thinking.

Not all the people who are sent to labor camps in China receive a trial beforehand. Many are arrested by the police and sent to labor camps without any trial. Sometimes people spend years in these camps without knowing if they are ever going to be free. It is not surprising, then, that most Chinese are careful to follow the rules laid down by the leaders of the Communist Party.

People reading wall posters on a street in Shanghai. The leaders of China use posters, loudspeakers, and other means of communication to spread government propaganda. What are some other ways in which the Communist leaders try to influence the thinking of China's people?

What Is Communism?

A word with several meanings. The word "communism" has several different meanings. First, it is used to describe the belief that all or most property should be owned by the entire community rather than by individual persons. In the past, various groups of people have tried to establish communities based on this idea. For example, the Oneida Community was started in New York State during the 1840's. In the Oneida Community, no one owned any private property. Instead, all goods belonged to the community as a whole.

"Communism" also refers to a set of ideas that were developed mainly by a famous German thinker named Karl Marx. When Marx was a young man, in the early 1800's, the Industrial Revolution was bringing great changes to Europe. (See page 164.) Marx was concerned about the hardships suffered by the hired workers in mines and factories. Many of these people had to work long hours at difficult or dangerous jobs for very little pay.

Marx believed that there were two main groups, or classes, in all industrial countries. One of these was the "working class." The other was the "ruling class," made up of wealthy people who owned the mines and factories. Marx predicted that the lives of the working people would become even harder as time went on. He believed the workers would finally revolt and overthrow the ruling class. They would establish a communist society, where land, factories, and other kinds of property would be owned by the people as a whole.

Many people accepted Marx's idea of struggle between classes. Among his followers was a Russian called V. I. Lenin. Lenin believed that the followers of Marx in each country should form a strong, well-organized political party that would take over the government by force and set up a communist society. In the early 1900's,

Karl Marx, a famous German thinker, is sometimes called the father of modern communism.

Russia was still mainly a farming nation. Most of the people were poor peasants who worked on the estates of rich landowners. In 1917, Lenin led a revolution in Russia that brought the Communist Party to power.

Today, Russia—now known as the Soviet Union—is still under the rule of the Communist Party. The country is governed by a powerful dictatorship* that has almost total control over people's lives. For example, the government controls farming, mining, manufacturing, and other ways of earning a living. It also controls education, sports, and the arts. No one in the Soviet Union is allowed to oppose the Communist Party. The people there lack many freedoms that are found in democratic countries like the United States. Among these are freedom of speech, freedom of the press, and freedom of religion. People now use the word "communism" to describe the kind of Communist dictatorship found in the Soviet Union.

The spread of communism. Until the 1940's, the Soviet Union was the only major

*See Glossary

country to have a Communist government. There were Communist parties in other countries, but they were not strong enough to seize power. In 1919, the Soviet leaders helped to form a worldwide organization called the Communist International, or the Comintern. The goal of this organization was to bring about Communist revolutions throughout the world. The Comintern was not very effective, and it was dissolved in 1943.

World War II* (1939-1945) helped provide opportunities for communism to spread to other countries. Near the end of this war, Soviet troops occupied a number of countries that had been under German or Japanese control. In some of these countries—such as Poland, Czechoslovakia, and Hungary—the Soviets helped to set up Communist governments. These governments needed the help of Soviet troops and weapons to stay in power. In several other countries, Communist parties took control of the government with little or no aid from the Soviet Union. Among these countries were China and Yugoslavia.

V. I. Lenin was a follower of Karl Marx. In 1917, he led a revolution that brought the Communist Party to power in Russia.

Since that time, a number of other countries have also come under Communist rule. They include the Asian nations of Vietnam, Laos, Kampuchea,* and Afghanistan. The island nation of Cuba has had a Communist government since 1960. In addition, the governments of some African countries are friendly toward communism.

The Cold War.* The rapid spread of communism at the end of World War II greatly alarmed people in the United States and other democratic nations. It seemed to them that the Communists were trying to take over the entire world by force. To protect themselves, some of the non-Communist countries began to form defense organizations such as NATO* and SEATO.* The Communist nations, in turn, formed alliances of their own.

The conflict between the Communist and non-Communist countries became known as the Cold War. Each side strengthened its armed forces and developed new weapons, such as nuclear bombs and long-range missiles. Sometimes fighting broke out between the two sides. For example, the Korean War* took place between 1950 and 1953, and the Vietnam War* lasted from 1957 to 1975. In these two terrible conflicts, millions were killed or wounded.

Is the Cold War still going on today? Many people would say that it is not. They point out that neither the Communist nor the non-Communist countries are as united as they once were. For example, the Communist nation of China has closer ties to the United States than it does to its Communist neighbor, the Soviet Union.

Other people feel that the Cold War has never ended. They say that the United States and Soviet Union are still the main rivals for world power. Both nations have weapons that are powerful enough to destroy civilization if a major war ever broke out. These people also note that Communist nations and Western democracies hold very different views about human freedom. As long as these differences remain, they say, the Cold War will continue.

Needs

The people of China, like all other people on the earth, must meet certain basic needs in order to be healthy and happy. Scientists who study human behavior tell us that these basic needs are almost exactly the same for all people, whatever their skin color, national origin, or religion may be. Whether people are rich or poor, they have the same basic needs.

There are three kinds of basic needs. They are: physical needs, social needs, and the need for faith.

Physical Needs

Some basic needs are so important that people will die or become very ill if they fail to meet them. These are physical needs. They include the need for:

1. air
2. water
3. food
4. protection from heat and cold
5. sleep and rest
6. exercise

Although all people share these needs, they do not all meet them in the same way. What are some ways in which you meet your physical needs? How do you think people in China meet their physical needs?

Social Needs

People also have social needs. They must meet these needs in order to have a happy and useful life. Social needs include:

1. Belonging to a group. All people need to feel they belong to a group of people who respect them and whom they respect. Belonging to a family is one of the main ways people meet this need. What can the members of a family do to show that they love and respect each other? How do the members of your family help one another? Do you think family life is important to the people of China? Why do you think this?

Having friends also helps people meet their need for belonging to a group. What groups of friends do you have? Why are these people your friends? Do you suppose young people in China enjoy doing the same kinds of things with their friends as you enjoy doing with your friends? Why? Why not?

2. Goals. To be happy, every person needs goals to work for. What goals do you want to reach? How can working toward these goals help you have a happy life? What kinds of goals do you think young people in China have?

3. A chance to think and learn. All people need a chance to develop and use their abilities. They need opportunities to find out about things that make them curious. What would you like to learn? How can you learn these things? How can developing your abilities help you have a happy life? Is it important for people in China to have a chance to think and learn? to help make decisions? Why? Why not?

4. A feeling of accomplishment. You share with every other person the need for a feeling of accomplishment. All people need to feel that their lives are successful in some way. What gives you a feeling of accomplishment? Can you imagine what life would be like if you never had this feeling?

The Need for Faith

In addition to physical and social needs, all people also have a need for faith. You need to believe that life is precious and that the future is something to look forward to. You may have different kinds of faith, including:

1. Faith in yourself. In order to feel secure, you must have faith in your own abilities. You must feel that you will be able to do some useful work in the world and that you will be generally happy. You must believe that you can work toward solving whatever problems life brings to you. How do you think you can build faith in yourself?

2. Faith in other people. You also need to feel that you can count on other people to do their part and to help you when you need help. What people do you have faith in? What do you think life would be like without this kind of faith?

3. Faith in nature's laws. Another kind of faith that helps people face the future with confidence is faith in nature's laws. The more we learn about our universe, the more certain we feel that we can depend on nature. How would you feel if you couldn't have faith in nature's laws?

4. Religious faith. Throughout history, almost all human beings have had some kind of religious faith. Religion can help people understand themselves and the world they live in. It can bring them joy, and it can give them confidence in times of trouble. Religion can also help people live together happily. For example, most religions teach people to be honest and to love and help their neighbors. In what ways do some people in China express religious faith?

A Chinese farm family. Which basic needs are these people meeting? Explain your answer.

Great Ideas

A Chinese typewriter must provide about two thousand different characters. As the feature on pages 182-183 explains, China's government is trying to simplify the written language. In what ways do you think this might be helpful to the Chinese people? In what ways might this affect community life in China?

Human beings have probably been living on the earth for more than two million years. During this long time, all people have met their needs in communities. They have found that only by living and working with other people can they have happy, satisfying lives.

In order to make community life successful, people have developed certain ideas and ways of living. We call these the "great ideas." Let us examine nine of these great ideas and see how they have made it possible for people to live in communities.

Language. In order to live and work together, people must be able to express their ideas and feelings to one another. The most important ways of communicating are by speaking and writing. Scientists believe that all human beings—even those who lived in earliest times—have had some form of spoken language. Writing was not developed until about five thousand years ago.

How does language help you to meet your needs? What would you do if you could neither speak nor write? Would you be able to think and to solve problems without using language? Explain your answer.

Education. Another great idea is education. In every community, the older people pass on certain ideas and skills to the younger people. Would it be possible to have a successful community without education? Why? Why not?

In early times, parents taught their children most of the things they needed to know in order to live successfully. Today, children in most parts of the world obtain a large part of their education in school. Do you think education is important for every person? Why do you think as you do?

Cooperation. In every community, people need to work together in order to accomplish their goals. Working together is called cooperation. Long ago, when most people were hunters, they had to cooperate closely to protect themselves from wild beasts and to get the food they needed. In what ways is cooperation important to communities today? What are some of the ways in which people cooperate with each other? What might happen to a community if people were not willing to work together?

Rules and government. Every community needs rules to guide the ways in which people act toward each other. Why is this true? What kinds of rules does your own community have? How do these rules make life safer and more pleasant for everyone? What would it be like to live in a community in which no one obeyed the rules?

In every community, there must be a person or a group of persons to make the rules and see that they are carried out. In other words, all communities need some form of government. In what ways are all governments alike? How do governments differ from each other?

Loyalty. In every truly successful community, most of the people are loyal to each other. They are loyal to the laws of their community and their country. They are also loyal to certain ideas and beliefs. In the United States, for example, most people are loyal to the principles of democracy. In addition, many people are loyal to their religious faith.

To what persons and ideas are you loyal? What are some of the ways in which you express your loyalty? How does loyalty help you to meet your needs?

Using natural resources. In order to meet their needs, people in all communities make use of soil, water, air, sunshine, wild plants and animals, and minerals. These gifts of nature are called natural resources. Would people be able to meet their needs for food, clothing, and shelter without using natural resources? Why? Why not?

In early times, people made little use of the natural resources around them. Today we use hundreds of natural resources in many different ways. How have changes in the use of natural resources affected your life?

Using tools. A tool is anything that people use to help them do work. What kinds of tools do you use every day? In all communities, people use tools to help them meet their physical needs. Would it be possible to have a successful community without tools? Why do you think this?

Tools that have a number of moving parts are called machines. Three hundred years ago, most machines were very simple. Then people began to develop more complicated machines. These could do many jobs that had formerly been done by hand. Today people use

A police officer directing traffic in Peking. What are some other kinds of rules besides traffic rules that are needed by a community such as Peking? Do you think it is more difficult to govern a community such as a nation or a state than to govern a city? Why? Why not?

many different kinds of machines to produce goods. How do modern machines help people to meet their needs more successfully?

Division of labor. In every community, not all the people do exactly the same kind of work. Instead, they work at different jobs. For example, some people earn their living by farming. Others work in factories or in offices. Dividing up the work of a community among people who do different jobs is known as division of labor.

By using division of labor, people are able to obtain more goods than they could if they tried to meet all of their needs by themselves. What do you think are the reasons for this? Would it be possible to have a successful community without division of labor? Why? Why not?

Exchange. Whenever people divide up the work of a community, they need to exchange goods and services with each other. In this way, they are able to obtain goods and services that they do not produce themselves. What would it be like to live in a community where people did not use exchange?

In early times, people did not carry on as much exchange, or trade, as people do today. We not only exchange goods and services within our own communities but we also carry on trade with people who live in communities far away. How does exchange help people everywhere to have a better way of life?

Buying ice cream in Anshan. How do you suppose these customers got the money for the ice cream? What are some ways in which the great idea of exchange helps people meet their needs?

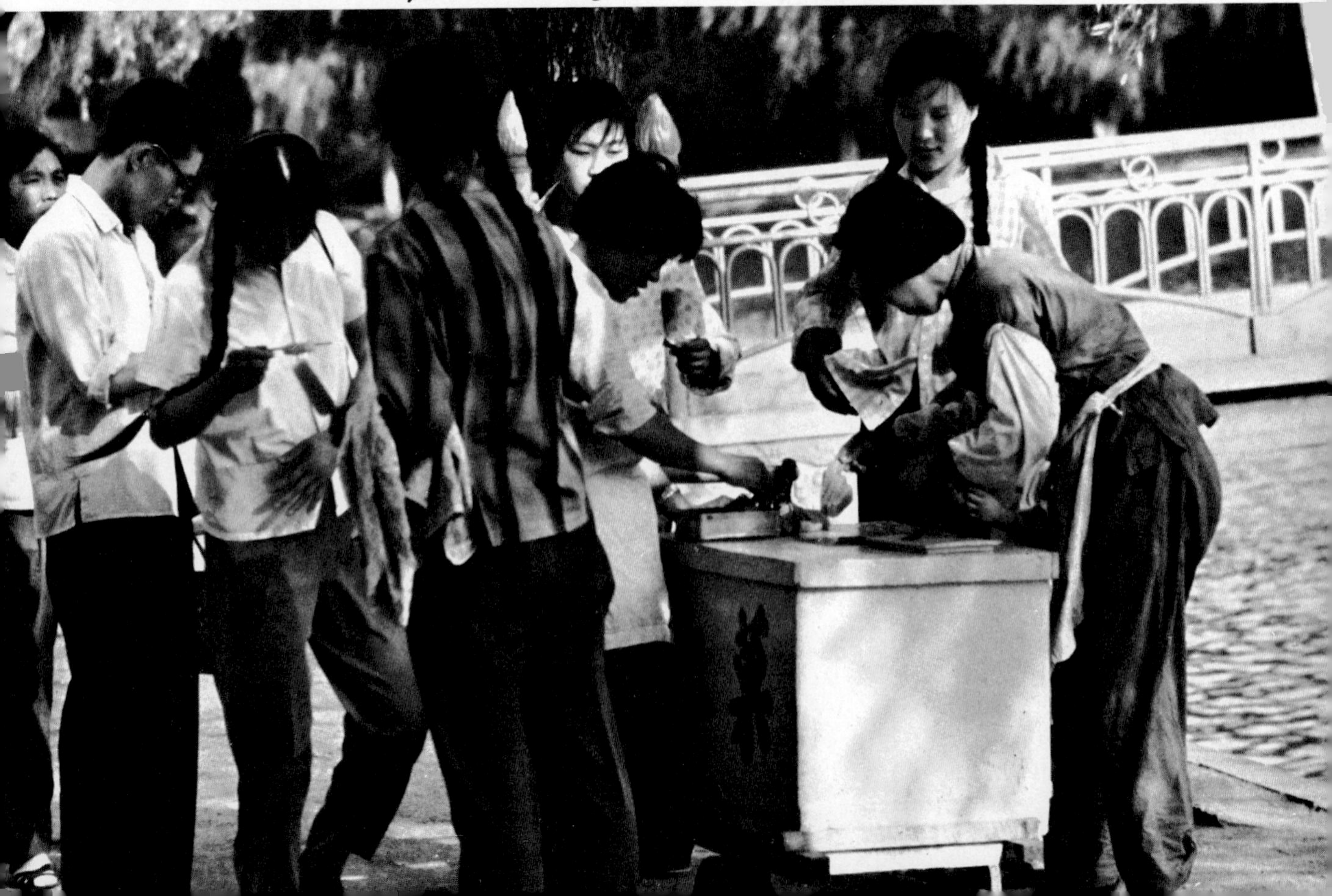

SKILLS MANUAL

CONTENTS

Thinking and Solving Problems

Why the social studies are important to you. During the next few years, you will make an important choice. You will choose whether or not you will direct your own life. Many people are never aware of making this choice. They drift through life, never really trying to understand what is going on around them or why things turn out the way they do. Without knowing it, these people have chosen not to direct their own lives. As a result, they miss many enriching experiences. Other people make a serious effort to choose a way of life that will bring them satisfaction. If you decide to live by choice instead of by chance, you will be able to live a more satisfying life.

You will need three types of knowledge to live by choice successfully. Living by choice will demand a great deal from you. You will have to keep growing in three different types of learnings — understandings, values and attitudes, and skills. As the chart on page 199 shows, the type of learnings we call understandings includes the kinds of information you need in order to understand yourself, your country, and your world. The type of learnings we call values and attitudes deals with the way you feel toward yourself and your world. The third type of learnings includes the skills you need to use in gaining understandings and developing constructive values and attitudes. Among these skills are those you need for obtaining and using knowledge, and for working effectively with other people.

The social studies can help you grow in the three types of learnings. Your social studies class is one of the best places in which you can explore the three types of learnings. Here you can obtain much of the information you need for understanding yourself and your world. You can practice many important skills. Through many experiences, you can begin to evaluate what in life is worthwhile to you.

The problem-solving method will help you achieve success in social studies. Since the social studies are of such great importance, you want to use the best possible study method. You could just read a textbook and memorize answers for a test. If you did so, however, you would forget much of the information soon after the test was over. Your thinking ability would not improve, and you would not gain new, constructive values and attitudes. You would not have the opportunity to use many important skills, either. We suggest that you use a special way of studying called the problem-solving method. You will want to use the problem-solving method as you do research. To use this method, follow these steps.

1. **Do some general background reading** in this book about a topic such as land, people, natural resources, or industry.

2. **Choose an important, interesting problem** that you would like to solve. Write it down so that you will have clearly in mind what it is you want to find out. (Look at the sample problem on page 200.) If there are small problems that need to be solved in order to solve your big problem, list them, too.

3. **Consider all possible solutions to your problem** and list the ones that seem most likely to be true. These possible solutions are called "educated guesses," or hypotheses. You will try to solve your problem by finding facts to support or disprove your hypotheses.

4. **Test your hypotheses** by doing research. This book provides you with four main sources of information. These are the pictures, the text, the maps, and the Glossary. To locate the information you need, you may use the Table of Contents and the Index. The suggestions on pages 201-204 of this Skills Manual will help you to locate and evaluate other sources of information.

Thinking and the Three Types of Learnings

THINKING

One of the main reasons you are attending school is to develop your ability to think clearly. Thinking includes seven different thought processes. (See definitions below.) If you learn to use your higher thought processes, rather than simply repeat information you have memorized, you will achieve greater success in school and in life. In fact, your ability to fulfill your obligations as a citizen will depend largely on how well you learn to think. Your ability to think clearly will also help you make progress in the three types of learnings included in the social studies. (See chart below.)

Seven Thought Processes

1. **Remembering** is recalling or recognizing information.
2. **Translation** is changing information from one form into another, such as words into pictures.
3. **Interpretation** is discovering relationships among facts, concepts,* and generalizations.*
4. **Application** is applying the appropriate knowledge and skills to the solution of a new problem.
5. **Analysis** is separating complicated material into its basic parts to see how those parts were put together, how they are related to each other, and how the parts are related to the whole.
6. **Synthesis** is putting ideas together in a form that is not only meaningful but also new and original.
7. **Evaluation** is judging whether something is acceptable or unacceptable, according to definite standards.

↕ ↕ ↕

THREE TYPES OF LEARNINGS

Understandings	Values and Attitudes	Skills
Concepts	Beliefs	Obtaining knowledge
Generalizations	Appreciations	Using knowledge
Facts	Ideals	Working with others

Understandings

You will truly gain an understanding of important concepts and generalizations when you use your thought processes to organize information in meaningful ways. In turn, the concepts and generalizations you develop will help you learn to think critically about new situations you meet.

Values and Attitudes

You will develop many constructive values and attitudes as you improve your thinking ability. Success in the higher levels of thinking will bring you faith that you can solve problems and make wise decisions. In turn, positive values and attitudes will help you to develop your thinking ability.

Skills

You will be more successful in developing the social studies skills when you use your higher thought processes described above. In turn, you will find that the social studies skills will help you do the critical thinking needed for solving the many difficult problems you will face during your lifetime.

*See Four Words To Understand, page 200

As you do research, make notes of all the information you find that will either support your hypotheses or disprove them. You may discover that information from one source disagrees with information from another. If this should happen, check still further and try to decide which facts are correct.

5. Summarize what you have learned. Have you been able to support one or more of your hypotheses with facts? Have you been able to disprove one or more of your hypotheses? What new facts have you learned? Do you need to do further research?

You may want to write a report about the problem. To help other people share the ideas that you have come to understand, you may decide to illustrate your research project with maps, pictures, or your own drawings. You will find helpful suggestions for writing a good report on pages 204-206 of this Skills Manual.

You can use the problem-solving method throughout your life. In addition to helping you to achieve success in the social studies, the problem-solving method can help you in another way. By using it, you will learn to deal with problems in a way that will be valuable to you throughout your life. Many successful scientists, business executives, and government leaders use this method to solve problems.

A sample problem to solve. As you make discoveries about China, you may wish to investigate problems about the country as a whole or about one region. The following sample problem is about the country as a whole.

> Climate in China varies greatly from one part of the country to another. How does climate in China affect the people who live there? In order to solve this problem, you will need to make several hypotheses about the ways in which the different climates affect the people. The following questions suggest some hypotheses.
>
> 1. What facts about differences in rainfall from place to place in China help to solve this problem?
> 2. What facts about differences in temperature help to solve it?
> 3. What facts about farming in China help to solve it?

Four Words To Understand

1. **A concept** is a big, general idea that includes many smaller, more specific ideas. An example of a concept is the idea of "trade." Many kinds of exchange are included in this idea. Two children who exchange marbles on the playground are carrying on trade. A person who pays money for a loaf of bread is also carrying on trade; so is a factory that buys raw materials from other countries and sells its manufactured products overseas. Only as you come to see the various things that the word "trade" includes do you grow to understand this concept. Another example of a concept is the idea of "climate."
2. **A generalization** is a general rule or principle that expresses a meaningful relationship among two or more concepts. It is formed by drawing a conclusion from a group of facts. For example, "Through trade, all people on the earth can have a better living," is a generalization drawn from facts about trade and the way people live in various parts of the world. It includes four concepts: "trade," "all people," "the earth," and "a better living." These have been put together to give a significant understanding about the world. The many facts you read about, hear about, or experience will make more sense if you think of them as statements that can be combined to form meaningful generalizations. Remember, however, that if a generalization is based on wrong or insufficient facts, or is carelessly thought out, it may be false. Make certain that you understand the concepts in a generalization, and judge carefully whether or not you think it is true.
3. **Values** are the things in life that a person considers right, desirable, or worthwhile. For instance, if you believe that every individual is important, we may say that one of your values is the worth of the individual.
4. **Attitudes** are the outward expression of a person's values. For example, if you truly value the worth of every individual, you will express this value by treating everyone you meet with consideration.

Learning Social Studies Skills

What is a skill? A skill is something that you have learned to do well. To learn some skills, such as swimming, you must train the muscles of your arms and legs. To learn others, such as typing, you must train your fingers. Still other skills require you to train your mind. For example, reading with understanding is a skill that requires much mental training. The skills that you use in the social studies are largely mental skills.

Why are skills important? Mastering different skills will help you to have a more satisfying life. You will be healthier and enjoy your leisure time more if you develop skills needed to take part in various sports. By developing artistic skills, you will be able to express your feelings more fully. It is even more important for you to develop skills of the mind. These skills are the tools that you will use in obtaining and using the knowledge you need to live successfully in today's world.

To develop a skill, you must practice it correctly. If you ask fine athletes or musicians how they gained their skills, they will say, "Through practice." To develop skills of the mind, you must practice also. Remember, however, that a person cannot become a good ballplayer if he or she keeps throwing the ball incorrectly. The same thing is true of mental skills. To master them, you must practice them correctly.

The following pages contain suggestions about how to perform correctly several important skills needed in the social studies. Study these skills carefully, and use them.

How To Find Information You Need

Each day of your life you seek information. Sometimes you want to know certain facts just because you are curious. Most of the time, however, you want information for some special purpose. If your hobby is baseball, for example, you may want to know how to figure batting averages. If you collect stamps, you need to know how to identify the countries they come from. As a student in today's world, you need information for many purposes. As an adult, you will need even more knowledge to live successfully in tomorrow's world.

You may wonder how you can possibly learn all the facts you are going to need during your lifetime. The answer is that you can't. Therefore, knowing how to find information when you need it is of vital importance to you. Following are suggestions for locating good sources of information and for using these sources to find the facts that you need.

Written Sources of Information

1. Books. You may be able to find the information you need in books that you have at home or in your classroom. To see if a textbook or other nonfiction book has the information you need, look at the table of contents and the index.

Sometimes, you will need to go to your school or community library to locate books that contain the information you want. To make the best use of a library, you should learn to use the card catalog. This is a file that contains information about the books in the library. Each nonfiction book has at least three cards, filed in alphabetical order. One is for the title, one is for the author, and one is for the subject of the book. Each card gives the book's special number. This number will help you to find the book, since all the nonfiction books in the library are arranged on the shelves in numerical order. If you cannot find a book you want, the librarian will be glad to help you.

2. Reference volumes. You will find much useful information in special books known as reference volumes. These include dictionaries, encyclopedias, atlases, and other special books. Some companies publish a book each year with statistics and general information about the

events of the preceding year. Such books are usually called yearbooks, annuals, or almanacs.

3. Newspapers and magazines. These are important sources of up-to-date information. Sometimes you will want to look for information in papers or magazines that you do not have at home. You can usually find the ones you want at the library.

The *Readers' Guide to Periodical Literature*, which is available in most libraries, will direct you to magazine articles about the subject you are investigating. This is a series of volumes that list articles by title, author, and subject. In the front of each volume is an explanation of the abbreviations used to indicate the different magazines and their dates.

4. Booklets, pamphlets, and bulletins. Many materials of this type are available from local and state governments, as well as from our federal government. Chambers of commerce, travel bureaus, trade organizations, private companies, and embassies of foreign countries publish materials that contain much information.

Many booklets and bulletins give accurate information. You should remember, however, that some of them are intended to promote certain products or ideas. Information obtained from such sources should be checked carefully.

Reading for Information

The following suggestions will help you save time and effort when you are looking for information in books and other written materials.

1. Use the table of contents and the index. The table of contents appears at the beginning of the book and generally is a list of the chapters in the book. By looking at this list, you can usually tell whether the book has the type of information you need.

The index is a more detailed list of the topics that are discussed in the book. It will help you locate the pages on which specific facts are discussed. In most books, the index is at the back. Encyclopedias often include the index in a separate volume, however.

At the beginning of an index, you will usually find an explanation that makes it easier to use. For example, the explanation at the beginning of the Index for *China* tells you that *p* means picture and *m* means map.

The topics, or entries, in the index are arranged in alphabetical order. To locate all the information you need, you may have to look under more than one entry. For example, to find out what pages in this book discuss cities, look up the entry for cities. Also, look up the entry for a specific city, such as Peking.

2. Skim the written material to see if it contains the information you need. Before you begin reading a chapter or a page, skim it to see if it has the information you need. In this way you will not run the risk of wasting time reading something that is of little or no value to you. When you skim, you look mainly for topic headings, topic sentences, and key words. For example, imagine you are looking for the answer to the question: "What are the main crops produced in South China?" In the Farming chapter of *China*, you might look for a topic heading that mentions South China. When you find such a topic heading, you would look for the key words "main crops".

3. Read carefully when you think you have located the information you need. When you think you have found the page that contains the information you are looking for, read it carefully. Does it really tell you what you want to know? If not, you will need to look further.

Other Ways of Obtaining Information

1. Direct experience. What you observe or experience for yourself may be a good source of information if you have observed carefully and remembered accurately. Firsthand information can often be obtained by visiting places

in your community or nearby, such as museums, factories, or government offices.

2. Radio and television. Use the listings in your local newspaper to find programs about the subjects in which you are interested.

3. Movies, filmstrips, recordings, and slides. Materials on a great variety of subjects are available. They can be obtained from schools, libraries, museums, and private companies.

4. Resource people. Sometimes, you will be able to obtain information by interviewing a person who has special knowledge. On occasion, you may wish to invite someone to speak to your class and answer questions.

Evaluating Information

During your lifetime, you will constantly need to evaluate what you see, hear, and read. Information is not true or significant simply because it is presented on television or is written in a book, magazine, or newspaper. The following suggestions will help you in evaluating information.

Learn to tell the difference between primary and secondary sources of information. A primary source of information is a firsthand record. For example, a photograph taken of an event while it is happening is a primary source. So is the report you write about a field trip you take. Original documents, such as the Constitution of the United States, are primary sources, also.

A secondary source is a secondhand report. For example, if you write a report about what someone else told you he or she saw, your report will be a secondary source of information. Another example of a secondary source is a history book.

Advanced scholars like to use primary sources whenever possible. However, these sources are often difficult to obtain. Most students in elementary and high school use secondary sources. You should always be aware that you are using secondhand information when you use a secondary source.

Find out who said it and when it was said. The next step in evaluating information is to ask, "Who said it?" Was she a scholar with special training in the subject about which she wrote? Was he a newsman with a reputation for careful reporting of the facts?

Another question you should ask is, "When was it said?" Changes take place rapidly in our world, and the information you are using may be out of date. For example, suppose you are looking for information about a country. If you use an encyclopedia that is five years old, much of the information you find will be inaccurate.

Find out if it is mainly fact or opinion. The next step in evaluating information is to decide whether it is based on facts or whether it mainly consists of unsupported opinions. You can do this best if you are aware of these three types of statements.

1. Statements of fact that can be checked. For example, "Voters in the United States choose their representatives by secret ballot" is a statement of fact that can be checked by observing how voting is carried on in different parts of our country.

2. Inferences, or conclusions that are based on facts. The statement "The people of the United States live in a democracy" is an inference. This inference is based on the fact that the citizens choose their representatives by secret ballot, and on other facts that can be proved. It is important to remember that inferences can be false or only partly true.

3. Value judgments, or opinions. The statement "It is always wrong for a country to go to war" is a value judgment. Since a value judgment is an opinion, you need to examine it

Seven Propaganda Tricks

People who use propaganda have learned many ways of presenting information to influence you in the direction they wish. Seven propaganda tricks to watch for are listed below.

Name Calling. Giving a label that is disliked or feared, such as "un-American," to an organization, a person, or an idea. This trick often persuades people to reject something they know nothing about.

Glittering Generalities. Trying to win support by using fine-sounding phrases, such as "the best deal in town" or "the American way." These phrases have no clear meaning when you stop and think about them.

Transfer. Connecting a person, product, or idea with something that people already feel strongly about. For example, displaying a picture of a church next to a speaker to give the impression that he or she is honest and trustworthy.

Testimonial. Getting well-known persons or organizations to announce in public their support of a person, product, or idea.

Plain Folks. Trying to win support by appearing to be an ordinary person who can be trusted. For example, a political candidate may try to win people's confidence by giving the impression that he or she is a good parent who loves children and dogs.

Card Stacking. Giving the wrong impression by giving only part of the facts about a person, product, or idea. For example, giving favorable facts, and leaving out unfavorable ones.

Bandwagon. Trying to win support by saying that "everybody knows that" or "everyone is doing this."

---

very critically. On what facts and inferences is it based? For example, what facts and conclusions do you think form the basis of the opinion: "It is always wrong for a country to go to war"? Do you agree or disagree with these conclusions? Reliable writers or reporters are careful to let their readers know which statements are their own opinions. They also try to base their opinions as much as possible on facts that can be proved.

Find out why it was said. The next step in evaluating information is to find out the purpose for which it was prepared. Many books and articles are prepared in an honest effort to give you accurate information. For example, scientists writing about a new scientific discovery will usually try to report their findings as accurately as possible, and they will be careful to distinguish between what they have actually observed and the conclusions they have drawn from these facts.

Some information, however, is prepared mainly to persuade people to believe or act a certain way. Information of this kind is called propaganda.

Some propaganda is used to promote causes that are generally considered good. A picture that shows Smokey the Bear and the words "Only *you* can prevent forest fires" is an example of this kind of propaganda.

Propaganda is also used to make people support causes they would not agree with if they knew more about them. This kind of propaganda may consist of information that is true, partly true, or false. Even when it is true, however, the information may be presented in such a way as to mislead you.

Propaganda generally appeals to people's emotions rather than to their reasoning ability. For this reason, you should learn to identify information that is propaganda. Then you can think about it calmly and clearly, and evaluate it intelligently.

Making Reports

There are many occasions when you need to share information or ideas with others. Sometimes you will need to do this in writing. Other times you will need to do it orally. One of the best ways to develop your writing and speaking skills is by making oral and written reports. The success of your report will depend on how well you have organized your material. It will also depend on your skill in presenting it. Here are some guidelines that will help you in preparing a good report.

Decide upon a goal. Have your purpose clearly in mind. Are you mainly interested in communicating information? Do you want to give your own viewpoint on a subject, or are you trying to persuade other people to agree with you?

Find the information you need. Be sure to use more than one source. If you are not sure how to locate information about your topic, read the suggestions on pages 201-203 of this Skills Manual.

Take good notes. To remember what you have read, you must take notes. Before you begin taking notes, however, you will need to make a list of the questions you want your report to answer. As you do research, write down the facts that answer these questions. You may find some interesting and important facts that do not answer any of your questions. If you feel that they might be useful in your report, write them down, too. Your notes should be brief and in your own words except when you want to use exact quotations. When you use a quotation, be sure to put quotation marks around it.

You will be able to make the best use of your notes if you write them on file cards. Use a separate card for each statement or group of statements that answers one of your questions. To remember where your information came from, write on each card the title, author, and date of the source. When you have finished taking notes, group the cards according to the questions they answer. This will help you arrange your material in logical order.

Make an outline. After you have reviewed your notes, make an outline. This is a general plan that shows the order and the relationship of the ideas you want to include in your report. The first step in making an outline is to pick out the main ideas. These will be the main headings in your outline. (See sample outline below.) Next, list under each of these headings the ideas and facts that support or explain it. These related ideas are called subheadings. As you arrange your information, ask yourself the following questions.

a. Is there one main idea that I must put first because everything else depends on it?
b. Have I arranged my facts in such a way as to show relationships among them?
c. Are there some ideas that will be clearer if they are discussed after other ideas have been explained?
d. Have I included enough facts so that I can complete my outline with a summary statement or a logical conclusion?

When you have completed your first outline, you may find that some parts of it are skimpy. If so, you may wish to do more research. When you are satisfied that you have enough information, make your final outline. Remember that this outline will serve as the basis of your finished report.

Example of an outline. The author of this feature prepared the following outline before writing "Making Reports."

I. Introduction
II. Deciding upon a goal
III. Finding information
IV. Taking notes
    A. List main ideas to be researched
    B. Write on file cards facts that support or explain these ideas
    C. Group cards according to main ideas
V. Making an outline
    A. Purpose of an outline
    B. Guidelines for arranging information
    C. Sample outline of this section
VI. Preparing a written report
VII. Presenting an oral report

Special guidelines for a written report. As a guide in writing your report, use the outline you have prepared. The following suggestions will help you to make your report interesting and clear.

Create word pictures that your readers can see in their minds. Before you begin to write, imagine that you are going to make a movie of the subject you plan to write about. What scenes would you like to show on the screen? Next, think of the words that will create these same pictures in your readers' minds.

Group your sentences into good paragraphs. It is usually best to begin a paragraph with a topic sentence that says to the reader, "This is what you will learn about in this paragraph." The other sentences in the paragraph should help to support or explain the topic sentence.

A sample paragraph. Below is a sample paragraph from this book. The topic sentence has been underlined. Notice how clear it is and how well the other sentences support it. Also notice how many pictures the paragraph puts in your mind.

> We fly northward across the Yunnan-Kweichow Plateau until we come to the bed of a great lake that dried up millions of years ago. This ancient lake bed is like a huge basin scooped out of the earth. It is bordered on the south by the plateau we just crossed. Mountain ranges surround it on the other sides. Because the rocks and soil of this great basin are purplish red in color, it is called the Red Basin. The floor of the Red Basin is very hilly. We see terraced rice fields on the slopes of these hills.

Other guidelines. There are two other things to remember in writing a good report. First, use the dictionary to find the spelling of words you are doubtful about. Second, make a list of the sources of information you used, and include it at the beginning or end of your report. This list is called a bibliography.

Special guidelines for an oral report. When you are going to give a report orally, you will also want to organize your information in a logical order by making an outline. Prepare notes to guide you during your talk. These notes should be complete enough to help you remember all the points you want to make. You may even write out portions of your report that you prefer to read.

When you present your report, speak directly to your audience. Pronounce your words correctly and distinctly. Remember to speak slowly enough for your listeners to follow what you are saying, and use a tone of voice that will hold their interest. Stand up straight, but try not to be too stiff. The only way to improve your speaking skills is to practice them correctly.

Holding a Group Discussion

One of the important ways in which you learn is by exchanging ideas with other people. You do this frequently in informal conversation. You are likely to learn more, however, when you take part in the special kind of group conversation that we call a discussion. A discussion is more orderly than a conversation, and it usually has a definite, serious purpose. This purpose may be the sharing of information or the solving of a problem. In order to reach its goal, the discussion group must arrive at a conclusion or make a decision of some kind.

A discussion is more likely to be successful when those who take part in it observe the following guidelines.

1. **Be prepared.** Think about the topic to be discussed ahead of time. Prepare for the discussion by reading and taking notes. You may also want to make an outline of the ideas you want to share with the group.

2. **Take part.** Contribute to the discussion; express your ideas clearly and concisely. Be sure that the statements you make and the questions you ask deal with the topic being discussed.

3. Listen and think. Listen thoughtfully to others. Encourage all of the members of the discussion group to express their ideas. Do not make up your mind about a question or a problem until all of the facts have been given.

4. Be courteous. When you speak, address the entire group. Ask and answer questions politely. When you disagree with someone, point out your reasons calmly and in a friendly way.

Working With Others

In school and throughout life, you will find that there are many projects that can be done better by a group than by one person working alone. Some of these projects would take too long to finish if they were done by a single individual. Others have different parts that can be done best by people with different talents.

Before your group begins a project, you should decide several matters. First, determine exactly what you are trying to accomplish. Second, decide what part of the project each person should do. Third, schedule when the project is to be completed.

The group will do a better job and reach its goals more quickly if each person follows these suggestions.

1. Do your part. Remember that the success of your project depends on every member of the group. Be willing to do your share of the work and to accept your share of the responsibility.

2. Follow the rules. Help the group decide on sensible rules, and then follow them. When a difference of opinion cannot be settled by discussion, make a decision by majority vote.

3. Share your ideas. Be willing to share your ideas and talents with the group. When you submit an idea for discussion, be prepared to see it criticized or even rejected. At the same time, have the courage to stick up for a principle or a belief that is really important to you.

4. Respect others. Remember that every person is an individual with different beliefs and talents. Give the other members of the group a chance to be heard, and be ready to appreciate their work and ideas.

5. Be friendly, thoughtful, helpful, and cheerful. Try to express your opinions seriously and sincerely without hurting others or losing their respect. Listen politely to the ideas of others.

6. Learn from your mistakes. Look for ways in which you can be a better group member the next time you work with others on a project.

Building Your Vocabulary

When you do research in many different types of reading materials, you are likely to find several words you have never seen before. If you skip over these words, the chances are that you will not fully understand what you are reading. The following suggestions will help you to discover the meanings of new words and build your vocabulary.

1. See how the word is used in the sentence. When you come to a new word, don't stop reading. Read on beyond the new word to see if you can discover any clues to what its meaning might be. Trying to figure out the meaning of a word from the way it is used may not give you the exact definition. However, it will give you a general idea of what the word means.

2. Sound out the word. Break the word up into syllables, and try to pronounce it. When you say the word aloud, you may find that you know it after all but have simply never seen it in print.

3. Look in the dictionary. When you think you have figured out what a word means and how it is pronounced, check with the dictionary. Have you pronounced it correctly? Did you decide upon the right definition? Remember, most words have several meanings. Do you know which meaning should be used?

4. Make a list of the new words you learn. In your own words, write a definition of each word you include in your list. Review this list from time to time.

Learning Map Skills

The earth is a sphere. Our earth is round like a ball. We call any object with this shape a sphere. The earth is, of course, a very large sphere. Its diameter* is about 8,000 miles (12,874 kilometers*), and its circumference* is about 25,000 miles (40,233 kilometers). The earth is not a perfect sphere, however, for it is slightly flattened at the North and South poles.

A globe represents the earth. The globe in your classroom represents the earth. Since the globe is a sphere, it has the same shape as the earth. The surface of the globe shows the shapes of all the landmasses and bodies of water on the earth. By looking at the globe, you can see exactly where the continents, islands, and oceans are located. Globes are made with the North Pole at the top, but they are usually tilted to represent the way the earth is tilted.

When you use a globe or a map, you need to know what distance on the earth is represented by a given distance on the globe or map. This relationship, which is called the scale, may be expressed in numbers. For instance: 1 inch = 400 miles (644 kilometers). Another way of expressing the scale is to include a small drawing that shows how many miles or kilometers on the earth are represented by a certain distance on the globe or map. (See map F on page 210.)

Locating places on the earth. Travelers, geographers, and other thoughtful people have always wanted to know exactly where certain places are located on the earth. Over the years, a very accurate system has been worked out for giving such information. This system is used by people in all parts of the world.

A location system needs starting points and a unit of measurement. The North and South poles and the equator provide the starting points for the system we use to locate places on the earth. The unit of measurement is the degree, which is used in mathematics to measure circles. Any circle may be divided into 360 equal parts, called degrees.

Parallels show latitude. In order to locate a place on the earth, we first find out how far it is north or south of the equator. This distance, when measured in degrees, is called north or south latitude. The equator is the line of zero latitude. Since the North Pole is one fourth of the way around the earth from the equator, its location is one fourth of 360 degrees, or 90 degrees north latitude. Similarly, the South Pole is located at 90 degrees south latitude. A line that connects all points on the earth that have exactly the same latitude is called a parallel. This is because such a line is parallel to the equator. (See illustration A, below.)

Meridians show longitude. After we have determined the latitude of a place, we need to know its longitude. This is its location in an east-west direction. The lines that show longitude, called meridians, are drawn so as to connect the North and South poles. (See illustration B, below.) Longitude is measured from the meridian that passes through Greenwich, England. This line of zero longitude is called the prime meridian. Distance east or west of the prime meridian is called east or west longitude.

*See Glossary

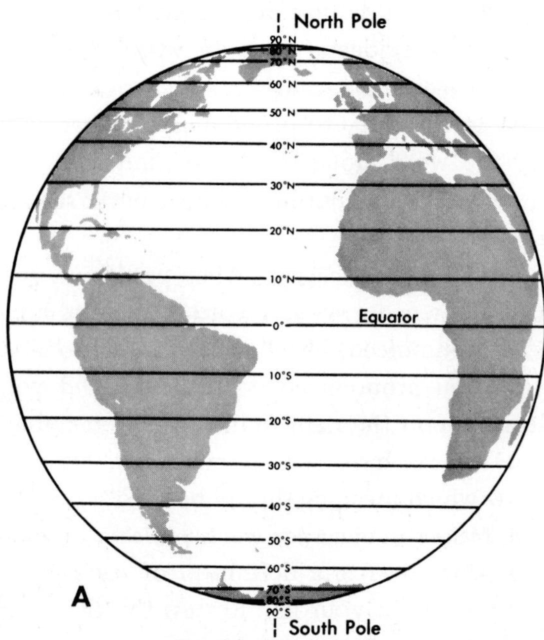

A
Parallels Show Latitude

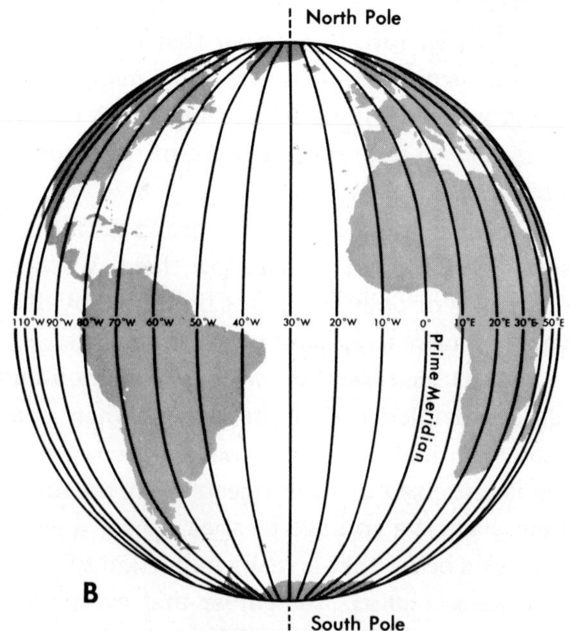

B
Meridians Show Longitude

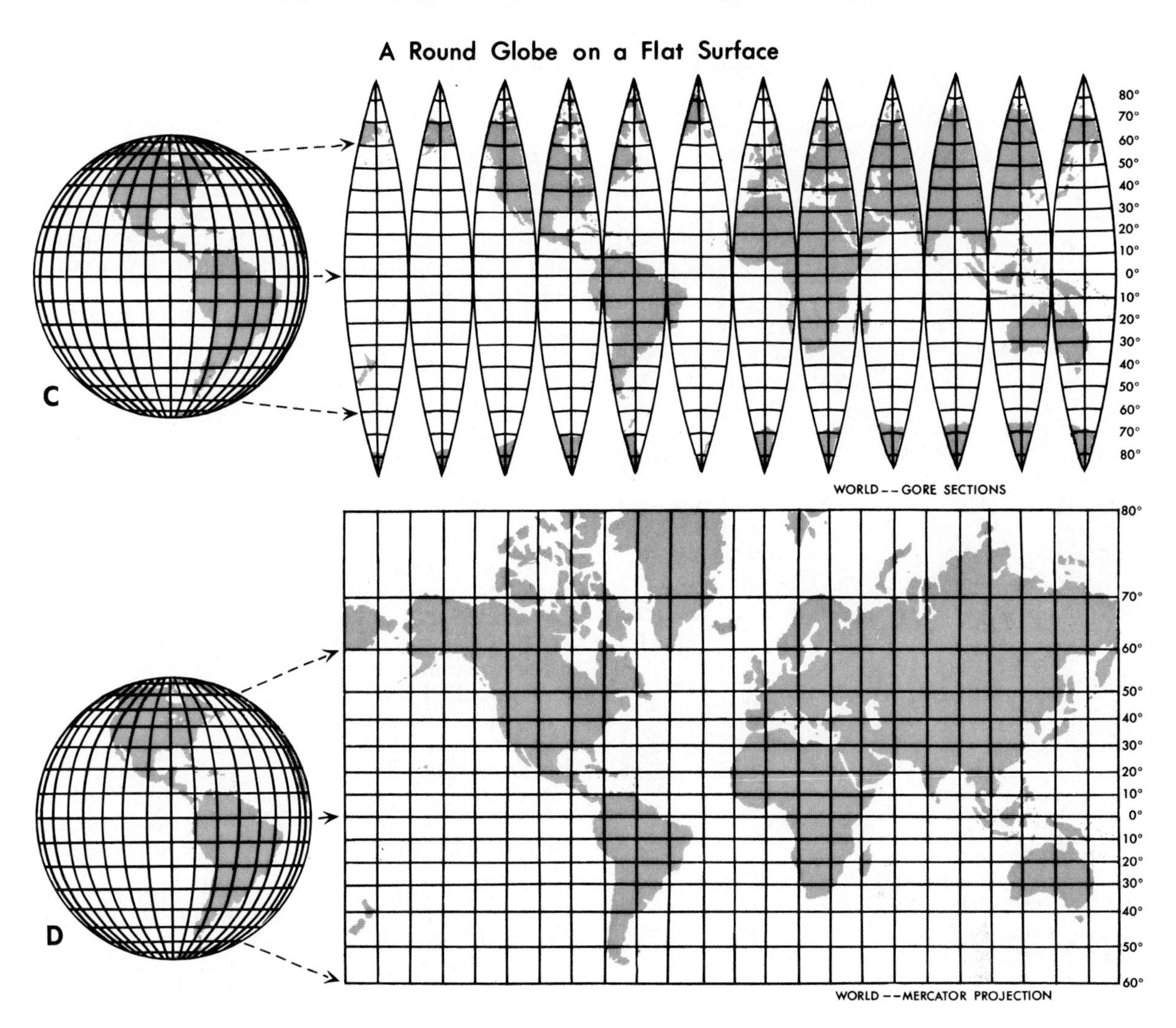

Locating places on a globe. A parallel or a meridian can be drawn to represent any degree of latitude or longitude. On a globe, parallels and meridians are usually drawn every ten or fifteen degrees. The exact location of a place may be indicated like this: 30°N 90°W. This means that the place is located 30 degrees north of the equator, and 90 degrees west of the prime meridian. See if you can find this place on a globe.

The round earth on a flat map. An important fact about a sphere is that you cannot flatten out its surface perfectly. To prove this, you might perform an experiment. Cut an orange in half and scrape away the fruit. You will find that you cannot press either piece of orange peel flat without crushing it. If you cut one piece in half, however, you can press these smaller pieces nearly flat. Next, cut one of these pieces of peel into three sections, or gores, shaped like those shown in illustration C, above. You will find that you can press these small sections almost completely flat.

A map like that shown in illustration C can be made by cutting the surface of a globe into twelve pieces shaped like the smallest sections of your orange peel. Such a map would be fairly accurate. However, an "orange-peel" map is not an easy map to use, because the continents and oceans are split. It would be difficult to measure distances across the splits.

A flat map can never show the earth's surface as truthfully as a globe can. On a globe, shape, size, distance, and direction are all accurate. Although a single flat map of the world cannot be drawn to show all four of these things correctly, a flat map can be made that will show one or more of these things accurately.

Illustration D, above, shows a world map drawn on a Mercator* projection. When you compare this map with a globe, you can see that the continents have almost the right shape. On this map, however, North America seems larger than Africa, which is not true. On Mercator maps, lands far from the equator appear much larger than they really are. These maps are useful to navigators because they show true directions.

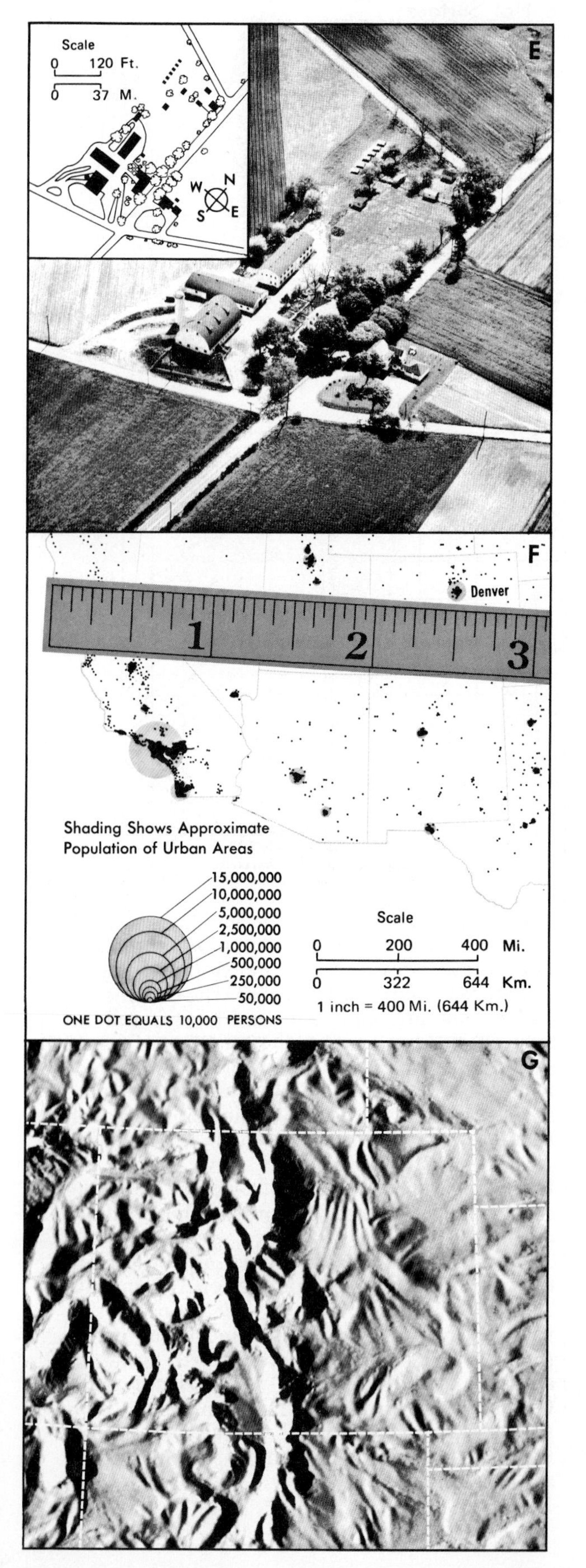

SPECIAL-PURPOSE MAPS

Maps that show sections of our earth. For some purposes, we prefer maps that do not show the entire surface of the earth. A map of a very small area can be drawn with greater accuracy and can include more details than a map of a large area can.

Illustration E, at left, shows a photograph and a map of the same small section of the earth. Drawings on the map, called symbols, show the shape and location of things on the earth. The scale makes it possible to determine size and distance. Since north is not at the top of this map, a compass* rose has been drawn to show directions.

Maps for special purposes. Maps can show the location of many different kinds of things. For instance, a map can show what minerals are found in certain places, or what crops are grown. A small chart that lists the symbols and their meanings is usually included on a map. This is called the legend, or key.

Symbols on some geography maps stand for the amounts of things in different places. For instance, map F gives information about the number of people in the southwestern part of the United States. The key tells the meaning of the symbols, which in this case are dots and circles.

On different maps, the same symbol may stand for different things and amounts. For example, each dot on map F stands for 10,000 persons. On other maps, a dot might represent 5,000 sheep or 1,000 bushels of wheat.

There are other ways of giving information about quantity. For example, various designs or patterns may be used on a rainfall map to indicate the areas that receive different amounts of rain each year.

RELIEF MAPS

Some globes and maps show the roughness of the earth's surface. From a jet plane, you can see that the earth's surface is irregular. You can see mountains and valleys, hills and plains. For some purposes, globes and maps that show these things are needed. They are called relief globes and maps.

Since globes are three-dimensional models of the earth, you may wonder why most globes do not show the roughness of the earth's surface. The reason for this is that the highest mountain on the earth is not very large when it is compared with the earth's diameter. Even a very large globe would be almost perfectly smooth.

In order to make a relief globe or map, you must use a different scale for the height of the land. For example, you might start with a large flat map. One inch on your flat map may represent a distance of 100 miles (161 kilometers) on the earth. Now you are going to make a model of a mountain on your map. On the earth, this mountain is two miles (3.2 kilometers) high. If you let one inch represent this height on the earth, your mountain should rise one inch above the flat surface of your map. Other mountains and hills should be modeled on this same scale.

By photographing maps or globes with raised relief, we can make flat maps that show landforms. Map G, on page 210, is a photograph of a molded relief map. Photographs such as this help us to see what land areas really look like.

Topographic maps. Another kind of map that shows the earth's relief is the topographic, or contour, map. On a topographic map, lines are drawn to show different elevations of the earth's surface. These are called contour lines. The illustrations on this page help to explain how a topographic map is made.

Illustration H is a drawing of a hill. Around the bottom of the hill is our first contour line. This line connects all the points at the base of the hill that are exactly twenty feet above sea level. Higher up the hill, another contour line is drawn connecting all the points that are exactly forty feet above sea level. A line is also drawn at an elevation of sixty feet. Other lines are drawn at intervals of twenty feet until the top of the hill is reached. Since the hill is generally cone shaped, each contour line is shorter than the one just below it.

Illustration I shows how the contour lines in the drawing of the hill (H) can be used to make a topographic map. This map gives us a great deal of information about the hill. Since each line is labeled with the elevation it represents, we can tell how high different parts of the hill are. It is important to remember that land does not rise in layers, as you might think when you look at a topographic map. Wherever the contour lines are far apart, we know that the land slopes gently. Where they are close together, the slope is steep. With practice, you can imagine the land in your mind as you look at such a map. Topographic maps are especially useful to people who design roads and buildings.

On a topographic map, the spaces between the contour lines may be filled in with different shades of gray. On map J, at right, black and four shades of gray were used to show differences in height of forty feet. The key box shows the height of the land represented by the different shades. On some topographic maps, colors are used to represent different heights of land.

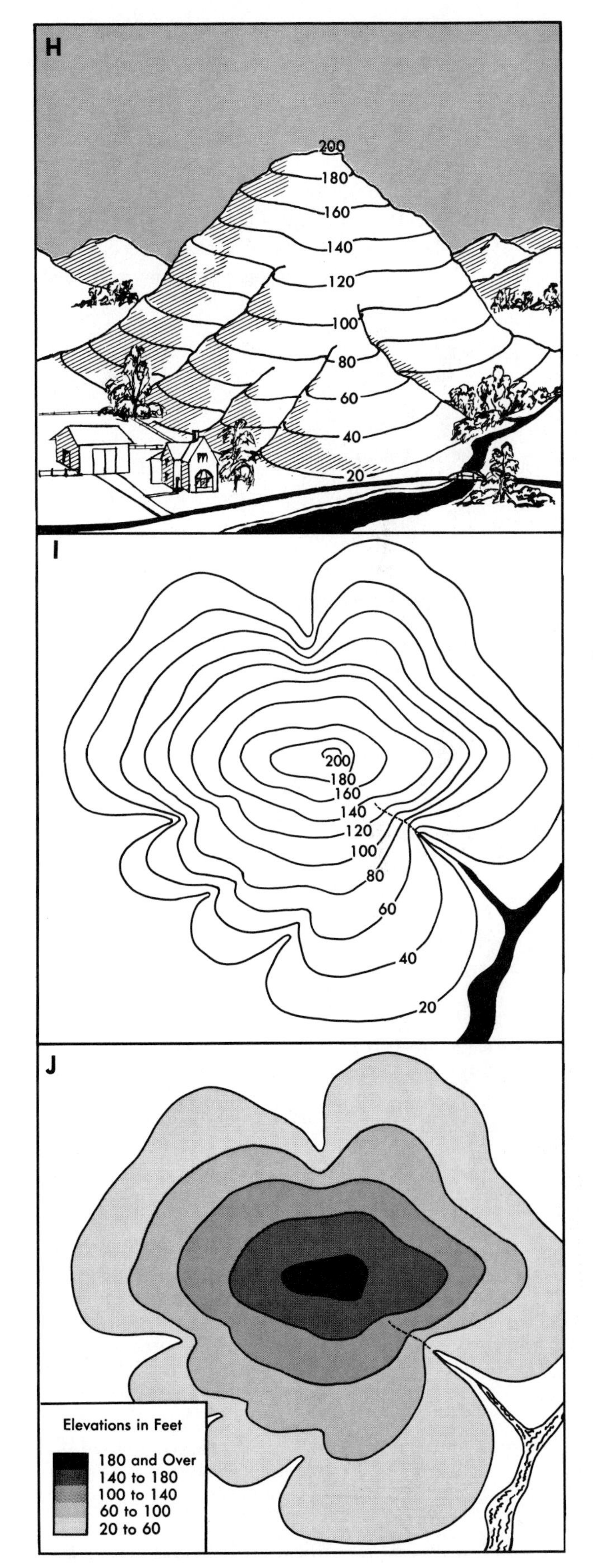

GLOSSARY

Complete Pronunciation Key

The pronunciation of each word is shown just after the word, in this way: **equator** (i kwā'tər). The letters and signs used are pronounced as in the words below. The mark ' is placed after a syllable with a primary or strong accent, as in the example above. The mark ' after a syllable shows a secondary or lighter accent, as in **hydroelectric** (hī' drō i lek' trik).

a	hat, cap	j	jam, enjoy	u	cup, butter
ā	age, face	k	kind, seek	u̇	full, put
ã	care, air	l	land, coal	ü	rule, move
ä	father, far	m	me, am	ū	use, music
b	bad, rob	n	no, in		
ch	child, much	ng	long, bring	v	very, save
d	did, red	o	hot, rock	w	will, woman
		ō	open, go	y	young, yet
e	let, best	ô	order, all	z	zero, breeze
ē	equal, see	oi	oil, voice	zh	measure, seizure
ėr	term, learn	ou	house, out		
		p	paper, cup		
f	fat, if	r	run, try	ə	represents:
g	go, bag	s	say, yes	a	in about
h	he, how	sh	she, rush	e	in taken
		t	tell, it	i	in pencil
i	it, pin	th	thin, both	o	in lemon
ī	ice, five	ŦH	then, smooth	u	in circus

abacus (ab' ə kəs). A very old device used for doing arithmetic. The abacus consists of a rectangular frame with counters or beads that slide back and forth on wires.

aborigines (ab' ə rij' ə nēz). The earliest known inhabitants of a country or area, or descendants of these people.

acre. A unit for measuring land. One acre is about three fourths as large as a football field.

alloy. A metallic substance made by combining two or more metals, or a metal with a nonmetal. For example, brass is an alloy of copper and zinc, and steel is an alloy of iron and carbon.

ancestor worship. The religious practice of honoring one's ancestors by placing offerings of food, incense, and other items at shrines and graves. Although ancestor worship was probably practiced in China before Confucius, it is closely connected with the Confucian teaching that a person should honor his or her parents.

antimony (an' tə mō' nē). A hard, brittle, silvery white metal. It is often mixed with other metals to harden them.

Arctic (ärk'tik) **Circle.** An imaginary line around the earth, about 1,600 miles south of the North Pole. (See map, pages 6-7.)

asbestos (as bes' təs). A grayish or greenish mineral fiber that will not burn. It is used chiefly in making fireproof textiles and building materials.

atomic energy. Energy that is stored in atoms. All matter is made up of atoms, which are much too small to be seen except with a special microscope. When atoms are split or combined in certain ways, great amounts of energy are released. This energy can be used for many purposes, including the production of electricity.

autonomous (ô ton' ə məs) **region.** Autonomous means self-governing. In China autonomous regions were established so the minority peoples could run their own affairs. However, these regions are controlled by the national government.

barbarian (bär bãr' ē ən). A person, usually from a foreign country, thought of as fierce or uncivilized.

barefoot doctor. In China, a health worker in a farming village who treats minor injuries and illnesses. A farm worker who is chosen to become a barefoot doctor receives several months of training in a city hospital. The barefoot doctors are called this because farm workers in China so often go barefoot.

barge. A flat-bottomed boat used mainly to carry freight on rivers and canals.

bearings. Objects, such as metal balls and rollers, that enable one part of a machine or a mechanical device to slide smoothly over or around another part. For example, ball bearings are used in roller-skate wheels.

bituminous (bə tü′ mə nəs) **coal.** The most plentiful and important type of coal. It is used as a fuel, especially for the production of electric power. High-quality bituminous coal can be made into coke. See **coke.**

blast furnace. A cylinder-shaped furnace in which iron is made from iron ore. It is called a blast furnace because a strong blast of air is blown into the bottom of the furnace. The air rises through a mixture of iron ore, coke, and limestone. It makes the coke burn at the high temperature needed for producing iron.

Buddha (bůd′ ə). The title, meaning "Enlightened One," given to the founder of the Buddhist religion. Buddha, whose name was Siddhartha Gautama (sid där′tə gou′tə ma), lived in India about 2,500 years ago. He taught that selfish desires are the cause of all sorrow, and that by getting rid of these desires a person can gain perfect peace and happiness.

Buddhist (bůd′ ist). The religion founded by Buddha, and its followers. See **Buddha.**

cabinet. A group of leaders who serve as advisors to the head of a government. Usually the cabinet members are in charge of various government departments.

cadres (kad′ rēz). Commonly, a group of trained persons who can be put in charge of others and train them in some special kind of work. In China, cadres are people who have been trained to do special work for the government. They are usually members of the Chinese Communist Party.

calligraphy (kə lig′ rə fē). Handwriting as a form of art, especially the painting of Chinese, Japanese, or Persian characters with a brush.

Canton. A large city in South China. In Chinese it is known as Kwangchow or Guangzhou (Pinyin spelling). Canton lies along the Pearl River, about eighty miles from the South China Sea. It is a leading seaport and manufacturing city.

capitalist. Favoring an economic system called capitalism. In this system, individuals or private companies own land, factories, and other property used for producing goods. The United States and Canada are examples of capitalist countries.

catty. Plural, **catties.** A Chinese unit of weight equal to a little more than one pound.

censor. To examine materials such as books and magazines before they are published, or radio and television programs before they are broadcast. The purpose is to remove or change anything that government officials or some group might consider harmful.

census. A government survey taken to find out the population of a country or region, as well as other important facts.

centimeter (sen′ tə mē′ tər). A unit in the metric system for measuring length. It is equal to about .39 inch. See **metric system.**

Chiang Kai-shek (ji äng′ kī′ shek′), 1887-1975. Chief political and military leader of the Chinese Nationalists from the 1920's until his death. When the Communists took over the mainland of China in 1949, Chiang moved the Nationalist government headquarters to the island of Taiwan.

Chin Ling Shan (chin′ ling′ shän′). The mountain range which forms much of the boundary between North and South China. (See map, page 25.)

circumference (sər kum′ fər əns). The distance around an object or a geometric figure, especially a circle or a sphere.

citronella grass. A fragrant grass from which a pale yellow oil, called citronella, is obtained. Citronella is used in making perfumes, soaps, and insect repellents.

civilians (sə vil′ yənz). Usually, persons who are not on active military duty.

coke. A fuel made by roasting coal in special airtight ovens. Coke, which burns at a very high temperature, is needed for the production of iron and steel from iron ore.

Cold War. A conflict between Communist and non-Communist nations that began in the 1940's. It was called "cold" because it was fought largely with propaganda and other non-violent methods rather than with guns and bombs. But actual fighting did take place in certain countries, mainly Korea and Vietnam.

collective. A farm, factory, or other organization that is owned and operated by a group of people working together. The members of a collective share in the profits that are left after taxes and other expenses have been paid.

colonialism (kə lō′ nē ə liz′ əm). Refers to the control or rule of a territory by a foreign power. When a nation seeks such control, it usually expects to gain land, resources, or other economic benefits.

communism. A system in which all land and other property used for producing goods is owned by the community as a whole. It also refers to the teachings and actions of the Chinese Communist Party and of the Communist parties in other countries. (See pages 189-190.)

compass rose. A small drawing included on a map to show directions. A compass rose is often used as a decoration. Here are three examples of compass roses:

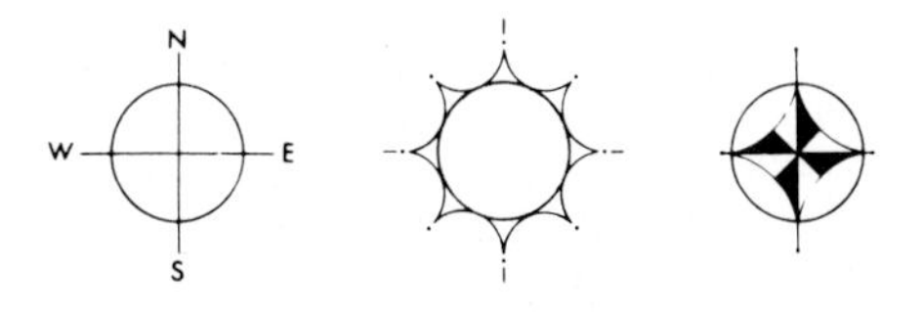

Confucius (kən fū′ shəs), 551?-479 B.C. Name used in English-speaking countries for the Chinese philosopher K'ung Fu-tzu (ku̇ng′ fü′ dzu′). His teachings were the main laws by which China's people lived for more than two thousand years.

consumer goods. Food, clothing, furniture, and other goods that people buy and use to meet their everyday needs.

crude oil. Petroleum as it comes from the ground, before it has been refined.

cymbals (sim′ bəls). A musical instrument consisting of two brass plates. They are crashed against each other to make a ringing sound.

Dairen (dī′ ren′). The Japanese name commonly used for the seaport city of Talien in North China. Dairen is now part of the city of Luta. See **Luta.**

Dalai Lama (dä lī′ lä′ mə). The chief priest of a branch of Buddhism called Lamaism. In earlier times, the Dalai Lama was the ruler of Tibet. The present Dalai Lama now lives in India.

deciduous (di sij′ ü əs). Refers to trees that shed their leaves each year, such as maples and elms.

delta. A triangular area of land formed by deposits of mud and sand at the mouth of a river.

Deng Xiaoping. See **Teng Hsiao-ping.**

density of population. The average number of people per unit of land area. Density of population can be figured by dividing the total number of people in a given area by the number of square miles or square kilometers in the area.

developed countries. Highly industrialized countries, in which most of the work is done by power-driven machinery. In the developed countries, natural resources are used extensively, and the general standard of living is high. (See map on page 165.)

dialect (dī′ ə lekt). A local form of a language.

diameter (dī am′ ə tər). A straight line that passes through the center of a figure, such as a circle or a sphere, and joins the opposite sides. Also, the length of such a straight line.

dictatorship. A government in which all ruling power is held by a single leader or by a small group of leaders.

drought (drout). A long period of time when little or no rain falls.

dynasty (dī′ nə stē). A series of rulers descended from the same ancestor.

economic (ē′ kə nom′ ik). Having to do with the way in which goods and services are produced, distributed, and consumed. The scientific study of this topic is known as economics.

electronic (i lek′ tron′ ik). Refers to certain devices, such as transistors and silicon chips, or to products that make use of such devices. Radios, television sets, and computers are examples of electronic products.

Empress Dowager. See **Tzu Hsi.**

equator (i kwā′ tər). An imaginary line around the earth, exactly halfway between the North Pole and the South Pole.

export (ek spôrt′). To send goods from one country or region to another, especially for the purpose of selling them. These goods are called exports (eks′ pôrts).

famine. An extreme shortage of food in an area.

Formosa (fôr mō′ sə). A name formerly used by people in Western countries to refer to the island of Taiwan. (See **Taiwan.**) Sailors from Portugal who visited Taiwan in the 1500's called it Formosa, which means "beautiful" in Portuguese.

gorge (gôrj). A narrow passageway, as between two mountains. (See picture, pages 32-33.)

PRONUNCIATION KEY: **hat, āge, cãre, fär; let, ēqual, tėrm; it, īce; hot, ōpen, ôrder; oil, out; cup, pu̇t, rüle, ūse; child; long; thin; ᴛʜen; zh, measure; ə represents a in about, e in taken, i in pencil, o in lemon, u in circus.** For the complete key, see page 212.

Grand Canal. A canal in China that connects Tientsin and Hangchow. (See map on page 21.) It was constructed in several stages. One section was completed late in the fifth century B.C. In the seventh century A.D., the canal was lengthened and improved by an emperor of the Sui dynasty. Later, additional improvements were made by the Mongols under Kublai Khan, and by the Ming emperors. In recent years, more improvements have been made in the Grand Canal.

growing season. The period of time when crops can be grown outdoors without danger of being killed by frost.

Han (hän) **Chinese.** The nationality group to which more than nine tenths of the people in China belong. This group got its name from the Han dynasty, which ruled China from 206 B.C. to A.D. 220. However, people of the Han group had been living in China long before that time.

Himalaya (him′ ə lā′ ə) **Mountains.** A mountain system about 1,500 miles long that stretches through southern Asia. (See map, page 7.) It includes Mount Everest, the highest peak in the world.

Hong Kong. A British colony, located along the coast of China about ninety miles southeast of Canton. (See map on page 21.) Hong Kong, which is made up partly of islands, has a deep natural harbor. It is an important trading and manufacturing center. Textiles, plastics, and electronic equipment are manufactured here and exported, mainly to the United States. Hong Kong also carries on much trade with China and Japan. There are two large cities in Hong Kong. These are Victoria, the capital, and Kowloon. The population of Hong Kong is about 5,250,000. Almost all of these people are Chinese.

hydroelectric (hī′ drō i lek′ trik). Refers to electricity produced by waterpower. The force of rushing water is used to run machines called generators, which produce electricity.

import (im pôrt′). To bring goods into a country or region from another country or region, especially for the purpose of selling them. These goods are called imports (im′-pôrts).

inflation (in flā′ shən). Refers to a time of rapidly rising prices. During a period of inflation, a given amount of money, such as a dollar, buys fewer goods and services than it did before.

irrigation. The process of supplying farmland with water by ditches, canals, sprinklers, pipelines, or other means.

Islam (is′ ləm). The religion founded by a prophet named Mohammed, who was born in Arabia in A.D. 570. According to this religion there is only one God, and Mohammed is his prophet. Followers of Islam are called Moslems.

ivory. A hard, white substance that comes from the tusks of elephants, walruses, and certain other animals. Ivory is used in making piano keys, billiard balls, and many other articles.

Kampuchea (kam pü chē′ ə). A small nation in southeastern Asia. (See map, pages 6-7.) It is also known as Cambodia.

kaoliang (kä′ ō lē ang′). Any one of several kinds of grain plants. The stalks of kaoliang grow eight to ten feet tall and are used for fuel, thatch, and animal feed. The kernels of grain grow in clusters at the top of the stalk. They are used as food by people.

kilometer (kə lom′ ə tər). A unit in the metric system for measuring length. It is equal to .62 mile. See **metric system.**

kitchen god. One of the most important gods worshiped by the Chinese people before the Communists discouraged religion. Families kept a picture of this god on the chimney. They believed he rose to heaven every year to report their good and bad deeds.

Korean War. A conflict, lasting from 1950 until 1953, between Communist and non-Communist forces in Korea. In 1950, Communist troops from North Korea unexpectedly invaded South Korea. United Nations forces, consisting largely of Americans and South Koreans, but also including troops from many other countries, forced the North Koreans back. The cease-fire agreement that ended the Korean War set the boundary between North and South Korea approximately along the 38th parallel.

Kuomintang (gwō′ min dang′). The Chinese name for the Nationalist Party of China. See **Nationalist Party of China.**

lacquer (lak′ ər). Any one of several types of tough, glossy varnish. In Japan and China, lacquer is made from the sap of the lacquer tree.

landlord. A person who owns land or a building and rents it to another person. Until the Communists took control of China in 1949, much of the farmland there was owned by landlords.

Lao-tzu (lou′dzə′). A Chinese philosopher who is supposed to have lived during the sixth century B.C. He is considered the founder of Taoism. See **Taoism.**

Lhasa (läs′ ə). Capital of the autonomous region of Tibet. Founded in the seventh century A.D.

limestone. A common rock, usually formed from the shells and skeletons of sea animals. Limestone is used for making cement and in the production of iron and steel. It is also used as a building stone.

Li Po (lē′ bô′), 701-762. A famous writer of the T'ang dynasty, considered by many people to be China's greatest poet.

lunar calendar. Any calendar based on the time from one full moon to the next, which is about 29½ days. The lunar calendar formerly used in China divided the year into twelve months of 29 or 30 days each. An extra month was added every thirty months, in much the same way that an extra day is added to our calendar every four years.

Luta (lü′ dä′). A large city in North China that includes the important seaports of Port Arthur and Dairen. The name Luta comes from the Chinese names for these seaports, Lushun and Talien.

Macao (mə kou′). A Portuguese territory that is located along the southern coast of China, near the city of Canton. It covers about six square miles. (See map, page 21.)

Manchuria (man chu̇r′ ē ə). A name formerly used for the part of northeastern China that now includes the provinces of Heilungkiang, Kirin, and Liaoning. (See map, page 82.)

Manchus (man′ chüz). A group of people who have lived for many centuries in Manchuria and nearby areas. The Manchus conquered China in the seventeenth century and ruled it until 1912. See **Manchuria**.

manganese (mang′ gə nēs). A grayish white metal that is used mainly in producing steel. Small amounts of manganese are added to the steel to make it stronger.

Mao Tse-tung (mou′ dzə′ du̇ng′), 1893-1976. For many years chairman of the Communist Party of China and the country's most important leader. He helped to form the Communist Party of China in 1921, and led the Chinese Communist army to victory in the civil war against the Chinese Nationalist forces.

Mercator (mėr kā′ tər) **projection.** One of many possible arrangements of meridians and parallels on which a map of the world may be drawn. Devised by Gerhardus Mercator, a Flemish geographer who lived from 1512 to 1594. On a Mercator map, all meridians are drawn straight up and down, with north at the top. The parallels are drawn straight across, but increasingly far apart toward the poles.

metric system. A system of measurement used in most countries and by scientists throughout the world. In this system, the meter is the basic unit of length. It is equal to 39.37 inches. In the metric system, 100 centimeters equal one meter, and 1000 meters equal one kilometer.

migration. The movement of people from one region or country to another, for the purpose of settling there.

millet (mil′ it). Any one of several kinds of plants that produce clusters of grain. It is raised as food both for people and animals.

minority (mə nôr′ ə tē). Less than half. Usually a minority group consists of people who differ in race, religion, or national origin from the group that makes up the largest part of a country's population.

missionary. A person who is sent out by a religious group to persuade other people to follow that religion.

molybdenum (mə lib′ də nəm). A silvery white metal that melts at a very high temperature. It is used to strengthen and harden steel.

Mongolia (män gōl′ yə). An area in east central Asia that was the original home of the Mongols. Mongolia was part of the vast territory under the control of the Mongol emperor Genghis Khan in the thirteenth century A.D. Today, Mongolia includes an independent country called the Mongolian People's Republic. (See map on pages 6-7.) It also includes an autonomous region of China called Inner Mongolia (see map on page 82) and a small section of the Soviet Union.

Mongolian People's Republic. See **Mongolia**.

monsoons. Winds that reverse their direction from season to season.

municipality. Plural, **municipalities.** A city, town, or other unit of local government. In China, there are three special municipalities that are not part of any province or autonomous region. These three are Shanghai, Peking, and Tientsin.

PRONUNCIATION KEY: **hat, āge, cãre, fär; let, ēqual, tėrm; it, īce; hot, ōpen, ôrder; oil, out; cup, pu̇t, rüle, ūse; child; long; thin; ᴛʜen; zh,** measure; **ə** represents **a** in about, **e** in taken, **i** in pencil, **o** in lemon, **u** in circus. For the complete key, see page 212.

Nationalist Party of China. A Chinese political party, also known as the Kuomintang. It grew out of a revolutionary group formed by Sun Yat-sen to overthrow China's Manchu rulers. After the emperor was overthrown, the Nationalists gradually gained control of much of China. In 1949, following a civil war with the Chinese Communists, the Nationalist Party leaders were forced to flee to the island of Taiwan. (See pages 179-181.)

Nationalists. Members of the Nationalist Party of China. See **Nationalist Party of China.**

NATO. The North Atlantic Treaty Organization, an alliance formed in 1949 by the United States, Canada, and ten European nations for the purpose of defense against possible attack by the Soviet Union. Greece, Turkey, West Germany, and Spain were later admitted as members.

navigation (nav′ ə gā′ shən). Travel by boat on a body of water such as a river, lake, or ocean.

nomad (nō′ mad). A member of a tribe or group of people without a permanent home. Nomads move from place to place to find food or to locate pasture for their livestock.

nomadic (nō mad′ ik). Referring to the way of life followed by nomads. See **nomad.**

nuclear (nü′ klē ər). Refers to the production or use of atomic energy. A nuclear reactor is an apparatus for splitting atoms to produce atomic energy. See **atomic energy.**

oasis (ō ā′ sis). Plural, **oases** (ō ā′sēz). A fertile area in a desert, in which there is enough water to permit plants to grow.

opera (op′ ər ə). A play in which the characters usually sing their lines rather than speak them. Operas often include ballet or other forms of dance.

pavilion (pə vil′ yən). A somewhat open building that can be used as a shelter in places such as gardens or parks.

Pearl River. A river in South China that flows from the city of Canton to the South China Sea. (See map, page 21.)

peasant. In some parts of the world, a person who owns a small farm or works as a farm laborer.

pedicab (ped′ ə kab′). A small three-wheeled vehicle that is pedaled like a bicycle. Pedicabs can be used for carrying either passengers or freight.

philosopher (fə los′ ə fər). A person who thinks deeply about important questions and tries to find answers to those questions through the use of reasoning.

phosphate rock. A kind of rock that contains chemicals needed by plants. It is ground up and used in making fertilizer.

plateau (pla tō′). A large, generally level area of high land.

porcelain (pôr′ sə lin). A very fine type of pottery, first developed in China. It is made from a white clay called kaolin.

Port Arthur. English name commonly used for the seaport town of Lushun in North China. The British gave it this name in the nineteenth century when they used it as a naval base to fight China. It is now part of the city of Luta. See **Luta.**

premier (pri mir′). In China, the official who is in charge of the day-to-day operations of the national government. The premier is elected by the National People's Congress for a term of five years.

propaganda (prop′ ə gan′ də). Information that is spread in an organized manner to influence people's thoughts or make people act in a certain way.

province (prov′ əns). In China, a political division that is somewhat similar to a state in the United States.

rapeseed. The seed of the rape plant, which belongs to the mustard family. The leaves of the rape plant are used as food for sheep and hogs. A useful oil is obtained from the seeds.

republic. A nation in which the people govern themselves through elected representatives. The United States of America is a republic.

retail. Refers to stores that sell goods directly to the persons who will use the product. Grocery stores and clothing stores are examples of retail stores.

revolution. A complete change, such as the overthrow of a government or an important change in people's way of living.

sabotage (sab′ ə täzh). The destruction of machinery or other property that belongs to one's employer, to the enemy in time of war, or to a government with which one disagrees.

SEATO. The Southeast Asia Treaty Organization, an alliance formed in 1954 by the United States, Great Britain, France, Australia, New Zealand, Pakistan, Thailand, and the Philippines. The purpose of SEATO was to defend countries in Southeast Asia from possible attack by Communist nations. Pakistan withdrew from SEATO in 1972, and the organization was disbanded in 1976.

seedbed. A small piece of ground that has been prepared for planting seeds. The young plants are allowed to grow in the seedbed until they are large enough to transplant into a larger field.

Shenyang (shən′ yäng′). Modern Chinese name for the city of Mukden in Liaoning Province. Mukden is the Manchu name for the city. See **Manchus**.

Shih Huang Ti (shir′ hwäng′ tē′), 259-210 B.C. The Ch'in ruler who founded the Chinese Empire. He undertook the building of the Great Wall to keep out invaders.

shuttlecock. A cork ball with feathers, used in games such as badminton.

silt. Fine soil or earth. Especially particles of soil carried by a river or some other body of water.

Southwest Asia. A part of Asia that includes Turkey, Iran, Iraq, Syria, Lebanon, Israel, Jordan, part of Egypt, countries on the Arabian Peninsula, and the island of Cyprus. (See map on page 9.)

Soviet (sō′ vē et) **Union.** Another name for the Union of Soviet Socialist Republics. (See map, pages 6-7.) Until 1922, the official name of this country was Russia.

soybean. A bushy plant of the pea family. Soybeans are raised as a farm crop in many parts of the world. The beans and oil from the beans are used to make foods, paint, and many other products. The green plants are used as feed for livestock. They may also be plowed into the soil to make it more fertile.

square inch. A unit for measuring area, equal to the area of a square that measures one inch on each side.

square mile. A unit for measuring area, equal to the area of a square that measures one mile on each side. One square mile contains 640 acres. See **acre**.

standard of living. The average level of conditions in a community or country, or the level of conditions people consider necessary for a happy, satisfying life. In countries with a high standard of living, many different goods and services are considered to be necessities. In countries with a low standard of living, many of these same items are luxuries enjoyed by only a few people.

state farm. In China, a large farm that is owned and operated by the national government. Profits from the farm go directly to the government, which hires workers to plant and harvest the crops. On a state farm the fields are usually very large. These permit the use of large farm machines such as tractors and combines.

steel. A strong, hard metal that consists mainly of iron, mixed with a small amount of carbon. Different kinds of steel contain different amounts of carbon, but always less than 2 percent. Special steels also contain other substances. For example, stainless steel may contain as much as 18 percent chromium and 8 percent nickel.

suburb. An outer part of a city, or a smaller community near a city.

Sun Yat-sen (sůn′ yät′ sen′), 1866-1925. A Chinese statesman and revolutionary leader. Sun attended mission schools in Hawaii and graduated from the College of Medicine in Hong Kong. He organized a revolutionary group, later known as the Nationalist Party, which helped to overthrow China's Manchu emperor. See **Nationalist Party of China**.

synthetic (sin thet′ ik). Refers to certain artificial substances, such as plastics and nylon, developed to replace similar natural materials.

tai chi chuan (tī′jē′chwän′). An ancient Chinese form of exercise and self-defense. The graceful movements of *tai chi chuan* emphasize balance and coordination rather than strength.

Taiwan (tī′ wän′). A large, mountainous island in the Pacific Ocean, about ninety miles off the coast of China. Its name means "terraced bay" in Chinese. Taiwan is usually considered part of China. However, it has a separate government.

Taoism (tou′ iz əm). A philosophy and religion, supposedly founded by a Chinese thinker named Lao-tzu during the sixth century B.C. The philosophy of Taoism was based upon the idea of living close to nature. Over the years witchcraft and magic ceremonies became an important part of Taoism.

technician (tek nish′ ən). An expert in the details of some subject, or a worker who is especially skilled in a particular occupation.

Teng Hsiao-ping (dung′shou′ping′), 1904-
In recent years, the most powerful government leader in China. Teng was the son of a well-to-do landowner in the province of Szechwan. He joined the Communist Party while living in France during the 1920's. Later he took part in the revolution that brought the Communists to power in China.

PRONUNCIATION KEY: hat, āge, cãre, fär; let, ēqual, tėrm; it, īce; hot, ōpen, ôrder; **oi**l, **ou**t; cup, pu̇t, rüle, ūse; **ch**ild; lo**ng**; **th**in; ᴛʜen; **zh**, measure; ə represents **a** in about, **e** in taken, **i** in pencil, **o** in lemon, **u** in circus. For the complete key, see page 212.

textile. Refers to woven or knit cloth, or the yarn used to make cloth.

three-dimensional (də men′ shə nəl). Having height, width, and length.

thresh. To separate kernels of grain from the stalks on which they grew.

Tibet (tə bet′). Autonomous region in Outer China. (See maps, pages 25 and 82.) As long ago as the A.D. 600's, Tibet was an independent kingdom. In the centuries that followed, it was sometimes independent and sometimes under the control of foreign rulers. The Tibetan people followed a religion called Lamaism, which is a branch of Buddhism. In the 1600's, the chief priest of this religion, called the Dalai Lama, became Tibet's ruler. Later, Tibet came under the control of China's Manchu rulers. However, it remained more or less self-governing, under a series of religious leaders. In 1950, Tibet was invaded by the Chinese Communists. It is now governed in the same way as China's other autonomous regions. See **autonomous region.**

Tien An Men (tē en′ än′ men′) **Square.** A large square in Peking, the capital city of China. Located outside the south gate of the Forbidden City, where the emperors used to live. (See map, page 106.) Its name means "Gate of Heavenly Peace."

topographic (top′ ə graf′ ik). Refers to the physical features of an area, such as lakes, rivers, and hills. A topographic map shows the elevation of these features and their location in relation to each other.

topsoil. The top layer of soil on the earth's surface. It is seldom much more than one foot deep. Normally, topsoil is more fertile than the soil beneath it, because it contains a larger amount of decayed plant material.

treaty. An agreement between two or more nations.

tropical. Typical of the tropics, the part of the earth that is closest to the equator. The weather in the tropics is generally hot all year round.

Tu Fu (dü′ fü′), 712-770. An important Chinese writer of the T'ang dynasty, famous for his beautiful poems.

tung nuts. Seeds of the tung tree. A pale yellow, quick-drying oil produced from tung nuts is used in paints, varnishes,and similar products.

tungsten (tung′ stən). A grayish white metal used in making high-quality steel, wires for electric light bulbs, and other products.

typhoon. A destructive tropical storm that forms over the Pacific Ocean. When this type of storm forms over the Atlantic, it is called a hurricane. Typhoons and hurricanes are made up of violent winds that whirl around a calm center called the eye. The eye is usually about fifteen miles in diameter, and the entire storm may be as much as five hundred miles across. The whirling winds blow at a speed of seventy-five miles an hour or more, but the storm itself travels rather slowly, at about fifteen or twenty miles an hour. Usually, several typhoons form over the Pacific each year. Some of these storms remain over the ocean. Others strike the coasts of China, Japan, or the Philippines.

Tzu Hsi (tsü′ shē′), 1835-1908. Empress Dowager Tzu Hsi was one of the most powerful women in China's history. As the mother of the child emperor T'ung Chih (tung′-jir′), Tzu Hsi helped to rule the country for him until he died in 1875. Then she chose her nephew Kuang Hsü (gwäng′ shü′), to be the next emperor. When he displeased her, she had him imprisoned and ruled the country herself.

United Nations. An organization formed in 1945 to work for world peace. About 155 nations are members. Agencies related to the United Nations work to solve problems in fields such as health, agriculture, and labor.

urban area. A city and the heavily populated area around it.

Urumchi (ů rům′ chē), also called Tihwa. Capital city of Sinkiang Uighur in Outer China. (Compare maps on pages 82 and 20.)

Vietnam War. A war that took place in the country of Vietnam between 1957 and 1975. (See map, pages 6-7.) On one side was the non-Communist government of South Vietnam, aided by the United States and several other countries. On the other side was the Communist government of North Vietnam and a force of South Vietnamese rebels known as the Viet Cong. The war ended in 1975 when the Communist forces gained control of Saigon, the capital of South Vietnam. During this long conflict, several million people were killed or wounded.

warlord. A military leader who rules an area or a political division by force.

Western. In this book, refers to Europe, and to the United States and other countries whose civilization developed from that of Europe.

Whampoa (hwäm′ pō′ ä′). A seaport and manufacturing city in southeastern China. It is located on the Pearl River about nine miles from Canton.

wholesale. Refers to companies that sell large quantities of goods to smaller companies and stores, which in turn sell the goods to the people who actually use them. In China, most wholesale trade is carried on by government-owned companies. For example, the China Cotton and Textile Company buys large amounts of cloth from textile factories. Then it sells the cloth to retail stores throughout China. See **retail**.

World War II, 1939-1945. The second war in history that involved nearly every part of the world. The Allies, which included China, the United States, the United Kingdom, the Soviet Union, and many other countries, defeated the Axis. The Axis included mainly Germany, Italy, and Japan.

Wuhan (wü′ hän′). A large city on the Yangtze River. (See map on page 21.) This city, which has a population of about four million, was formed in 1950 from three smaller cities—Hankow, Hanyang, and Wuchang.

Yangtze (yang′ tsē) **River.** The third longest river in the world. It begins in the mountains of Tibet and flows eastward across China for over 3,400 miles, emptying into the East China Sea. In China the Yangtze is usually known as the Chang Chiang or Chang Jiang (Pinyin spelling), which means "Long River."

Yellow River, known as the Hwang Ho or Huang He (Pinyin spelling) in Chinese. The second longest river in China. It begins in the province of Tsinghai and flows generally eastward for nearly 3,000 miles, emptying into the Yellow Sea.

yuan (yü än′). The unit of money in the People's Republic of China.

Yüan Shih-k'ai (yü än′ shir′ kī′), 1859-1916. Chinese military leader and government official who was a friend of Empress Dowager Tzu Hsi. After the Manchus were overthrown and China became a republic, he was named president.

PINYIN SPELLINGS

Spellings used in this book	Pinyin Spellings
Brahmaputra River	Yarlung Zangbo Jiang
Chiang Ching	Jiang Qing
China, People's Republic of	Zhonghua, Renmin Gongheguo
Chin Ling Shan	Qin Ling Shan
Chou En-lai	Zhou Enlai
East China Sea	Dong Hai
Formosa Strait	Taiwan Haixia
Grand Canal	Da Yunhe
Great Khingan Mts.	Da Hinggan Ling
Great Wall	Wanli Changcheng
Hua Kuo-feng	Hua Guofeng
Kunlun Shan	Kunlun Shan
Lao-tzu	Laozi
Lin Piao	Lin Biao
Li Po	Li Bai
Loess Plateau	Loess Gaoyuan
Manchurian Plain	Dongbei Pingyuan
Mao Tse-tung	Mao Zedong
Mekong River	Lancang Jiang
Mongolian Plateau	Monggol Gaoyuan
Pearl River	Zhu Jiang
Po Hai Gulf	Bo Hai Wan
Red Basin	Yuan Pendi
Salween River	Nu Jiang
Si River	Xi Jiang
South China Sea	Nan Hai
South Yangtze Hills	Nan Chang Qiuling
Sungari River	Songhua Jiang
tai chi chuan	taijiquan
Takla Makan Desert	Taklimakan Shamo
Tarim River	Tarim He
Teng Hsiao-ping	Deng Xiaoping
Tibetan Plateau	Qing Zang Gaoyuan
Tien An Men	Tiananmen
Tien Shan	Tian Shan
Tu Fu	Du Fu
Yangtze River	Chang Jiang
Yellow Plain	Huang Pingyuan
Yellow River	Huang He
Yunnan-Kweichow Plateau	Yunnan-Guizhou Gaoyuan

PRONUNCIATION KEY: hat, āge, cãre, fär; let, ēqual, tėrm; it, īce; hot, ōpen, ôrder; **oil**, **out**; cup, pu̇t, rüle, ūse; **ch**ild; lo**ng**; **th**in; ᴛʜen; **zh**, measure; ə represents **a** in about, **e** in taken, **i** in pencil, **o** in lemon, **u** in circus. For the complete key, see page 212.

INDEX

Explanation of abbreviations used in this Index: *p* — picture *m* — map

---

PRONUNCIATION KEY: **hat, āge, cãre, fär; let, ēqual, tėrm; it, īce; hot, ōpen, ôrder; oil, out; cup, pu̇t, rüle, ūse; child; long; thin; ᴛʜen; zh,** measure; **ə** represents **a** in about, **e** in taken, **i** in pencil, **o** in lemon, **u** in circus. For the complete key, see page 212.

Maps and Special Features

Acknowledgments

Grateful acknowledgment is made to the following for permission to use the illustrations found in this book.

A. Devaney, Inc.: Page 90
Alpha: Pages 152-153 by Terry Qing
American Museum of Natural History: Page 39
Authenticated News International: Page 73
Bettmann Archive, The: Page 164
Bibliotheque Nationale: Page 47
Black Star: Page 86 by Emil Schulthess
Brown Brothers: Pages 49, 57 (left), and 59
Camera Press-Pix: Page 8 by Alfred Gregory
Carl E. Östman: Pages 14-15 by S. E. Hedin; pages 34-35 by Ralp Herrmans
Contact Press Images: Pages 70-71 by Liu Heung Shing
Design Photographers International: Pages 140-141
Eastfoto: Pages 28-29, 32-33 (upper), 52-53, 79, 113, 144, 145, 146, 156, 166, 168-169, 184-185, and 186-187; page 29 by Yang Ping-wen
East-West Photo: Page 192
Ewing Galloway: Pages 4-5 and 32-33 (lower)
Freelance Photographers Guild, Inc.: Pages 81, 96-97, and 148-149; page 68 from the Andy Bernhaut Archive; page 138 by Richard Harrington
Globe and Mail: Pages 36-37 by Burns; page 97 by Oancia
Globe Photos: Pages 130-131
Harrison Forman: Pages 60-61, 101, 102-103, 120, 141, and 173
Historical Pictures Service: Page 189
J. Allan Cash: Pages 154-155, 160, and 170-171
Katherine Young: Pages 150-151 by Joel Morwood
Leo de Wys, Inc.: Page 112 by Steve Vidler
Magnum Photos, Inc.: Pages 76, 91, 106-107, 118-119, 134-135, and 136-137; pages 12-13, 22-23, 50-51, and 62-63 by Marc Ribaud; pages 30-31 and 142-143 by René Burri
Metropolitan Museum of Art: Page 44 (left and right)
Museum of Fine Arts, Boston: Page 121
Peabody Museum of Salem: Pages 54-55 by Mark Sexton
Photo Researchers, Inc.: Page 16
Popperfoto: Pages 57 (right) and 161
Rapho Guillumette Pictures: Pages 24-25 and 188; pages 18-19 by Brian Brake; pages 84-85 by Audrey Topping; pages 104-105 by Roland and Sabrina Michaud; pages 194-195 by Paolo Koch
Shostal Associates, Inc.: Pages 10-11, 42-43, 100, 109, 125, 126-127, 183, and 196
Sovfoto: Page 190 painting by V. A. Serov
Stock, Boston, Inc.: Pages 2-3, 26-27, 89, 128-129, 132, 172-173, and 177 by Richard Balzer; page 162 by Ethan Signer; page 180 by James R. Holland
United Press International: Pages 40, 129, and 175
Van Cleve Photography: Pages 110-111 and 158-159
Wide World Photos: Pages 38-39, 57 (middle), 66-67 (left), 67 (right), 75, 92, and 157
Zentrale Farbbild Agentur: Pages 114-115; page 78 by Dr. Hans Kramarz; pages 94-95 and 98-99 by J. Bitsch; pages 117, 122-123, and 193 by Kurt Göbel

Grateful acknowledgment is made to Scott, Foresman and Company for the pronunciation system used in this book, which is taken from the Thorndike-Barnhart Dictionary Series.

Grateful acknowledgment is made to the following for permission to use cartographic data in this book: Nystrom Raised Relief Map Company, Chicago 60618: Page 9 and bottom map on page 210; Panoramic Studios: Pages 6 and 17; Rand McNally & Company: Pages 6-7; United States Department of Commerce, Bureau of the Census: Center map on page 210.